WO
DEA

Edited by Mike James

True Crime Library — No. 7
A Forum Press Book
by the Paperback Division of
Forum Design,
P.O. Box 158, London SE 20 7QA.

An Imprint of True Crime Library

Reprinted 1995, 1997, 1998

Typeset by Techniset,
1 Back Cross Lane, Newton-le-Willows, Merseyside WA12 9YE.
Printed and bound in Great Britain

ISBN 1 874358 06 0

To Stuart, Joanna, Jeanette,
Roy, Bill and Ted.
The team

CONTENTS

FOREWORD

Edward T. Hart

Feminists have brought us to a pretty pass. If all men and all women are equal — as indeed they should be — then they should surely have an equal share of the pleasure and the pain encountered along life's rollercoaster ride. There should be no special privileges when things go wrong. So if a man and a woman become equally involved in capital murder, justice surely demands that they suffer the same fate ... even if this means that the woman also endures the grisly ritual of execution.

That's what logic says. The heart says something else. Like me, I suspect, most men find the notion of a woman dangling at the end of a rope, head grotesquely askew, unacceptable. I am equally disconcerted by the thought of a woman being strapped securely into an electric chair and then shocked to death.

Mohammed Ali's trainer Angelo Dundee, speaking of his weird and wonderful assistant Bundini Brown, once said: "I've stopped making the mistake of trying to understand him. The more I tried, the more confused I became."

The stories told in this excellent book have the same effect upon me. Only in this case, it's my own feelings that I find so hard to understand. My heart comes up with appealing points designed to help save the female denizens of Death Row from their awesome fate. And then my alter ego promptly demolishes those arguments.

For instance …

Point One: The execution of a mother — taking her away from the children she may love deeply while being loved in return — is surely an affront to civilisation.

Alter Ego: That is doubtless so … but haven't male murderers been known to love their children too?

Point Two: Doesn't the basic nature of women entitle them to a separate set of judgements? Sociologists assure us that women are the gentler sex, more loving, more caring than the male. "If the world was run by women," said Mahatma Gandhi, who knew a thing or two about peace, "there would be no wars."

Alter Ego: All probably true. And yet the murderesses you'll meet in this book match the murderers in terms of sheer sadism, blow for bloody blow. The Fraus of Dachau are not yet extinct.

During my Fleet Street days, I saw my share of murderesses at the Old Bailey. Their faces are still there, in the backrooms of my mind. And more often than not, they were the sort of faces that you'd trust to baby-sit, to care for an infirm aunt … and maybe partner you into the sunset of your days.

It's the same in this book. Few of the faces match up with their deeds. Mike James, fast becoming the king of crime anthologists, has chosen accounts written by some of the very best reporters in America, veterans of their trade who have seen more than their fair share of human drama. The result is thought-provoking, to say the least.

Turn the pages and you'll meet:

Ruth Snyder, the beautiful doe-eyed blonde who led her husband like a Judas Sheep to the slaughter.

Judith Neeley, the teenager with film-star looks who tortured her victims before killing them.

Ada Le Boeuf, the society queen who shocked the Bayou.

Louise Peete, the heart-breaker who drove four of her lovers to suicide.

Anna Antonio, the devout Catholic who hugged her

three-year-old son on her execution day, telling him, "I'm going away. I'm going away for a long time."

Betty Lou Beets, the blonde barmaid who made her husbands dig their own graves before shooting them.

Martha Place, the martinet housekeeper who wielded an axe.

Eva Coo, the roadhouse owner who walked casually to the electric chair as though strolling down the avenue on a Sunday afternoon.

Mary Creighton, the demure housewife and impatient poisoner.

Anna Hahn, the blonde charmer who became a serial killer.

And Karla Tucker, the sweet-faced innocent, who killed with a pickaxe and enjoyed every blow.

This book comes as yet another startling reminder of the capacity for sheer evil which exists in the human heart, regardless of gender. And yet despite all this, half of me was still hoping to read that the telephone had rung on Death Row ... and that the warden in true Hollywood style had stayed the executioner's hand in the nick of time.

All of which only goes to show one thing. I'm clearly a confused old chauvinist at heart.

EDITOR'S NOTE

Mike James

I once dreamed that I was walking down a prison corridor, flanked by warders, with the chaplain reading from the Good Book and the executioner waiting to greet me. I woke in mortal terror. I was so shaken that I went downstairs, made a pot of tea and read until dawn. Even then, I was scared to go back to sleep in case the dream returned.

If a nightmare can have this effect upon the mind, just imagine what the reality can do to a man or — as in the instances cited in this book — a woman caged up on Death Row for a year or more, hoping against hope that she'll be reprieved ... but fearing all the while that, in Sing Sing vernacular, she will one day be forced "to walk the Last Mile and ride the lightning". An experience far, far worse than any nightmare we can ever know.

Different Death Rows have different ways of spinning murderesses into eternity. In Sing Sing they'll place you in 'Old Sparky' — pictured on the cover of this book — and secure you tightly with heavy straps around the legs, forearms and body. They'll apply electrodes to a bare patch on your leg, fit the metal helmet on to your head (having previously shaved a patch to ensure good contact) and slip on the hood. Then in front of a window full of witnesses, the executioner will pull the lever which sends two thousand volts coursing through your body.

In California, you will again be strapped into a chair in

front of silent witnesses. The chamber will be cleared, the doors sealed and then the cyanide pellets will drop. If you follow the executioner's advice — "Count to ten, breathe deeply and don't fight the gas" — you'll probably be pronounced dead within a couple of minutes.

On a few Death Rows, hanging is still employed. You'll stand on the scaffold, hands tied behind your back, legs strapped together, a hood over your head, a noose around your neck. Then the trap-door will clang and you'll be plunged into eternity. The speed of your demise will depend upon the expertise of the hangman ... but (an alarming thought for the condemned) the hangmen of America are out of practice. They will soon, I suspect, become as extinct as the Dodo.

When given the chance to choose the manner of their death, most killers opt for lethal injection, a comparatively merciful form of execution. Sodium thiopental is first used to induce a deep sleep; then pancuronium bromide, a muscle relaxant, is used to help stop the breathing.

All the other execution methods used on Death Row are deliberately barbaric, for it has long been argued that it's not the fear of death that does most to deter the would-be murderer; it's the manner of the dying!

Nevertheless the Death Rows of America must surely concern all of us with heads to think and hearts to feel, simply because of the long drawn-out delays between sentence and execution. This form of mental torture is no longer tolerated in any other civilised nation.

Defenders of the system will tell you that this is democracy at work ... that the condemned are simply being given every chance. But Death Row is not a democratic place. Its residents don't include makers and shakers of industry, top-ranking politicians or power brokers.

Those with the kind of money capable of hiring the very best lawyers may not necessarily buy their freedom; but they can normally be expected to escape the harsher penalties of the law.

Politics too plays its part. Round about election time,

state governors become notoriously hawk-like. With law and order such a high priority in the States, it takes political courage to grant a reprieve when the voters are baying for blood.

This book isn't really concerned with the rights and wrongs of capital punishment ... only with its application to the women of Death Row.

Some of the murders recounted are chillingly evil, proving that men have no monopoly of cruelty. And then at the other end of the spectrum, we have the cruelty of the state ... which all too often appears to be playing a legal game of cat and mouse with the convicted, alternately raising and dashing hopes.

The long drawn-out delays affect everyone.

Consider Warden Lawes, a strong opponent of capital punishment, who nevertheless had the task of leading Ruth Snyder down the corridor towards the waiting executioner. Words of comfort couldn't have come easily.

Consider the matrons who had established a kind of friendship with the prisoner. They also walked the Last Mile beside her, helped her into the chair and said their goodbyes. They had been told to remain calm and dry-eyed during the execution. They wept instead.

Consider the relatives, friends and Ruth Snyder's daughter Lorraine, whose hopes must have risen and fallen with each passing day.

Then consider Ruth Snyder herself, who was told on her execution day that she had been reprieved ... only to learn a few hours later that the report was untrue.

My own nightmare went away with the daylight, banished by the knowledge that it was only a dream. But for the women of Death Row, such nightmares never go away. They are a constant reminder of the fate that awaits them.

1

RUTH SNYDER

Edward T. Hart

"What do you think they'll give me if I talk?" Ruth Snyder asked Detective James Smith. "A couple of years?"

Even in the glamorous surroundings of Tiffany Studios, Ruth Brown stood out from the crowd. With her blonde hair, blue eyes, film-star looks and voluptuous figure, she was a magnet for men. They would find excuses to linger beside the switchboard she operated, to engage her in conversation, building up the courage to make a pass.

One such admirer distracted Ruth enough to cause her to dial a wrong number ... a misdial setting up a train of events that would lead to one of the most memorable murders in the history of New York.

Asked by her employer to call the boss of another studio, she had mistakenly rung Albert Snyder, art editor of *Boating News* and a man with a notoriously short fuse.

"Look, young lady," roared Snyder, "I'm far too busy to be bothered by other people's mistakes. If you can't do your job properly, get out and let someone else take over."

Ruth was amused by the outburst. "I'm sorry if I upset you," she said. "But everyone makes a mistake just once in a while. Maybe even you!" And so saying, she broke the connection.

Intrigued by her husky, seductive voice, Snyder waited 10 minutes and then rang her back. "Look," he said, "I want to apologise for my rudeness. I've been having a bad day, but I had no right to take it out on you."

Still mildly amused, Ruth shrugged. "That's all right,"

she said. "We all have bad days. There's no need for apologies."

"Oh, but there is," said Snyder. "Why don't you let me take you out to dinner, so that I can apologise properly?"

She had heard that line before, a time or two. "You're making too big a thing of it," she said. "I really do understand; so let's just forget it."

"Please," said Snyder in a voice surprisingly humble, "please come and dine with me. There are no strings, I promise you." He paused and added cleverly, "Look upon it as a business meeting, if you prefer. I'm looking for an assistant, and with your voice, you could be ideal. The money's good."

It was the money rather than the man that persuaded Ruth to accept. Nevertheless, she dressed with care, choosing a low-cut dress that showed off her full figure to advantage.

Snyder was 32, a bachelor and not overly experienced in the ways of women. From his first glimpse of the 19-year-old Ruth, he was totally bewitched. She read the desire in his eyes and played him with skill, speaking demurely and appearing to be the soul of respectability. But every now and then, she would lean forward rather carelessly and give him a glimpse of cleavage capable of checking him in mid-sentence.

By the end of dinner he was ready to give her the moon. Instead he gave her a job which immediately doubled her present salary. As he had a well-earned reputation for being frugal the offer tells its own story.

Snyder had hitherto been staid in his ways, a man old before his time. But now suddenly he changed. Night after night, he would be out on the town with Ruth. He would take her to restaurants, the theatre, night clubs and dance halls.

It wasn't a lifestyle that he particularly enjoyed, but he sensed that it was the only one that gave him any chance of capturing this blonde enchantress. Ruth, for her part, was relishing a life she had never known before. Yet although still in her teens, she was smart enough to reel in this catch with care.

She could have become his mistress without any trouble, but she wanted more than that. She wanted the security of marriage. So at the end of the evening, she would thank him politely and permit only a goodnight kiss. As the weeks rolled by, they advanced to cuddles and careless hands. But until the engagement ring was slipped on her finger just before Christmas, this was as far as the love-making was allowed to go.

They were married on July 24th, 1915, but now that he had netted his bride Albert went back to his old ways. The need to woo was over; so were the nights on the town. He just wanted to spend his evenings by the fireside.

They were hopelessly mismatched; and it wasn't just the 13-year age gap that separated them. Ruth had a desperate desire for excitement. She wanted gaiety, a touch of wildness, the chance occasionally to dance the night away ... This was something that Albert couldn't, or wouldn't understand.

In November 1917 she gave birth to a daughter, Lorraine, but this only widened the divide. Albert hadn't wanted children. He resented having his sleep disturbed, and for a while stubbornly refused even to acknowledge the existence of his child.

In 1923 the Snyders moved up in the world, buying a house in Queens Village, Long Island; and because they now had spare bedrooms Ruth's mother, Josephine, came to live with them and help look after Lorraine.

For Ruth, opportunity beckoned. With Albert absent from the house from eight in the morning until six in the evening, and her mother in residence, it was a chance to enjoy the good times again. The Twenties, the age of the Charleston and the flapper, could have been designed with Ruth in mind. She was a spectacular dancer and a spectacular woman. She was also a natural flirt, well aware of her power over men. There was hardly a man in the neighbourhood who didn't envy Albert his bride.

She mixed with a happy-go-lucky circle of young women who were pleasure-seekers, with their equally young husbands and boy friends. They knew her as "Tommie", and one of the men later questioned by the police described Ruth as a "red-hot momma".

In June 1925, she was dining with her friends, Karin Kaufman and Harry Folsom, in Henry's Restaurant in Manhattan when a lightly-built man wearing tortoise-shell spectacles approached.

"Ruth," said Harry Folsom, "meet Judd Gray." The newcomer sat down next to Ruth and, once Folsom and Kaufman were talking to one another, he was soon deep in conversation with her.

It was an attraction of opposites from the start. Ruth, effervescent and strong, liked to dominate men. The 31-year-old Judd was shy, with a weak personality. He longed for excitement, but lacked the courage to pursue it. Within minutes the couple were so engrossed in conversation that they barely noticed when Folsom and Kaufman laughingly made their excuses and left them alone at the table.

Ruth ordered more drinks and the words flowed freely, as each learnt about the other's life. She told Judd that she was married with a daughter and lived in Queens. There was just the barest hint of marital trouble, as she mentioned that her husband Albert was away on holiday.

Judd, too, admitted that he was married and had a daughter and lived in East Orange, New Jersey. He said that his wife Isabel was a virtuous and respectable woman who apparently had no desire to enjoy life ... and that consequently the marriage had become a sham.

"And what sort of job do you have?" asked Ruth, whose interest in men's earning power had never waned.

"I'm a travelling salesman in ladies' underwear," said Judd.

"Don't you find it uncomfortable?" said Ruth, rocking with laughter. Then, as her giggles subsided, she continued: "I'm sorry. I know it's a comedian's joke, but I've never actually heard anyone say it before."

Judd shrugged resignedly. "It's all right," he said, "I hear that crack at least once a day. I guess it goes with the job." He paused. "I also sell corsets. Maybe one day I'll sell you one. Or better still, maybe I'll give you one. I have the feeling we're going to be friends."

They talked right through into the late afternoon; and by the time they parted, each knew they'd found what they'd been looking for.

Judd had been given the chance to escape from what had become a boring existence ... the chance to engage in a passionate affair with a beautiful woman. For the shy salesman, it was the stuff of which dreams are made.

On July 14th, Ruth went away on holiday with Albert and her daughter Lorraine, and the days were filled with quarrels. After one particularly violent row she left Albert behind and went back to New York with the child.

On the evening of her return, August 4th, Judd phoned, inviting her to have dinner with Harry Folsom and himself at Henry's Restaurant. Ruth left Lorraine in her mother's care and went.

The wine was poured freely and Folsom several times suggested that Judd should give Ruth a corset from his company's stock. This was heavy-handed humour; a saleman's joke. Intimate garments such as corsets were never really given freely. The donor would always expect to receive some equally intimate token of gratitude from the lady.

Folsom eventually left them alone, after making one final quip about the corset, accompanied by a lewd wink.

Judd refilled Ruth's glass. "I really would like to give you a corset," he said. "It would give me pleasure to know that you were wearing my gift each day. It would help to put a seal on our friendship."

Ruth's eyes met his over the rim of her glass. "I would like that too," she said.

A few minutes later they left the restaurant and headed for the Bien Jolie Corset Company on Fifth Avenue. The building was in darkness. Judd opened the door with his key and together they went into the showroom.

He took her bust, waist and hip measurements with a tape and she noticed that his hands were shaking. Then, timidly, he asked: "Would you like me to help you fit it? I would like to be sure it's perfect."

Ruth smiled secretly to herself. "That would be kind," she said. "If you're sure it wouldn't be too much trouble."

"No trouble at all," he assured her hastily, and hurried off to the stock room to fetch a selection of all shapes and sizes.

The fitting of a corset is inevitably a fairly intimate affair. The woman concerned first needs to remove her dress, slip and existing corset … and is thus left wearing little more than a bra and panties.

Ruth took it a bit further than that. By the time Judd returned, his arms full of corsets, she had removed everything, including her stockings. She was standing there, totally nude.

Judd dropped the corsets and wrapped his arms around her. The fitting could wait. For other corset salesmen, if their stories were to be believed, this would have been quite a common occurrence. But for the shy Judd Gray this was something entirely new; a moment he had often dreamed about, but never expected to happen … particularly with a woman as beautiful as Ruth Snyder.

He started to take off his tie, but his hands were shaking so badly that he couldn't undo the knot. Ruth, laughing, undid it for him; and then, setting the pattern for their future relationship, she took command and undressed him.

Once more he wrapped his arms around her, but she pushed him away gently. "Just be patient a moment longer," she said.

She walked down the showroom, took some very expensive fur coats off their hangers and threw them on the floor to form a makeshift bed. It was to be their first love-nest of many.

In September they spent their first night together in the glamorous Waldorf-Astoria hotel where Judd normally stayed when he was on business trips. It was the start of a passionate affair that would continue for the next 18 months.

Ruth would tell Albert that she was staying with girl friends and, although such overnight absences became increasingly frequent, he never seemed to suspect anything. Sometimes when Ruth couldn't get away for the night, she would visit Judd at the hotel in the afternoons. She would even take Lorraine with her as camouflage, leaving her sitting in the lobby while she made love in Judd's room.

Throughout the affair, Ruth and Judd were in constant touch with one another by letter. Ruth would sign hers "Momie" or "Momsie" (Judd's nicknames for her). Sometimes he would sign his simply "Bud".

This was far more than a casual fling, for they had a genuine need of one another. Judd's wife, Isabel, was frigid and so their sex-life had virtually ceased to exist. By comparison, the ever-inventive Ruth came from another world. And Albert Snyder, too, had proved to be a cold and unemotional lover, quite incapable of satisfying the wild passions of his wife.

As their relationship developed, Ruth became increasingly dominant and Judd increasingly besotted. He even began visiting Ruth at her home where he met with the disapproval of her mother. Anxious to ensure that Albert shouldn't find out about the affair, Ruth begged Josephine not to mention Judd's visits; and Judd, ever obliging, supplied Josephine with corsets at a discount in the hope of winning her over.

From the very beginning, Ruth had hinted to her lover that her marriage was an unhappy one. Now, playing on Judd's weakness in a way that she knew would ensnare him, she made repeated references to Albert's cruelty, saying that he beat and humiliated her.

A constant source of irritation to Ruth was Albert's obsession with Jessie Guishard, his former fiancée who had died. Every time they argued Albert would invariably compare her, unfavourably, with Jessie. She talked of this and of how wonderful life would be if she and Judd were both free.

She hadn't as yet said in so many words that she wanted Albert to be killed; but murder was already in her mind by the autumn of 1925.

She had talked to Leroy Ashfield, an agent from the Prudential Life Insurance Company, about taking out a policy on her husband's life, and in November she tricked Albert into signing three policies ... far more than he intended, or needed. She paid the first premiums without his knowledge, and instructed the postman to deliver all envelopes bearing the Prudential's stamp to her personally.

The highest policy — for $45,000 — contained a "double indemnity" clause which doubled the payment if Albert should die in an accident or be killed in the course of a crime. Ruth now stood to gain $96,000 by her husband's death. During the next six months she worked on Judd, hinting that she wanted Albert out of the way permanently.

At one meeting in a hotel room in June 1926 she produced two bottles of rye whisky and a packet of whitish powders which she asked Judd to sample. Judd drank one of the bottles of whisky and swallowed one powder. He was unconscious for the next 15 hours.

Shortly afterwards, during one of their assignations at the Waldorf-Astoria, she told Judd, "I am going to do away with the governor."

Judd was horrified. "You ought to go and see a doctor," he said.

He was nevertheless curious, and asked her how she was planning to do it. "By gas," Ruth replied, "or maybe with the sleeping powders I gave you." She went on to admit that she had already tried the powders — in a prune whip — but to no effect.

This was not the only time she told Judd about her attempts to murder Albert. She admitted having made at least four bids. The first was in August 1925, when she gave him some drugged whisky while he was working on his car in the garage. She closed the garage doors while the engine was running, but miraculously he escaped.

Almost a year later, she left the gas on while Albert was asleep on the living-room couch. In January 1927 she tried to poison him with bichloride of mercury, given under the guise of bismuth as a treatment for hiccups, and then a week later she again tried to gas him while he slept.

In October 1926, Ruth and Judd went away together on a 10-day holiday ... 10 days of passion during which she constantly reminded him that, once free of their marriage ties, life could always be like this.

Judd, who had a dry sense of humour, smiled and said, "I wouldn't be selling too many corsets, if I spent my days between the sheets."

To which Ruth chillingly replied, "Once we have Albert's insurance money, you won't need to work ever again. We will be in paradise."

Now for the first time, she appealed directly to her lover for help in murdering Albert. When Judd commented, "You are foolish to entertain such ideas," she persisted, asking him whether he knew anything about knock-out drops. When he insisted that he knew nothing about such matters, she still persevered, saying, "Could you get me something of the sort?"

"Absolutely not," was the reply. But although Judd recoiled from the idea of committing murder, he was quite willing to let her talk about it.

Ruth continued to chisel away at his resistance. In December she told him that Albert had bought a gun and that her life was constantly in danger. She complained, too, of her husband's treatment of Lorraine, saying that he beat and slapped her constantly.

When Judd weakly offered his sympathy she suddenly asked him whether he knew how to fire a revolver. Even when he told her he didn't, she implored him to shoot Albert.

Judd refused, saying, "I've never shot a man in my life and I'm not going to start with murder."

Ruth shrugged sadly. "In that case," she said, "I'll have to do it alone without your help. But at least discuss it with me, give me some suggestions."

Judd shook his head firmly, "No, I'm not getting involved in this. There has to be another way. Why don't we just move away and live together?"

But for Ruth it could never be that simple. Although she had come to enjoy her love sessions with Judd, she craved money even more. Now she wanted both.

She began to use all her wiles to persuade Judd to change his mind. She never said so in as many words, but there was always the implied threat that unless he helped her, sex between them could become a thing of the past. And for Judd, who had been transported into a world he'd hitherto only dreamed of, this would have been sheer tragedy.

By February 1927 his resistance had crumbled. As they spent a night at the Waldorf-Astoria, Ruth put forward a plan to render Albert senseless with chloroform and then to club him to death. She begged Judd to help her, omitting to say at this stage that he was to do the killing.

Intoxicated by passion, Judd found himself agreeing. "She got me in such a whirl that I didn't know where I was," he later explained.

At the beginning of March, having agreed to buy the various implements of murder, Judd went to Ruth's home for lunch to discuss the plan in detail. By now she had decided on chloroform followed by blows from some heavy instrument such as a hammer. "That way," she said, "he'll feel no pain."

Judd favoured a sash weight, while at the same time still refusing to have anything to do with the actual murder. Two days later while passing through Kingston, New York, he bought a bottle of chloroform in a chemist's shop. He then walked a few doors down the same street to a hardware store where he bought a sash weight about a foot long.

When they next met at Henry's he handed a parcel containing the sash weight and the chloroform to Ruth, who was with her daughter Lorraine. Undeterred by her presence, they discussed the murder of Albert by scribbling notes and passing them across the table.

Two days later, Ruth told Judd that she had practised with the sash weight and discovered that she wasn't strong enough to swing it effectively. He would have to help her.

In a strange statement of acquiescence, Judd said, "I can't do it alone. If I must do it, you'll have to help *me*." The tables had now been turned. It was he who would be the active participant in the crime, and Ruth the accomplice.

It was finally arranged that Judd would go to the Snyder home on March 7th to commit the murder. On that day, Ruth's mother would be away, as she often was, on a private nursing job. As soon as Albert had been drugged, Ruth would light a lamp in her mother's room to indicate that the coast was clear.

On the appointed day Judd reached the house at 9 p.m. He had needed to drink a quarter of rye whisky to pluck up the courage to come. And for two and a half hours he walked up and down the street, waiting for the signal light to show in the window. Finally, Ruth came out of the house to explain that Albert was still awake ... sleepy, but still conscious. At this, Judd lost his nerve. He promptly returned to New York City. Next morning took the train to Buffalo, where he had an appointment.

While he was away, Ruth sent him no fewer than nine letters and a telegram, all begging him to return to the house on March 19th, and to bring with him some rope. She, Albert and Lorraine would be out at a party, and her mother would be away. Ruth would leave the side door unlatched, so that he could enter the house, hide in her mother's room and await their return from the party.

On Friday, March 18th, Judd arrived in Syracuse, New York State, and booked into the Hotel Onondaga. While there he encountered an old friend, Haddon Gray, who shared Judd's surname but was no relation. In what seemed to Judd to be a flash of inspiration, he decided to use his unsuspecting friend as an alibi for the night of the murder.

Talking "man to man," he asked Haddon to disarrange

the bedclothes in his room and to hang a "Do Not Disturb" sign outside the door. He explained that he was going to spend the night with a girl and wanted to allay any suspicions his wife might have.

Having thus arranged his alibi (and in the process, established the fact that the crime was premeditated) Judd set off by train for New York City.

He arrived at Grand Central Station at 10.20 p.m. and bought a return ticket to Syracuse on the morning train. He then walked through the rain towards his destination, reaching Queens just after midnight, and continuing to the Snyder home, stopping occasionally to drink from a flask of whisky.

When he reached the house, he found the side door unlocked as Ruth had promised, and let himself in. On the kitchen table there was a packet of cigarettes ... the prearranged signal giving the "all clear". But due to the effects of the whisky, Judd had forgotten its meaning, and he waited for a quarter of an hour before going up as planned to the room of Ruth's mother, just behind the Snyders' bedroom.

Keeping his buckskin gloves on, he took off his hat and coat and placed them in the wardrobe. He then felt under the pillow where Ruth had said she'd leave the sash weight, a bottle of whisky and a pair of pliers to cut the telephone wires. Everything was there as planned.

Judd drank freely from the bottle of whisky, took off his jacket and put it on the bed; then he sat down on the floor, his head spinning from the drink he'd taken. Some 15 minutes later he opened his briefcase and laid out the contents on the bed. He had brought two strands of picture wire, a small bottle of chloroform, some cotton rags, a piece of cheesecloth, a handkerchief and, as an afterthought, an Italian newspaper he had found on the train.

Shortly before eight, the Snyders had left for a party given by some friends, Mr. and Mrs. Milton Fidgeon, who lived on Hollis Court Boulevard — just a few minutes' drive away. Drinking was already in progress when they arrived but Ruth — claiming to feel unwell — didn't drink at all … passing all her drinks to her husband. Unused to alcohol, Albert was fairly intoxicated by the time they gathered up their daughter and left the party.

It was now two o'clock in the morning. Restless from the whisky he'd consumed, Judd had started to walk downstairs when he heard the Snyders' car pulling up outside the house. He quickly retraced his steps and had a few more drinks to calm himself.

He heard footsteps on the stairs and the voices of Lorraine and Ruth. Shortly afterwards, Ruth slipped into his darkened room, whispering, "Are you there, dear?" When Judd replied, she said, "Wait quietly and I'll be back shortly."

Ruth entered her room, put on a nightdress, and then went into Lorraine's room. Albert, having put the car away, stomped heavily up the stairs to his bedroom. While he washed in the bathroom, Ruth rejoined Judd; and so it continued with her constantly slipping from the room her husband was in, to the room where Judd was waiting. If murder hadn't been on the menu, this would have had all the elements of a French farce.

Finally Albert went to bed and, his senses dulled by the effects of alcohol, immediately fell into a deep sleep. Ruth crept out of the bedroom and found Judd sitting on the floor, drinking even more whisky.

"You are going through with it tonight, aren't you?" she asked anxiously.

"I don't know whether I can or not," he replied. "I'll try."

They sat side by side, waiting for the right moment. Then at about 3 a.m. Ruth went into Albert's room, reappearing a few minutes later. "Now," she said, "now's the time."

Judd removed his buckskin gloves and put on rubber ones in their place. He took off his spectacles and gripped the sash weight, giving Ruth the chloroform, a coil of wire, the handkerchief and cotton rags.

Ruth took him by the hand and led him into the room

where her husband lay sleeping. Judd raised the sash weight with both hands. He aimed to smash Albert's skull with a single blow, but in his drunken state, he missed. The weight struck the bedhead, making a loud noise and inflicting only a glancing blow on Albert's head.

Now fully awake, Albert sat up and lashed out with his fists. Judd hit him again, and then climbed on top of him, trying to push the bedclothes over his face to muffle his cries. In the process he dropped the weight. Albert's hands reached around his attacker's throat, and Judd cried out to Ruth, "Momie, Momie, for God's sake, help me!"

Quick to respond, Ruth threw the chloroform bottle, handkerchief, wire and everything else on the pillow, and then picked up the sash weight and smashed it against her husband's head several times. Although Snyder was by now clearly dead, the panic-stricken Judd continued to straddle the body, squeezing Albert's throat with his right hand and covering his mouth with his left.

Realising finally that the struggle was over, Judd climbed off the bed. Ruth tied Albert's hands together with a towel and stuffed his mouth with cotton wool. Together, they tied his feet with a necktie, and then went into the bathroom.

As Judd washed his hands, Ruth noticed that his shirt and her nightdress were also soaked in blood. She told him to take off his shirt and gave him one of Albert's. She also changed her nightdress.

By now, Ruth and Judd were exhausted and in a state of shock. They returned to the living room and sat on the couch, speaking quietly. Ruth reminded Judd that they had agreed to ransack the house to make it look as if there had been a robbery.

They returned to Albert's bedroom. Terrified that her husband might still be alive, Ruth asked, "Is he dead? He's got to be dead. This has got to go through or I'm ruined."

She asked Judd to pull the picture wire tight around Albert's neck. He tried, but his shattered nerves could take no more. In need of another drink, he left the room. By the time he returned, the wire had been wound tightly around

Albert's neck.

Overcome with guilt, Judd shouted, "I'm through with you!" as he helped Ruth overturn the furniture and scatter the contents of various drawers around the floor. In their confusion the couple scattered everything as they imagined burglars might do. Ruth emptied her husband's wallet and stuffed the notes (about $70 in all) into Judd's pocket.

She asked him to take her jewellery, but Judd refused. "Hide it somewhere and they probably won't know anything about it," he said.

In an equally futile attempt to destroy the evidence, Ruth went down to the cellar, burned the bloodstained shirt and nightdress in the furnace, and hid the sash weight.

She noticed that her pillow case was flecked with blood and changed it, throwing the soiled one into her dirty-clothes basket. She gave Judd a bottle of whisky, saying he might need it on the train, and finally asked him to knock her unconscious, so that it would look as though she had been the victim of a burglar's attack.

The gentle Judd couldn't bring himself to do this, but he tied her hands and feet with cheesecloth. Placing the Italian newspaper he had picked up on the train in a prominent position, he left her lying, tied and gagged, on her mother's bed.

"It may be two months, it may be a year, and it may be never, before you see me again," were his parting words as he staggered down the stairs and out into the rain.

Dawn was breaking as he left the scene. He returned to Syracuse that morning, making a series of further blunders that would wreck his alibi. Later that evening he dined with his friend, Haddon Gray, and told him that he had been at Ruth's house when two intruders had burst in and murdered her husband.

"After they'd gone," explained Judd, "I bent over Albert's body to see whether he was still alive, and got blood on my clothes."

Haddon believed him, and helped him to destroy his bloodstained coat.

Ruth, meanwhile, had stayed on the bed for several hours, waiting for the right moment to make a move. Just before 7.45 in the morning, she dragged herself to her daughter's room and knocked on the door.

Lorraine, having gone to bed late the night before, was tired and not easy to wake. But the tapping became louder and more persistent, and eventually she rolled out of bed and went to investigate.

She opened the door to discover Ruth lying on the landing, hands and feet still bound, but only partially gagged. She was moaning, pleading with her daughter to get help. Terrified, Lorraine didn't even stop to untie her, but ran across the road to the home of the Mulhausers, friends of her parents who lived opposite. She returned to the house a few minutes later with Louis Mulhauser and his wife Harriet.

Louis picked Ruth up with some difficulty — she was a statuesque lady — and carried her into Lorraine's room. He placed her on the bed and undid the ropes that bound her.

"Would you call the police, Louis?" she said. "But first look in the bedroom. See whether Albert's all right."

Louis went into the master bedroom and one quick glance was enough to tell him that Albert was far from all right. He lay on the bed, the covers piled high on top of him. His head was buried deep in the pillow and the nape of his neck was exposed ... a strand of picture wire embedded in the flesh, a metallic noose. The wire had been doubled and a metal pencil had been inserted into the loop to serve as a tightening key. There were deep wounds in his scalp. Louis shuddered, left the room and picked up the hall telephone.

Although the Mulhausers were upset by the tragedy, they were hardly surprised. Just a week earlier, Louis had spotted a sinister-looking stranger prowling round the neighbourhood and peering into Ruth's kitchen window.

He had told Ruth about this, believing that the man might well have been a burglar gauging his chances of a break-in. Louis's fears now seemed to have been realised: the prowler had broken into the house to commit a robbery, been discovered by Albert and had then killed in panic.

The first policemen on the scene were inclined to agree. For the moment it seemed to be the most logical explanation. But when the big guns of the force arrived, they were not so readily convinced.

Police Commissioner George V. McLaughlin began to question Ruth in the presence of several other officers. She explained that the family had returned home from a party at two o'clock, and then continued: "While my husband was putting the car away, I helped my daughter get ready for bed and then went to bed myself. Soon afterwards I heard footsteps in the hall. I was worried that Lorraine might be feeling sick from something she'd eaten at the party, so I went out into the corridor. As I passed the room normally occupied by my mother, two strangers appeared in the doorway, grabbed me and threw me on the bed. I felt a blow on my head and must have fainted away. I don't know what else happened until daylight when I woke in the hall."

The only description she was able to give of her assailants was that they were dark and foreign-looking, and had moustaches.

McLaughlin asked her what language they spoke and she replied, "It appeared to me like Italian," drawing attention as she said this to the Italian newspaper found in her mother's room.

The police were already sceptical about Ruth's story, and no one more so than Doctor Neail, the police surgeon. After he'd examined Ruth, he talked to James J. Conroy, the Assistant District Attorney for Queens County.

"What do you think of her story?" asked Conroy.

"Not much," replied the doctor. "If she really had received a blow heavy enough to have knocked her unconscious for several hours, there would have been something to show for it. There isn't even a bruise. Oh, there's no question about it. She's fabricating."

"Does she suspect you believe she's lying?" asked Conroy.

The doctor shrugged. "She knows it, and she knows I know she's lying. I told her flatly that her story of assault sounded ridiculous. Take my word for it ... that woman knows who did this job."

In fact, few murders can ever have been more bungled than this one. Ruth's story of a mystery intruder never really had a chance. Here are just some of the reasons why the police never took it seriously:

*There were no signs of a forced entry.

*The sash weight stained with dried blood was found in the basement.

*A professional burglar would have avoided murder at all costs.

*Ruth had been tied too loosely for this to have been the work of professionals.

*The bloodstained pillow case had been discovered in the dirty-clothes basket.

*The jewels which Ruth claimed to have been stolen were found hidden under her mattress.

*Although the house appeared to have been ransacked nothing seemed to have been taken.

*Despite Ruth's claim that she had been attacked, there were no signs of injury.

And possibly the most damaging feature of all had been her failure to call upon Albert for help. Why send Lorraine to neighbours when her husband was just a few yards away? There appeared to be only one possible solution to such a riddle. She knew he was already dead.

She was driven to Queens police station for further questioning in the custody of Detective James Smith, a handsome and shrewd officer. Her attitude on the journey alternated from friendly flirtation to indignation at being taken from her home. Almost immediately she was calling the detective by his first name.

"Jimmy," she said, "why must I go to the police station? I've told an honest story. Doesn't it sound convincing?"

Smith told her that it didn't, and he listed the reasons why. Ruth listened thoughtfully. Then she said, "I can't help it if the burglars hid my jewels. I really thought they'd stolen them. They must have hid them just to cause me trouble."

When Smith told her that she was now sounding even less convincing, she became indignant, speaking of her rights as a citizen. Smith noted that she still hadn't enquired about the fate of her husband.

At the police station, she relapsed into stony silence, refusing to elaborate on any of her previous answers. At four o'clock in the afternoon, she was officially told that her husband was dead. She uttered a sharp cry and screwed up her face. Smith observed that her eyes remained quite dry.

At 10.30 that evening the detective sat alone with Ruth in an interrogation room. She had become friendly again. "Tell me, Jimmy," she said suddenly, "how do you think I'm doing?"

"Badly," said Smith. "Why don't you tell us the truth? The whole department, from the commissioner down, is working on this case. We'll solve it sooner or later."

"What do you think they'll give me if I talk? A couple of years?"

Smith considered this a low estimate, but he felt that it might not be politic to say so. He asked, "Was it premeditated?"

Ruth nodded slowly. "I didn't do it alone, though," she said. "A man helped me — a married man."

Smith knew that several letters had been found in the Snyder house. They were love letters addressed to "Momsie", presumably Ruth. They had been signed by Judd Gray, and the detective now mentioned the name.

"Was that the man?" he asked. "Was that the man who helped you?"

Ruth nodded again. Smith said, "I think you should tell the commissioner about it."

"I'll be glad to," said the unpredictable Ruth. "I like him a lot and I'm sorry that I told all those lies." She took a handkerchief from her purse and began to cry. This time, she shed real tears. Ten minutes later, she began to dictate a 50-page confession before Commissioner McLaughlin.

This was her version of the murder:

"Judd walked into my husband's room. I stood in the hall. I saw him tie my husband's hands behind his back. I saw him use the chloroform. When he hit Al with the sash weight, I put my hands over my ears. I walked away from the door. A little later, Judd came out of the bedroom and said, 'I reckon that's it.'

"We hid the jewels. Judd wanted to take them with him, but I wouldn't trust him. Then he went away. I tied myself up and sent little Lorraine out to get help."

She said that Judd was currently booked into the Hotel Onondaga in Syracuse, and if the police wanted proof of her affair with him, her honeymoon bag was at present in the Waldorf-Astoria.

"Your what?" asked the commissioner.

"We called it our honeymoon bag," Ruth explained. "We always used it to register at hotels together. It's got a lot of Judd's love letters in it. I want you to pick it up in case he denies everything and tries to put all the blame on me."

The police were only too willing to retrieve the honeymoon bag. They also put a call through to Chief of Police Cadin in Syracuse, asking him to arrest Judd Gray. An hour later Syracuse returned the call.

"We've got Gray all right," said the chief. "But he's got a cast iron alibi. He can prove that he was in his hotel at 6.30 on Saturday night. The last train running from here to New York leaves a full hour earlier. He couldn't have been in Queens Village at the estimated time of the murder."

On the face of things, it appeared that Gray was telling the truth. He had registered at the hotel on Friday. On Saturday afternoon he had written several letters. Some of them had been received in Syracuse on Monday morning. They were all postmarked Saturday, 6 p.m. Moreover the hotel telephone operator confirmed that Gray had made several calls from his room on Saturday night. The latest had been recorded some time after 10 o'clock.

The Chief of Detectives for Queens, Inspector Gallagher,

was nevertheless still confident enough of his case to bring Judd back on the train to New York.

During the trip, Gray talked freely. He admitted the relationship between Ruth and himself. He said he loved her very much, but had never discussed with her the murder of her husband.

"What good would it have done me?" he asked. "We couldn't have married, even with Albert out of the way. I have a wife. Besides, I don't make a great deal of money. I couldn't possibly have supported Ruth and my own family. It's a ridiculous story. Anyway, I have an alibi."

"Have you?" said Gallagher quietly. He put a hand in his pocket and withdrew a small oblong of cardboard.

Judd glanced at it and paled. "What's that?" he asked.

"A ticket stub," replied Gallagher. "For the 5.30 train, Saturday evening, Syracuse to New York. We found it in your wastepaper basket."

Unfortunately for Judd, a chambermaid hadn't bothered to empty the basket on Sunday, and the police had found the stub.

"You faked those letters," said Gallagher. "You faked those phone calls, probably with the aid of a confederate. He shouldn't be too difficult to find. Now do you have anything to say?"

Judd had a great deal to say. He said it all before the train arrived at New York's Grand Central Terminal.

The difference between his story and that of Ruth wasn't great. The prime point of departure was that Judd insisted the murder had been all her idea.

"She hounded me into killing her husband," he said. "She drove me crazy. Finally we set the date for that Saturday night. I arrived in Queens Village at around midnight. I let myself in and hid in the guest room."

He claimed that Ruth had committed the murder over his protests. She had, he swore, administered the chloroform, used the picture wire and belaboured Snyder over the head with the sash weight. She hadn't used the gun, for fear of arousing the child.

"When she told me he was dead," said Judd, "I took a taxi to New York and caught the 8.45 train to Syracuse."

"What about this fake alibi?" asked Gallagher.

"It was done by a friend of mine," admitted Judd. "I asked him to stay in the room, make the phone calls, and post the letters. He thought it was only because I was trying to alibi a love affair to my wife."

The trial of Ruth Snyder and Judd Gray was set to begin on April 18th, 1927. The district attorney had two confessions which dovetailed neatly ... save for one detail. Each of the lovers branded the other as the motivating force to the murder of Albert Snyder.

The trial proved to be a sensation which dominated the world's headlines for weeks. The "Ruth versus Judd" debate raged across America. Ruth was generally perceived as the guilty party, a cold *femme fatale* who had instigated and planned her husband's death, bending Judd to her will for the actual enactment of the crime.

Her demeanour in court tended to support that view, as she answered questions coldly, with little apparent regret for what had happened ... a stance that earned her variously the titles of the Iron Lady, the Granite Woman, and the Iron Widow.

Judd was dubbed the Putty Man, the suggestion being that he was putty in the hands of this beautiful but dominating mistress. There was much sympathy for him, and some admiration as he admitted his guilt in court and gave evidence that was accurate and consistent.

The courtroom was packed each day, and at times the trial resembled a three-ring circus. On one occasion when Ruth broke down and wept, her tears brought jeers and laughter from the spectators. But she was undeniably the star of the show, and her personal magnetism remained powerful. During the trial she received more than 160 proposals of marriage; and the adjectives most frequently used to describe her were "voluptuous" and "statuesque".

The verdict was never really in doubt. The jury were out for an hour and 47 minutes before they returned to announce that they had found both Snyder and Gray guilty.

There was no recommendation for mercy, so the death sentence was mandatory. Judge Townsend Scudder sentenced them both to die in the electric chair, setting the date of execution for January 12th, 1928.

Ruth's chief counsel, Dana Wallace, began his fight for a new trial. It was a battle which was virtually lost before it began. There were no technical grounds for reversal, and there was no new evidence. Nevertheless, Wallace worked hard, hoping at least for a commutation of the sentence to life imprisonment.

But if the lawyer had little hope, Ruth had a great deal. She simply didn't believe that she would be executed. During the first few months of her imprisonment, she constantly asked her guards for news. She paced her cell restlessly, awaiting word from Wallace that there would be a new trial. When that word hadn't come by late September 1927, she became temporarily depressed.

Then one day, she asked to see Father Murphy, chaplain of the Queens County jail where she had first been imprisoned. When the priest arrived, Ruth told him that she wished to become a Catholic; and in embracing that faith, she appeared to gain a remarkable degree of fortitude.

The nation had already judged Ruth from a distance and found her to be ruthless and cold-hearted, but amongst those who really knew her, there was apparently no one with a bad word to say against her. The neighbours liked her, describing her as a good mother and a good cook. She had been immensely popular in her circle of friends, and the guards at Sing Sing came to like her too.

In particular she formed a close and remarkable friendship with the assistant matron of the prison, Lillian Hickey, who recalled: "I grew quite fond of her. She was never querulous, never inclined to argue, never impatient or restless. She would describe her crime at length, but never admit her guilt; and following her cues, I relieved her by pretending to believe in her innocence. She had delightful little mannerisms and bursts of generosity and was, on the whole, one of the most amiable and attractive young women I have ever known."

On another occasion, the matron would say, "Never ... from the moment Ruth Snyder entered the death house to the last, still moment when the lethal switch was thrown ... did she exhibit the slightest fear of her certain and ignominious death."

But can this be true? Other reports tell of Ruth being fearful to the point of hysteria. However, this is part of Mrs. Hickey's published account:

"Very often Ruth would sing in that sweet, rich voice of hers and I often thought that she was singing to Judd, for her clear notes would have carried easily to his cell. The song which she usually sang was some popular theme to which, she told me, she and her lover often had danced in the days before the murder.

"Of Judd, she once told me 'The happiest days of my life were those I spent with him.'

"Christmas of 1927 approached. Ruth had by now adopted the fatalistic attitude of the condemned. 'Well,' she would say to me, shrugging her pretty shoulders, 'I've got to die some time. Why shouldn't I die now?'

"When I was working on the night shift, I would report for duty at 10.30 p.m. Ruth, who slept well, usually would be asleep in her cell and she would still be sleeping when I left in the morning. Thus, for several days, we had no opportunity to talk. On one of those nights when I arrived at the prison, I found she had left a note for me. It read:

"My dear Mrs. Hickey: Ma! Where in heck have you been? I've tried to keep awake to say 'Howdy' but somehow I fall by the wayside and nap. Would you please call me some night and say 'Hello'?

"January 12th, 1928, the day set for the electrocution of Ruth Snyder and Judd Gray, arrived. When I got to the prison Ruth was eating her breakfast. With her invariable neatness she had taken her bowl of cereal, her plate of toast and her tin cup of coffee off the serving tray and placed each on the little wooden table from which she ate during those last days of her life.

"She greeted me cheerfully, for the possibility existed that word might be received that day from Governor Roosevelt at Albany, ordering a stay of execution. This possible word had not been denied by prison authorities, who wished to prevent last minute scenes, and even I could not say whether or not Ruth was to die that night. However I arrived at her cell with a depressing order. The order was to see that Ruth got a hot shower bath, a formula which usually precedes an electrocution at Sing Sing. I broke the news as gently as I could.

" 'Good morning, Ruthie,' I said. 'I think you'll have to take a hot bath.' "

" 'Oh why, Ma?' she asked. Her face clouded.

" 'I guess it's the doctor's orders,' I replied evasively.

"She began to cry quietly, without hysteria. All during her bath, she cried softly. Later that morning her mother and brother came and guards placed a mesh screen between Ruth and her visitors. Both objected to this customary procedure. 'I can't see why I can't kiss my mother goodbye. There's no harm in that.'

"I left the prison at 2.30 that afternoon with the instructions that if the execution took place that night I would be notified at my home to report back to work. At 6 o'clock I was called. The double electrocution had definitely been scheduled.

"When Ruth saw me she knew that her last hope was gone, that she was to die within a few hours. But she did not cry again. To spare her the pain she had not been told in advance, and officials had not asked her what she wanted for her last meal. Instead a chicken dinner with all the trimmings had been sent in to her and she ate heartily.

"When I greeted her with the customary, 'Hello, Ruthie', she was lying on her cot. She answered cheerfully, arose and came to the bars. 'I tell you what we'll do, Ma,' she said. 'We'll play cards.'

"Another matron and I joined her for a game of euchre. I am afraid neither the other matron nor myself concentrated on the last game, which Ruth won handily. We played until her attorneys arrived for a last visit.

"At about 10.30 p.m. we were instructed to remove Ruth from her cell to one adjoining the death chamber itself. As we took that last walk together, Ruth chatted casually. Approaching death failed utterly to move her. In the corridor we passed a guard whom Ruth had grown to know. She extended her right hand.

" 'Goodbye, Mr Phillips,' she said, 'and thank you.' Guard Phillips, a tall, almost lanky chap, closed one large hand over Ruth's. He patted the back of her hand with his other. 'Goodbye, Mrs Snyder.' He looked away from her as he said it.

"The door of the cell adjoining the death chamber was open. Without hesitation or nervousness, Ruth walked in. A few minutes later she was joined by her friend, Father McCaffrey.

"The State of New York was about to send this fair-haired woman to her death. It was an unpleasant, depressing business. The entire prison was a bit dazed by the horrible event that lay ahead. The other matron and I stepped into the cell as the priest came out. My cold hands trembled uncertainly as I pulled one of Ruth's stockings down to bare her leg for the deadly electrode of the chair. I couldn't bear to look into those large eyes of hers.

"Suddenly, impulsively, she reached down and gathered me in her strong arms. 'Don't cry, Ma,' she said softly, and kissed me farewell. My arms tightened around her, then I pulled myself away. I was closer, much closer at that moment, to a breakdown, than she."

Perhaps Lillian Hickey saw a braveness in Ruth that male colleagues either failed to notice or chose to ignore when selling exclusives to news-hungry reporters. Or, as assistant matron, she was duty bound to report an emotionless, pain free end for Ruth.

Certainly, newspaper headlines screamed that Ruth was already in a "death-like" stupor. Her hair gone grey; eyes sunken. She chattered madly, wept and prayed.

Another report of Ruth's last day recalls:

On the morning of January 12th, 1928, Ruth Snyder arose at 9.30 in the morning. She dressed and ate breakfast with good appetite. Her spirits were high, almost buoyant. No condemned prisoner, a noted penologist had observed, ever believes he is going to die until the final moment of his life. Ruth Snyder's behaviour on this last day of her life was characteristic in that respect.

She knew that there was an open and direct telephone line from the office of Warden Lewis Lawes to Governor Roosevelt. At 11.20 a.m. a wild rumour spread through the prison that the governor had, indeed, granted a stay of execution. A guard repeated the rumour to Ruth Snyder. She became wildly elated. She fell to her knees and incoherently thanked Heaven for her life.

At 1 o'clock she was told that the report of the stay was untrue. This she flatly refused to believe. She denounced the guard who gave her the news as cruel and heartless. He was guilty of torturing a helpless woman, she cried.

When 5 o'clock came she was calm. She spoke to a guard. "You see," she said, "that wasn't a rumour after all. I've been reprieved. At least, I have a stay of execution."

The guard, who knew better, asked upon what this opinion was based.

"Because," Ruth Snyder said triumphantly, "it's almost supper time and the warden hasn't been here to ask me what I want to eat. If I were to be executed I'd have my choice of a menu."

This was partly true and the guard knew it. The warden had not asked Ruth Snyder what she wished for her last meal. There was a reason for it. After consulting with Father Murphy and the prison doctor, the warden had decided not to ask her to select her menu. This would kill all her hope and, in the physician's opinion, probably promote hysteria.

On the other hand, Judd Gray, whose behaviour was almost phlegmatic, ate a hearty meal of broiled chicken, mashed potatoes, celery, olives and ice cream. After this repast, he puffed on an expensive cigar. At 7.30 p.m., he was moved into the pre-execution chamber.

An hour later, the warden, accompanied by his principal keeper and Father Murphy, arrived at Ruth Snyder's cell. She greeted them with a flashing smile. "My reprieve," she said. "You've come to tell me about the reprieve."

They had not. They had come to move her to the pre-execution cell, Father Murphy gravely informed her.

She stared incredulously at the priest and the warden. She burst into a sudden fit of sobbing. "No!" she cried. "No! No! I'm too young to die. You can't kill me. And what about my baby? Who's going to look after my baby?"

It was rather late to think of little Lorraine's future, but no one was tactless enough to mention it. Still sobbing, Ruth was escorted from her cell to another, only 30 feet removed from the chamber where her lover, Judd Gray, waited calmly for his death.

At 9 o'clock, Ruth's attorney, Dana Wallace, came to her cell. Gravely, he told her that there was no more hope. This was the end. There was no chance at all.

She wept uncontrollably. "It's terrible," she moaned. "It's terrible. Are you sure there's no hope at all?"

Wallace told her that the telephone line to Albany remained open. If the governor changed his mind, the warden would be immediately apprised.

Ruth Snyder asked Wallace for a pencil and a piece of paper. In a trembling hand she wrote her last message to the world:

"I am very, very sorry I have sinned and I am paying dearly for it. I can only hope that my life — that I am giving up now — will serve as a lesson to the world."

Then, for the first time in months, she mentioned the name of Judd Gray. "Judd and I sinned together," she said. "And I suppose we'll go together. God knows where."

Wallace left her cell at 10 o'clock. She still wept. Father Murphy and the prison chaplain, Father McCaffrey, came in to comfort her. What she may have said to the priest in her final hour is, of course, not a matter of record.

When double executions are scheduled at Sing Sing, it

is the policy of the warden to bring the prisoner most likely to hysteria first to the death chamber. In this case it was decided that Ruth Snyder was far from being as stoical as Judd Gray. Hence her execution was scheduled before that of Gray. The reason was not, as an irreverent newspaper man put it, "Ladies first."

At 10.45, a crowd had gathered outside the prison. The state executioner Robert Elliott had passed anonymously among them and entered the prison gates. Now he was in the death chamber, carefully examining the lethal machinery.

The 28 legal witnesses were assembled by Warden Lawes, who cautioned them to remain utterly silent while in the chamber. He admonished the reporters not to take any photographs. At ten minutes before 11 p.m., the witnesses walked quietly, almost tiptoeing, across the crunchy gravel of the prison yard to the round death chamber and silently took their places facing the electric chair. The dazzling light almost blinded them as they entered the room.

Dana Wallace spoke softly to his neighbour, Assistant District Attorney James Conroy. "Ruth's going to hold up pretty well," he said. "She won't need any assistance."

Warden Lawes, an opponent of capital punishment for many years, stood at the side of the electric chair, facing the witnesses. "Do not talk," he said. "Be as quiet as possible. Do not leave the chamber until you are told that you may do so."

The silence was almost solid. The witnesses sat tense and waiting, staring at the door which opened at the rear of the chair, the last door any condemned person walks through in this life.

The door was flung suddenly open. Father Murphy, Father McCaffrey and the Protestant chaplain, the Reverend Mr. Arthur Peterson, entered the room, their heads bowed in prayer. They were followed by Ruth Snyder, accompanied by two matrons, Mrs. Mary Mann and Mrs. Lillian Hickey. Ruth no longer seemed statuesque. Her figure appeared shrunken. Her formerly bright golden hair was now dull. She was clad in an unpressed, brown cotton smock. On her feet were a pair of shapeless carpet slippers.

She sat in the lethal chair and, at that moment, she seemed more self-possessed than the two matrons, who wept as they retired from the chamber. Robert Elliott, the executioner, emerged from the smaller chamber at the right of the chair. His face was pale and he looked like a man about to perform a most distasteful duty. The attendants strapped her wrists to the chair arms, adjusted the leather helmet to her head.

Suddenly she shrieked:

"Oh, Father, forgive them, for they know not what they do!"

Father McCaffrey stood before her, a golden crucifix upraised. Ruth Snyder kept her startled eyes riveted on the form of the dying Christ.

Once more she cried out:

"Father, forgive *me*! Oh, Father, forgive *me*!"

Elliott had moved towards the woman, but he stepped back once more as she shrieked.

Now he took another step.

"Father, forgive them! Father, oh Father, forgive them!" and she broke into a fit of hysteria.

Carefully Elliott adjusted the head cap. He worked slowly, because his fingers trembled. His hair down over his eyes, he stooped to adjust the leg electrode underneath the rough grey skirt which the state gave Ruth as her death shroud.

As they made ready to drop the death mask over Ruth's face her lips moved in desperate prayer. The mask lowered, Elliott plunged one hand into his hip pocket, and strode towards the small cubicle where the switch is housed. The witnesses sat as if turned to stone.

Elliott was poised at the switch, watching Warden Lawes for the signal to send Ruth Snyder to her death. For some seconds they stood there, then Lawes raised his hand.

Elliott threw the switch.

The current crackled. The woman's legs strained back against the leg bar. Her arms wrenched stiff against their fastenings. Elliott watched her and worked the current up, then down.

The woman's chest rose and fell.

A photographer there in the death chamber had a hidden camera strapped to his leg. As Ruth's body lurched against the straps he took the famous photograph of Ruth dying.

For a minute or so the current ate all that was life from Ruth Snyder's body, then Warden Lawes raised his hand again, and Elliott threw off the switch. He stood aside. He seemed to be looking into space. His fists were clenched.

Prison physicians stepped forward and listened with the stethoscope. Her heart was still.

The straps were undone. The body fell forward limply onto the white enamelled steel stretcher held by two attendants. The stretcher and its burden, with gaping mouth and protruding tongue, were lifted to a carriage and wheeled into the adjoining room where the autopsies are held.

Five minutes later, Judd Gray was escorted through the door. He wore black trousers and a white shirt open at the throat. He peered round the room. Without his horn-rimmed glasses his eyes looked darker, larger.

He spoke not a word. He sat in the chair, staring directly ahead while the straps and helmet were adjusted. He was dead in less than 60 seconds. His body was moved to a stretcher. He was wheeled into the adjoining room. The doctors followed.

Now, the lovers were close together, lying side by side upon white tables. Less than a foot separated them. Now, there was no one, nothing, to keep them apart. The law was done with them; so was the world.

The witnesses filed quietly from the execution chamber. Their faces were sober. Most of these were reporters, lawyers and others who had often gazed upon the sordid side of life. Now they were obviously shaken. No one spoke as the newspapermen made their way to the telephones and filed their stories.

Ruth Snyder and her drab lover were dead. Old Testament justice had been done. Albert Snyder was avenged. His widow lay lifeless at the side of her dead lover. Man's law, relentless, slow-moving, and inexorable, had taken its course.

2
THE SAD GOODBYE

David Feldon

"Let's make believe it isn't going to happen. Let's pretend I'll still be here tomorrow, and the next day and the next." — Anna Antonio on her execution day.

You could tell that she must have been a very attractive girl, even though the months of strain while the forces of the law pondered her fate had taken their toll. Dark shadows had been etched under her large, luminous brown eyes, and her shapely figure had lost its roundness. She was only twenty-eight, but under the harsh lights of her cell she could have passed for forty. She sat on her bed, rosary in hand, and as her fingers moved nervously over the beads she mumbled her *aves* over and over again. Finally she finished praying, slipped the beads into the pocket of her kimono, and said, "If God wills that I must die, then it is God's will."

Now a shadow of her former attractive self, she stood up and ran a hand through her stringy black hair. Her long, wavy hair had once been her great pride; many an hour had she spent before the mirror in the privacy of her bedroom, brushing the tresses vigorously, pinning them up to form an elaborate frame for her round, pretty, dimpled face. Now her hair felt coarse under her fingers. She shuddered when she touched the round bald patch at the rear of her skull.

Within 30 minutes the gaunt woman would exchange the kimono for a black cotton dress. Within one hour, she was scheduled to die — in Sing Sing's electric chair. An Albany housewife, Mrs. Anna Antonio had been convicted with two men of the savage murder of her husband, Salvatore Antonio. The state contended that she had offered the men $800 to kill her husband for his insurance of $5,300.

Anna glanced once more, as she had a thousand times in the past few months, at the photograph of her three children — the two girls, aged nine and seven, and the little boy, who was only three years old. She had said goodbye to them, but she still dared to hope that she would live to see them again. Three times the governor of New York had granted her a reprieve. She kept telling herself that he would do it again, he must.

Two of those stays had come only minutes before the time set for her execution. The governor, she was certain, must have mercy in his heart. He would save her again. He must know that she had been tortured enough, that the agony of these months in jail was more than sufficient to pay for her sins.

Twice she had been moved from her cell in the Women's Wing to the pre-execution cell just outside the death chamber. Twice her head and her right leg had been shaved to provide a clean contact for the death-dealing electrodes. Twice she had said her last prayers with Father McCaffrey, the prison chaplain.

The date was August 12th, 1934. More than two years ago, on the eve of Easter Sunday, a car had screeched to a halt on a lonely section of the road between Hudson and Castleton, a few miles south of Albany. Three men were in the car. One was drunk. Salvatore Antonio, in fact, was very close to passing out. A railway worker, he had been "making the rounds" with his friends. By comparison, they were cold sober. Antonio felt sick, and he was glad they had stopped, so that he could get out of the car and get some air.

He stepped out and staggered to the side of the road, where he raised a hand to lean against a tree. The night was moonless and very dark, but a smell of spring was in the air. Antonio slumped against the tree and wished he hadn't drunk quite so much. One of his companions slipped out of the car and walked over to Antonio. The darkness obscured the gun in his hand. The third man emerged from the car and stood by the front bumper. The darkness concealed the hunting knife he held.

Suddenly, without warning, jets of flame stabbed through the night and five shots tore through the body of the drunken Antonio as he slumped to the ground. Astonishingly, he was still alive.

"Help me," he begged. "Help me. You are my friends. Why are you doing this to me?"

"I can't help you," his assailant said. "I must go through with this."

The other man sprang forward then and swung his knife hand in swift, downward strokes, stabbing Antonio fourteen times. The assassins then sped away in their car, leaving their victim by the road.

An hour later another car passed, and in the glare of the headlights two young law students from Albany saw Antonio. They quickly took him to Memorial Hospital, in Albany, but he died on the operating table.

The police probe into the murder moved rapidly into high gear. Anna, the victim's wife, tearfully disclosed her suspicions that her husband had been trafficking in narcotics and that he might also have been part of an arson ring.

"They took him for a ride," she told the police. "I'm sure of it. I warned him something like this might happen ... but he only laughed at me."

Anna was the perfect image of a grief-stricken widow at her husband's funeral, but detectives soon learned that there was more to this woman then met the eye. They learned that the couple frequently had furious quarrels, that Anna had complained that she was tired of her life with Salvatore Antonio, that she wanted no more children. She was, in short, sick of the drudgery of marriage to a labourer.

"I hope you die! I hope you die soon!" neighbours said they had heard her screaming at her husband.

"Me die?" they quoted his scornful reply. "I never die. I will live a long time and have many sons."

The police investigators contacted a score of Antonio's friends, but after intensive questioning all were eliminated as suspects except two — Samuel Feraci and Vincent Saetta. They earned the undivided attention of detectives when it was discovered that they had invited Antonio for a car ride on the evening of the savage murder.

Feraci and Saetta were taken into custody and questioned by relays of detectives, but they vehemently protested their innocence. They broke down only when they were confronted by the owner of an Albany hardware shop who identified the pair as the men who had bought a hunting knife from him a few days earlier.

But according to Feraci and Saetta, the murder plot had been engineered by Anna, the victim's wife. Feraci claimed that she talked him into it by promising to pay him $800 for killing her husband. Fearful that he could not pull it off alone, he had enlisted Saetta's aid, promising to pay him $200, which Saetta needed to buy a car. Feraci said he gave Saetta a down payment of $75, with the balance to be paid after Anna collected the $5,300 insurance.

On May 4th, nineteen days after the murder, Anna was arrested, but despite an overwhelming array of evidence against her, she vigorously denied everything. And she continued to deny all charges until detectives confronted her with a taxi driver who identified her as the woman he had driven to Feraci's house a few hours after the murder.

The surprise was too much for her. Quivering with rage, she screamed, "All right, all right! I'll tell you all about it!"

On the following April 15th, exactly one year after Salvatore Antonio had been murdered, a jury found Anna and her accomplices guilty of murder in the first degree. The jury had deliberated for six hours.

The jury had heard Saetta testify, "We took Antonio for a good ride towards Hudson. I brought a gun, Feraci a knife, to let him have it on the way back. Antonio had his hands in his hip pocket. I pulled my gun. I fired the shots."

And Feraci had said: "I hear bang, bang, bang! Then Saetta runs around the car and points to the knife. Antonio was lying in the road. He said to me, 'Sam, please, I never did anything to you.' I said I can't help it. I got to do it. So

I did the stabbing."

The three killers were taken to Sing Sing and the vigil of death began. Routine appeals were filed and the hand of the executioner was stayed for month after month. After her thirteenth month on Death Row, the state revealed that it had cost the taxpayers an extra $3,900 for three matrons to attend Anna round the clock. The final appeal was turned down shortly after this announcement and the date with death was set for the week of June 24th. It was customary at Sing Sing that executions were performed on Thursday, beginning at 11 p.m. If it followed this pattern, Anna and her accomplices would have their rendezvous with death on the evening of June 28th.

In many quarters, however, it was felt that Anna would never keep this date. The pressure of public opinion was mounting hourly in protest at the taking of a woman's life, particularly a woman who was the mother of three children. Only once before had New York State executed a woman — Ruth Snyder. Now editorial writers and civic leaders joined in demanding clemency for Anna Antonio.

But when the State Lunacy Commission declared on June 17th that she was sane, it seemed that the last legal escape route had been blocked. "My children, my poor children," Anna was quoted as saying in her cell in the death house when she was advised of this. "I'm only sorry for them."

The newspaper sob sisters had a field day with these piteous words and public opinion rose even higher. As a result, she won a clemency hearing before the governor at the gubernatorial mansion in Albany, on June 20th. Present with Anna and her attorney were the condemned woman's three children.

Anna's attorney, Daniel Prior, pleaded for mercy. "Must these little ones suffer so?" he asked, pointing to the little children. It was a difficult decision indeed for the governor. The children were innocent pawns, certainly, and their lives had been blighted by the actions of their mother. But she had killed deliberately. A jury had already agreed upon that after due deliberation, and the presiding judge had imposed the death sentence.

Six days passed without word from the governor, and Anna Antonio, the sands of her tragic life rapidly running out, had 48 hours to live. She sat on her bed, numbed by the enormity of the fate that awaited her and told her beads over and over.

One of her matrons stopped by the cell to look in on her. Anna paused in her prayers and looked up.

"Surely somebody will help me ... w-won't they?" she asked hopefully.

"I'll help you, Anna," the matron said, and Anna shrugged. The matron knew it wasn't the answer she wanted to hear, but it was not within her power to do more.

"Will they let me see the baby again?" Anna asked abruptly. She had seen her son for thirty minutes the day before. She had hugged him close, pressing his soft cheeks against her own. His uncle had brought him, and the little boy had pleaded to be allowed to stay with his mother. The uncle had promised him two ice-cream cones if he wouldn't cry.

On June 27th, the day before the execution was due to take place, the warden went to see the governor. The warden had often expressed his opposition to capital punishment. He told the governor that Anna was a very young woman, that she had married when she was only 16, and that according to reports her husband had frequently beaten her severely.

The governor replied that he had no choice under the law but to allow the sentence to stand.

In a talk with reporters the warden said that the governor had indicated that he did not feel it was fair to let two murder conspirators die and commute the sentence of the third, even though the third was a woman. It was feared that a precedent might be established if a woman found guilty of deliberate murder was granted a commutation of her sentence solely because she was a woman.

In the death house Anna told her attorney, "I know I'm

going to die. I don't mind now. There never was any real hope."

Gone now were the tears and the hysteria. Finally Anna was resigned to her fate. A caged canary in her cell began to sing. The bird had flown into the prison and a convict who caught it had asked that it be given to Anna. Before her lawyer left Anna wrote out her will, bequeathing her few meagre possessions to her children.

On the morning of June 28th Anna awoke from an all but sleepless night. She put on a pink cotton dress with a white collar, then picked at the food on her breakfast tray with no appetite.

"I'm discouraged, ill and heartbroken," she said to one of her matrons. "There is so much to live for, and I will not live. Only a few months ago I was young. Now, very soon I will die. What have I done?"

The matron did not have the heart to remind the doomed woman of her awful crime, of how she had plotted the death of her husband, the father of her own children.

The grey day dragged its way into night. By 6 p.m. all preparations for the triple execution had been completed. The executioner had arrived and taken up his post in the chamber where, before that night was over, he would earn $450—$150 for each of the condemned upon whom he would carry out the law's sentence. Up the hilly road from Ossining, small groups of people walked quietly towards the prison gates, where they gathered in clusters to maintain a death vigil.

At 9 p.m. Anna's brother emerged from the prison gates and was at once surrounded by reporters. He had stayed an hour beyond the last visiting deadline.

What did she have for her last dinner?

"Nothing, nothing at all," he said. "She didn't even give an order. She couldn't eat ... She is so brave. She prays, but she is not afraid to die. She made me kneel down with her and pray. She gave me the gold cross from around her neck and told me to give it to her boy. I told her I would do that."

The brother of the doomed woman walked away, shoulders bowed in grief. Curious bystanders watched his departing figure till it disappeared.

Anna was now in the pre-execution cell, one of eight square iron cages in a long corridor adjacent to the death chamber. Her partners in murder, Saetta and Feraci, occupied two of the other cells, but none of the trio could see one another. No words were exchanged among them.

Accompanied by a guard and two matrons, a barber entered Anna's cell and shaved a circle two to three inches in diameter on the top of her skull. It was on this bare spot that the electrode of the death helmet would make contact.

Throughout the ordeal, Anna sat unmoved, numbly staring straight ahead of her. "My children, my children," she muttered. "What will they do now? I hope they won't judge me too harshly for anything I have done. I hope the girls will marry nice men — and my son a nice girl — when they grow up. I hope they will be happy. I hope — I hope ..."

At 10 p.m., Father McCaffrey went into Anna's cell and they conversed in low tones.

At 10.10, Vincent Saetta told a guard that he had to see the warden at once, and ten minutes later the warden hurried into the death house.

At 11 p.m., Anna asked the chaplain, "Is this the time?" He continued his prayers, without answering.

At 11.05, the warden called the governor, and at 11.15, the official witnesses were informed that there would be a 30-minute delay. Several reporters demanded to see the warden, but the guard said that was impossible; the warden was busy.

At 11.25, the warden entered the room where the official witnesses were waiting impatiently. "I have only this much to say," the warden said in the hush which greeted his entrance. "I have been in communication with the governor."

"A reprieve?" several reporters chorused.

"I cannot say at this time," the warden answered. In another moment he had left the room.

At midnight, Anna Antonio had expected to be dead, but she wasn't even aware of the time. She seemed to be in a trance-like state, numbed, almost indifferent to what went on around her. The priest sat beside her in her cell and they prayed together, Anna mumbling the responses to a litany in a dull, quiet monotone, devoid of inflection.

At 1.14 a.m., the warden returned to the room of waiting witnesses and bedlam broke loose as everyone tried to question him at once. He stood in rigid silence, and when at last it became obvious to all that he had no intention of speaking until there was absolute quiet, they simmered down. Finally, when he had their attention, he said: "I am authorised to release this statement from the governor: 'I have directed the warden of Sing Sing prison to postpone the executions of Anna Antonio, Sam Feraci and Vincent Saetta for 24 hours to study and consider a long statement made by Saetta just before 11 p.m. tonight, the general substance of which has been repeated to me over the telephone by the warden.' "

Anna Antonio did not learn of the reprieve until 3.15 a.m. She had collapsed in a faint at 1 a.m.

Saetta had attempted to shoulder all responsibility for the crime in his eleventh-hour statement. He claimed that he had quarrelled with Antonio over money, and insisted that Anna had had no prior knowledge of the murder. "Mrs. Antonio is absolutely innocent of this crime," he declared.

Saetta said that his fight with Antonio had been the result of a debt of $75 owed to him by the latter. Not only had Antonio refused to pay him, Saetta said, but he became angry when Saetta confronted him and threatened him with a knife. Added to that, Saetta continued, he learned that Antonio had told mutual friends that he intended to take Saetta "for a ride." Saetta said that he then decided to beat Antonio to the punch, and that Feraci had helped him do so.

So Anna lived another day on borrowed time, passing dreamlike once again through the routine of a day that preceded that last walk on earth. Again she refused food;

again she seemed oblivious to all around her.

At 7.45 p.m., with little more than three hours left before the time set for the executions, Anna's attorney appealed to the governor for time to request a new trial. The district attorney who had prosecuted the case was hastily summoned, and after a conference which lasted about an hour, the governor announced: "In the interests of justice, another reprieve must be granted, this time for ten days. Attorney Prior will be given his opportunity to request a new trial before the trial judge, Earl H. Gallup."

The district attorney observed: "Saetta's statement is an absolute fabrication of lies. It does not square with anything brought out at the trial or during the investigations." And, at Sing Sing a clerk disclosed that when the trio were admitted to the prison over a year earlier, Saetta had said that he expected to get a commutation because a woman was involved. "We'll beat this case yet," the clerk quoted Saetta. "If not, I'll make a statement at the last minute."

When the matron informed Anna of the new reprieve, she exclaimed, "Thank God! I still live. I still have time to see my children again."

Judge Gallup denied the appeal for a new trial on July 5th, but Anna was granted a third reprieve in order that her attorney might have time to refer the ruling to the Court of Appeals.

Despite her previous despair, Anna now became a much happier woman. Suddenly she was imbued with confidence that her life would be spared. She began to take nourishment again, and take an interest in her personal appearance. Once more she began to brush her long, black hair.

The Court of Appeals, on July 16th, sustained the lower court's refusal of a new trial, but Anna's attorney was able to make yet another move on her behalf.

He went before Supreme Court Justice Bryon Brewster, in Albany, on August 2nd, and made still another request for a new trial, on the grounds that he had uncovered new evidence. But, on August 8th, just four days before the latest date scheduled for the execution, Justice Brewster denied the motion.

"I am painfully aware of the gravity of my decision," he said. "But I cannot find that the new evidence is ground for a new trial, or that it would have changed the rendered verdict."

Later that day a guard beckoned to the matron who accompanied Anna as she walked in the tiny yard outside the death house. The guard whispered a few words to the matron, and when they had returned to Anna's cell, the matron said, as gently as possible: "I'm afraid I have bad news for you, Anna. The judge has denied a new trial."

Anna stared at her in disbelief, a cold fist of horror clutching at her heart. She had been so confident. She turned to her bed and sank to the floor beside it. Her lips moved in prayer, her shoulders shook with sobs that racked her whole body.

Three times she had been reprieved — virtually in the shadow of the chair. Surely no other condemned person ever executed at Sing Sing suffered such mental torture. Towards the end, she told one of her matrons, "I've been through enough to kill a million people. I am almost dead now. I feel at times as though I am not breathing."

For several days she had eaten nothing, merely taking a few sips of coffee. During her confinement she had lost twenty pounds and now weighed less than six stone.

The night before her execution she was given sedatives in the hope that she would sleep. But she spent that long, last night sitting upright on her bed, staring blankly at the wall. Occasionally her eyes would droop and she would be on the point of drowsing; then she would come fully awake with a start and continue to stare at the wall.

The morning of August 12th dawned bright and clear. It was the kind of day on which it was good to be alive. Only for Anna this wasn't a good day at all. This was 'Black Thursday', the traditional day for executions in Sing Sing; and unless the governor could be persuaded to grant still another reprieve, she had just 15 hours left to live.

She knew that public sentiment was strong; and that

most people felt her life should be spared. Hadn't the state tortured her enough already, playing this cat-and-mouse game? Just how much suffering could a woman be expected to endure?

The governor, of course, had been made keenly aware of the height of public sentiment; but he was even more keenly aware of his responsibility as the chief executive. The facts brooked little argument. A person who knew the difference between right and wrong had cold-bloodedly planned a murder. A man's life had been taken. So far as the law was concerned, the fact that the killer was a woman was irrelevant.

On the governor's desk lay a new appeal for clemency, filed by Anna's attorney. The governor studied it intently …

At 8 a.m., a matron brought Anna a breakfast tray bearing hot cereal, rolls and coffee. Anna took a few sips of coffee, but left the food untouched. When asked whether there were any special things she would like for her last meal, she merely waved her hands helplessly … she didn't even want to talk about it.

But after a long silence she said listlessly, "It looks as if they've all turned me down. God alone can help me. I'm not thinking of myself so much. I'm thinking of what it will mean to the future of my children. Nobody can know how terrible it is to be here except someone who has gone through it."

At times during the course of her last day on earth, she aroused herself from her apathy and sobbed hysterically. Occasionally she would spring from her cot and utter a single, piercing scream. Once she said, "I don't think I'll be able to stand up at the end. They'll have to carry me."

At noon the governor, in response to reporters' questions, said, "I have taken no action."

Anna clenched her fists when she heard the news. "He knows everything there is to know," she said bitterly. "Why doesn't he say something?"

In the afternoon she was persuaded to come out of her cell for a while and sit in the corridor. There was a radio.

She listened to a humorous sketch and a musical programme. Suddenly the music was interrupted. A news commentator's voice broke in: "Latest flash from Albany! The governor has refused a further reprieve for Mrs. Antonio. She must die in the electric chair tonight."

A matron ran to the radio and switched it off. Anna stared around the corridor, her eyes wild. "They have all deserted me," she cried.

Shortly afterwards her brother, sister-in-law, nephew and a friend came to the prison and asked to see her, but she declined to receive them. "No," she said. "Just thank them. I want to be quiet."

Sadly, it was the seventh birthday of her daughter, Marie. She sent the child a dress she had made in her cell, and a box of candy. But it was decided that it would be better if only Frankie (at three, the youngest child) was brought to see her on this fateful day.

It wasn't often that the sound of a child's laughter was heard on Death Row; but it was that evening. Frankie was bouncing a ball in the corridor, and it got away from him.

"Here, Frankie," said Anna. "Here's another ball for you. It won't bounce, but it's a nice ball just the same."

She handed him an apple. He took it and shouted with glee. "Can't fool me. It's no ball, Mama. It's an apple!"

She took the small boy into her arms, caressed him, wept over him. "I'm going away," she said. "I'm going away for a long time."

Her last words to him were, "I hope you grow up to be a good man, Frankie."

Her brother took the boy away and returned alone at 7 p.m. He found her in quite a different mood.

"Let's make believe it isn't going to happen," she said. "Let's pretend I'll still be here tomorrow, and the next day and the next. Let's look forward to your visit with me the next time. There isn't going to be any end. Just try to remember that. No end at all. I shall be here the next time you call."

The man stared at his sister, the woman to whom he had

been virtually father and mother since their parents died 21 years earlier.

She seemed serene now, subdued, resigned. But her cheeks were sunken, her eyes — normally so luminous and bright — lacked sparkle. Her body was skin and bones, her hair in disarray.

"Don't say goodbye," she repeated. "Remember the good times."

"I'll see you tomorrow, my sister," he said, forcing a smile.

In the preparation for an execution, the most distressing detail is probably the visit from the prison barber. This serves as a grim reminder of what is soon to happen. The barber's chair is a plain affair made of old board just knocked together. But it does bear an unfortunate resemblance to that other, grimmer chair.

There have been instances when men were so irrational by the time that the barber came to trim them that they mistook the barber's chair for the electric chair, and the barber for the executioner. In the early days of electrocutions it was the practice to shave a spot on the top of the head; but this was later to be found unnecessary. Hair is a good conductor, so the barber merely needs to trim.

When he arrived at her cell, Anna turned to the matron by her side and said, "It's going to be, I guess." That was all.

After he'd gone she put on the dress in which she was going to die ... the dress she had made in her cell. It was a blue dress (about the same shade as the keepers' shirts) with blue trimmings. One of the matrons had freshly washed, starched and ironed it for her.

Just as one of her stockings was being slit, to make a place for the leg electrode, she said, "I'm not afraid to die. I have nothing on my conscience. I never killed anyone."

She continued to talk for several moments, rambling, almost incoherent. She said one of the co-defendants had told her he was going to kill her husband, and that she replied, "I don't care what you do."

As for killing him herself, she said that she could have done it easily, any time ... for "there were always plenty of guns and dope in the house to do it with."

That was as close as she ever came to confessing to the murder.

A few minutes later, she was kneeling and praying alongside Father McCaffrey. At 11 p.m. the guards came to the door of her cell.

"Are you ready, my child?" the priest enquired.

Anna nodded. She rose to her feet and stood for a moment, taking a long look around her cell. She studied the picture of her children, picked it up and kissed it.

The principal keeper led the way from the women's wing, on through the 'dance hall', the central corridor upon which were the condemned cells of the men.

It was a long 'Last Mile', but Anna walked it firmly. The priest remained by her side, giving responses to her prayers. Two matrons walked behind her ready to assist if she faltered; but they weren't needed. From somewhere she had found a new strength.

She walked past the cells of Saetta and Feraci, but didn't give them so much as a glance. She had walked one hundred paces before she reached the brown door of the death chamber.

The door opened upon a room flooded with bright light. From white faces, the eyes of the witnesses stared at her. She saw the chair, and just as the principal keeper motioned to her, she stepped forward quickly. In front of the chair she paused. She turned, backed two short paces and sat down.

The matrons stepped forward and fastened the strap around her chest. They held her thin white arms while other straps were tightened by the male guards. Even after the hood had been placed over her head, she continued to pray ... and so still was the room that her soft voice filled it.

The two matrons, with a guard between them, stood in front of the chair, not over four feet away, blocking the view of the witnesses. Only these three, two women and one man, actually saw her die.

An official gave the signal by dropping his arm. The executioner pulled the switch. The current coursed through Anna's body. The executioner manipulated his controls for a second, and then there was a third shock of electricity.

The prison doctor stepped forward, placed a stethoscope against Anna's chest, then stepped back. "I pronounce this woman dead," he said.

It was 11.17 p.m. on August 12th, 1934. During the next fifteen minutes, Feraci and Saetta followed Anna in death.

Just after her death, Governor Herbert H. Lehman issued the following statement:

"The case has received my most painstaking and careful consideration from the time the Court of Appeals affirmed the conviction of Mrs. Antonio and her co-defendants.

"The responsibility of carrying out the death penalty on a woman is so distressing that frankly I sought to find any fact which would justify my interference with the course of justice.

"I have studied the record with the greatest of care. I reprieved all three defendants so that the case of Anna Antonio could again be submitted and considered in the courts of the state.

"I have not found any circumstances which would, under my oath of office and the duty I owe to all of the people of the state, justify the commuting of her sentence.

"I am certain that in the history of the state there are very few instances where the case of any person tried for murder in the first degree has been given greater study and examination.

"In the case of Mrs. Antonio the trial jury found her guilty. The Court of Appeals unanimously affirmed that verdict. Motions for a new trial, on newly discovered evidence, were made in the County Court and in the Supreme Court. Both were denied. The Court of Appeals has also denied an appeal and a motion for a re-argument.

"After the most careful scrutiny of the record and of all of the other papers in the subsequent proceedings and from my very deliberate consideration of all aspects of these cases, I am convinced that each of the three defendants is guilty.

"Appeals have been made to me to grant executive clemency to Anna Antonio on account of her sex, but the law makes no distinction of sex in the punishment of crime; nor would my own conscience or the duty imposed upon me by my oath of office permit me to do so. Each of the defendants is guilty. The crime and manner of its execution are abhorrent. I have found no just and sound reason for the exercise of executive clemency.

"The administration of criminal law should be fair and just. I am satisfied that it has been in these cases. Likewise, the administration of justice must be definite and certain, so that society may be protected and respect and observance of the law maintained."

During the time that Mrs. Antonio was in the death house, the state spent a total of $4,650 upon her supervision and maintenance — more than was ever spent upon an inmate of the condemned cells at Sing Sing. One might suppose that it would be difficult to find women willing to take the jobs as matrons in the death house, but such was not the case. When Mrs. Antonio was first sentenced to death, numerous applications were received by the warden from substantial housewives in Ossining who wanted one of the three positions as matron. Although somewhat distressing, to say the least, the work is not tedious, and the pay is unusually good.

3
A HIT-WOMAN'S DREAM

John Read

"Oh, God, it hurts! If you're going to kill me, please hurry up!" — The dying words of victim Debra Thornton.

On the morning of June 13th, 1983, George Turner knocked on a door in an apartment complex in northwest Houston. Turner was at the residence of Jerry Lynn Dean to find out why his co-worker had not picked him up that Monday morning. Dean and Turner had been sharing rides each day since they began working for a Houston cable company.

"Jerry must have overslept, or is ill, or his car won't start," were some of the thoughts that ran through Turner's mind. When he didn't see Dean's car parked in front of the apartment he wondered if he had already gone to work.

However, since Turner was there, he went up to the door of Dean's apartment. He knocked, but received no answer. Automatically, his hand tried the door. To his surprise, it was unlocked.

Turner stuck his head in and called Dean's name. The utter silence gave no hint of the ugly, sickening sight he was to see once he entered the bedroom of the small apartment. The grisly scene caused Turner almost to lose his breakfast as he stumble from the room and ran to the nearest telephone to call the police and report the tragedy.

His call, logged at 7.30 a.m., brought Detectives Bill Owen and Chet Thomas speeding to the address. Both officers were more than familiar with gruesome sights in the crime-ridden city of Houston — the largest city in Texas and fourth largest in the United States. But when George Turner met officers at the door and pointed to the bedroom, they were quiet for a moment as they looked on one of the bloodiest scenes they had ever encountered.

The ceiling and walls were spattered with fresh, still wet, blood. The corpses lay on a blood-soaked bed. One of them had a long-handled axe-type weapon protruding from its chest.

A male, identified by Turner as Jerry Dean, lay on his back, completely naked. His upper torso bled from multiple gaping wounds. The other victim of the ruthless killing was a woman, whom Turner could not identify.

Still stuck in her bosom was the pickaxe, which police believed was the one used to hack at the two unfortunate victims. The three-foot handle of the implement pointed grotesquely to the ceiling. The woman wore only a blood-soaked T-shirt.

Looking round the room, the detectives saw signs of ransacking. Neither wallet nor purse belonging to the dead pair was found. Then Turner informed Detective Owen that Dean's 1974 blue El Camino was missing from the parking area.

Also missing were items he usually saw when he visited Jerry, including parts of an unassembled motorcycle that Dean was constructing in his apartment. The bike was something that Dean treasured, Turner said, adding that Dean had spent a fortune on parts.

Owen immediately called police headquarters and gave a description of the missing car. An all-points bulletin was radioed to patrolmen, asking them to be on the lookout for the vehicle.

The crime lab crew arrived and removed the axe from the chest of the female victim — carefully, so as not to smudge any fingerprints. Other tools of a similar nature lay on the floor beside the bed. Turner told the detectives that they used such tools in their work to loosen dirt and cut roots. The pickaxe was a mattock-like tool, with a sharp pick on one end and a hoe blade on the other.

Ruth Brown (above) before her marriage to Albert Snyder

Ruth's lover and accomplice in murder, Judd Gray

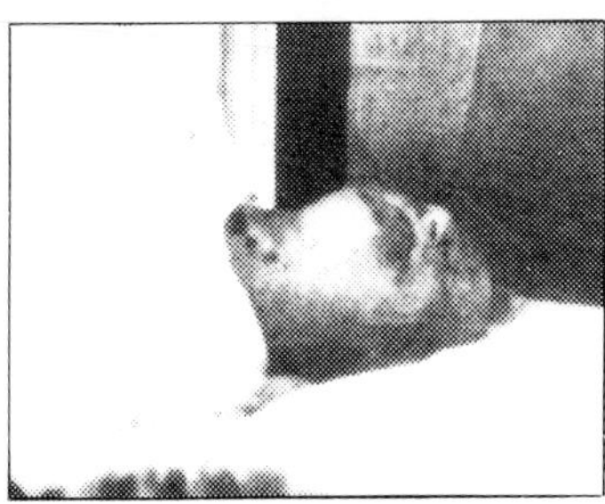

Albert Snyder had been brutally bludgeoned and strangled

The chilling view of Old Sparky that greeted condemned killers as they approached Sing Sing's death chamber

A camera strapped to a photographer's leg snapped this picture of Ruth Snyder's execution

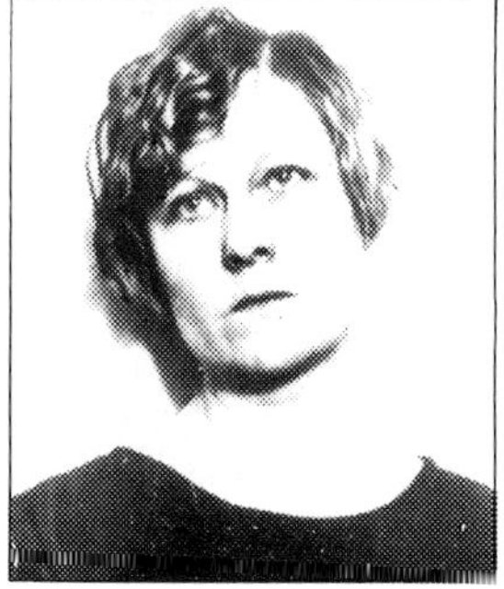

Left, Ruth Snyder shortly before execution. Above, matron Lillian Hickey who walked Ruth to the chair

"I've been through enough to kill a million people. I am almost dead now. I feel at times as though I am not breathing," Anna Antonio told a prison matron after two years on Death Row

Vincent Saetta (far left) and Samuel Feraci (left) followed Anna to Sing Sing's electric chair

Karla Tucker and the pickaxe (arrowed) she used on her helpless victim

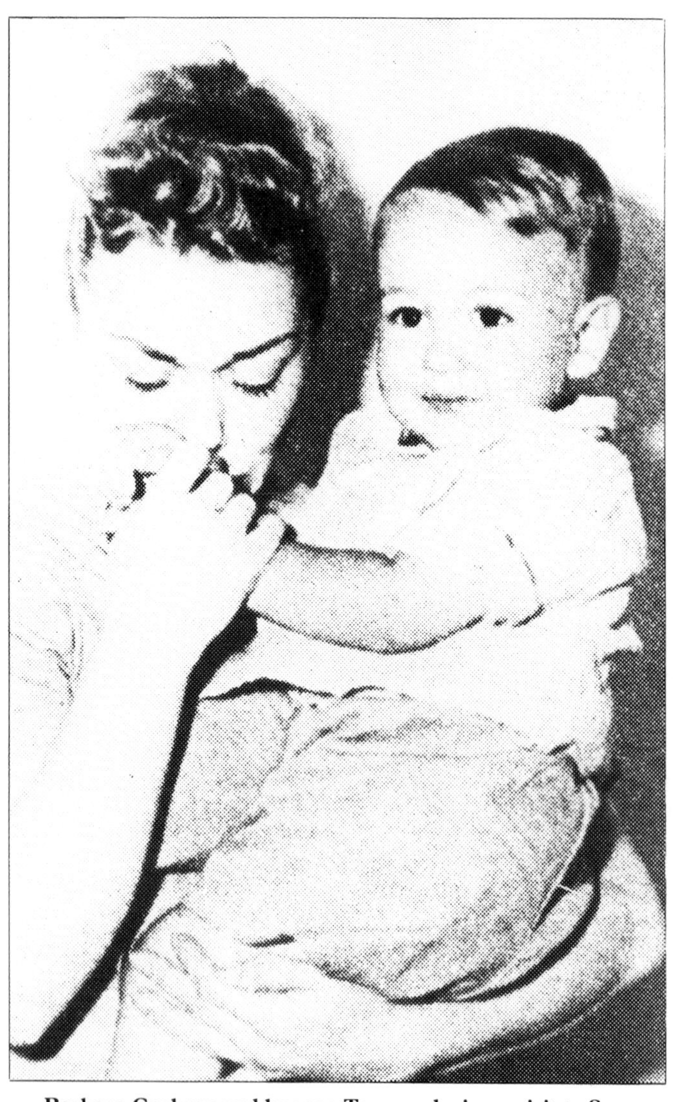

Barbara Graham and her son Tommy during a visit to San Quentin's Death Row. "I wish I could see him grow up, but I won't, so what's the use of wishing - of thinking"

Even when seated in the electric chair, Eva Coo (above) kept her poise. To the prison matrons who had escorted her there she called: "Goodbye, darlings!"

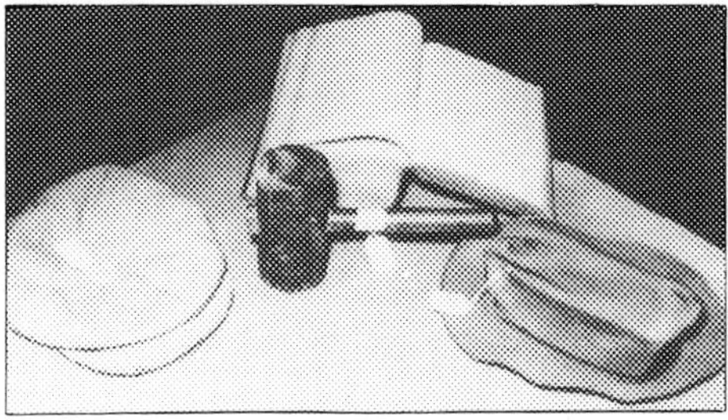

Stained mallet, Bible with a date changed, and an old felt hat were the exhibits at the trial

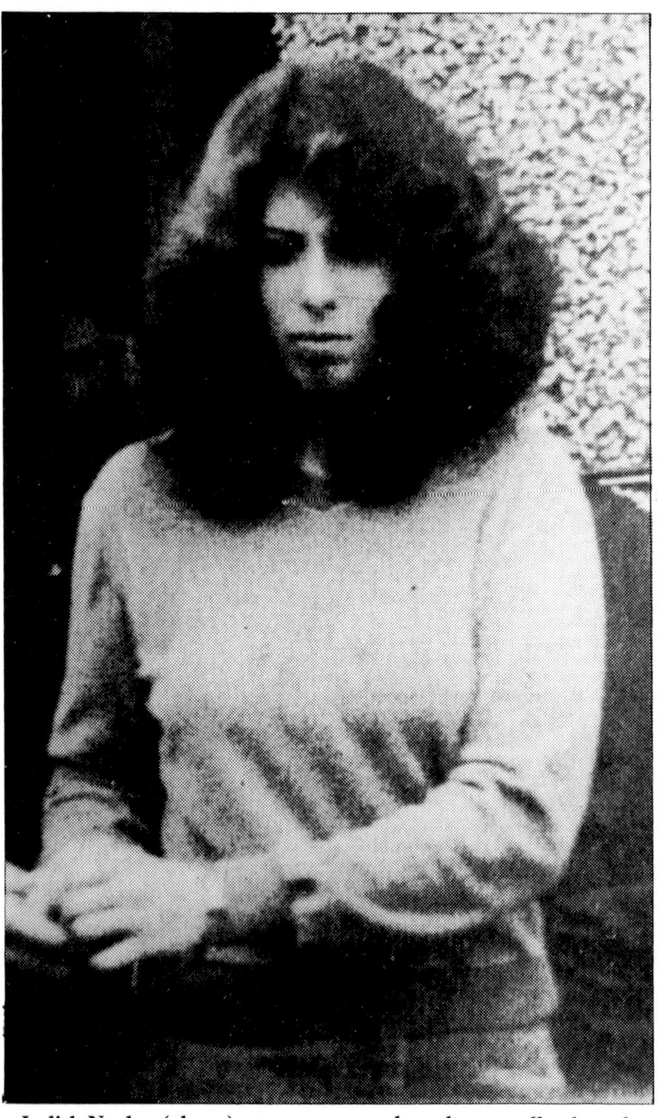

Judith Neeley (above) was pregnant when she sexually abused, then tortured her victims to death

Detectives Owen and Thomas found no one who had heard anything, or seen anyone during the night which could shed light on the merciless killings. Nor were the officers able to find anyone acquainted with the female victim.

The medical examiner set the approximate time of death at only three to four hours before Turner rapped on the door of Dean's apartment. He had the bodies taken to a morgue, where autopsies would be performed after the woman was positively identified. And that came about soon after news of the shocking double slaying appeared in the newspapers. A relative identified her as Debra Ruth Davis Thornton, 32, of Houston.

On June 16th Dean's missing vehicle was found parked at the famous Astrodome. The El Camino was immediately taken to police headquarters, where experts examined it, looking for fingerprints and using a vacuum-cleaner to pick up hair and dirt that might provide clues.

Hopes for an early solution to the crime were dashed when the lab men gave their report to Detectives Owen and Thomas. There were no fingerprints on the vehicle. Even the axe handle had either been wiped clean of prints, or its wielder had worn gloves.

When the autopsy reports were available, the detectives theorised that the person they were looking for was someone who had harboured an intense hatred for the victims. The medical examiner told them that each had been struck 21 times. Some of the blows were inflicted on the pair while they were still alive. Dean had also been struck about the head with a heavy instrument that crushed his skull.

Detectives worked on the case with little success, though they questioned dozens of former offenders and sought out all the usual informants and the street people, who usually knew what was going on during the night hours. But then, in mid-July, Detective-Sergeant J. C. Mosier was checking a file on another unsolved murder when he ran across a name in the Dean-Thornton case that jumped out at him from the printed page. The name was Danny Garrett, one of the persons whom Owen and Thomas had questioned. Mosier had known Garrett for about eight years. Although he had recently lost contact with him, he still often talked to Garrett's former wife.

Mosier had taken a special interest in the June 13th slayings because Jerry Dean had once worked for one of Mosier's relatives. The familiar name spurred Mosier's interest in the unsolved case, so he phoned Danny Garrett's ex-wife and set up a meeting with her. At their meeting Mosier asked her if she was still on good terms with her former in-laws. She replied that she was. She consented to talk to one of them and see what she could find out, then report back to Mosier.

Mosier quickly got results. Just a few days later, he received a phone call from the woman. She told him that she had talked to her former brother-in-law and, according to the information she had gathered, Danny Garrett was definitely involved somehow in the June 13th slayings. She said that Garrett's relative was "very scared" and wanted to talk to someone, but he "didn't want to become involved".

"Tell him to call me," Mosier told her. Five minutes later, Mosier's phone rang again. The man who called was obviously shaken. He agreed to meet Mosier in a secluded place, but only if he would come alone.

"Don't bring no district attorney, or no other cops," the tremulous voice said. Mosier, promising to do as requested, then named an out-of-the-way meeting-place.

When Mosier met the man, he was surprised to find that he had brought a woman with him. He introduced her as a relative of Danny Garrett's girl friend. Then he told Mosier: "I don't want to be involved. But I just felt that it was my obligation to give this information".

It took quite a lot of persuasion from Mosier before he could convince the man that it was also his obligation to make a statement to the authorities. Eventually, though, the informant went willingly with him to the office of the district attorney, who persuaded the man to let officers equip him with a hidden microphone and recorder, which they taped to his person. Then he and the woman went with him to visit Danny Garrett and the latter's girl friend, Karla Faye Tucker.

Mosier informed his men of the time and place of the scheduled visit. A radio transmitter was rigged up, so that the waiting officers could hear the conversation taking place inside the house.

Mosier hoped that the conversation of the suspects and the informant would supply at least some of the necessary evidence to incriminate Garrett and Tucker. The informant, for starters, was heard to claim that the pair had become prime suspects.

"They're just digging!" Karla Tucker scoffed.

The informant then began some digging of his own. "Were the man and woman asleep?" he asked.

Garrett answered: "The guy woke up. The girl started waking up. I told her to stick her head under the covers."

During the conversation, Karla Tucker was asked if it was true that she became sexually aroused and if she had an orgasm with every stroke of the axe. Her answer was: "Hell, yes!"

On July 20th, a little more than a month after the terrible crime, Daniel Lynn Garrett was arrested by two detectives as he left his residence to go to work. Two other officers went to the house and placed Karla Faye Tucker under arrest. Then, as a third person ran from the house, one of the officers chased him on foot, catching up with him about two blocks away.

At police headquarters the three were taken to separate rooms to be questioned. Neither Garrett nor Tucker would answer any questions. But when the third person, whose name, officers learned, was Albert Sheehan, was questioned, they were surprised to be told that he'd gone to the apartment with Garrett and Tucker on the night of the slayings.

However, Sheehan convinced lawmen that he had taken no actual part in the killings, and that he left the apartment when he saw what the other two were about to do. He gave a full statement and agreed to testify against the suspects. And at the regular meeting of the grand jury, all three were indicted — Tucker and Garrett on two counts of capital murder, Sheehan for burglary.

Karla Tucker was the first to go on trial for the murder of Jerry Dean before Judge Patricia Lykos. Testimony began on April 11th, 1984, after a jury of eight women and four men was chosen. Prosecutor Joe Magliolo examined witnesses about the defendant's hatred of Jerry Dean, the motive leading to the horrendous crime and an eyewitness account of the visit to the crime scene. Magliolo played the tape-recording that lawmen believed was the most damaging testimony to feature in the case.

Albert Sheehan told the jury that he, the defendant and Garrett went to the apartment to collect some money from Dean. He said they had been drinking, smoking pot and taking pills all day. When they arrived there, he said, he went to look for Dean's car, while Karla and Garrett went into the apartment.

He testified that, a little later, he went to the apartment and heard a gurgling sound. He said he went to the bedroom where the noise was coming from and saw the defendant hacking at the victim. The gurgling sound was coming from the victim.

A crowded courtroom heard the gruesome details of the hackings to death from Albert Sheehan."Karla was standing over a body on the floor," he told the court. "She had a pickaxe buried in a body covered with a sheet. She was pulling on the axe, wiggling it and jerking it. She finally got it out and held it over her head. She turned and looked at me, smiled — and did it again."

Sheehan testified: "Next night, as we watched a television newscast about the killings, Karla was ecstatic. She was very proud of what she had done. She thought what they had done was something spectacular."

"Will you ever forget the sound and the way she looked and smiled at you before she struck the blow?" the prosecutor asked the witness.

"No, sir, I won't," Sheehan answered.

Next witness was the informant who was instrumental in recording the defendant's admission of guilt. He told how Tucker and Garrett came to his home at five o'clock on the morning of June 13th and told him that they had stolen Jerry Dean's car and some motorcycle parts, which they wanted to stash somewhere.

The two told him that they had "offed" Dean about two hours before. The witness told the court that Karla Tucker hated Dean because he had torn up the pictures that she had of her late mother. That was the reason she said, that she'd wanted to go over there and "whip his ass".

In testimony that established a motive for the crime, the witness stated that Dean didn't want his wife to run around with Karla — and it was for that reason that he'd destroyed Karla's pictures. Since that time Karla had harboured a bitter hatred for Jerry.

Due to the overwhelming evidence against his client, the defence counsel did not call any witnesses. In an unusual move, he asked the jury to find his client guilty, adding that he would seek life in prison for her, and try to save her from the death penalty. The two sentences are the only alternatives for a capital murder conviction in Texas.

It took only 70 minutes for the jury to return with the guilty verdict. Then, in an all-out effort to save Karla Tucker from the death penalty, her counsel — during the punishment phase of the trial before the same jury — called a woman psychiatrist as a witness.

The doctor testified that she'd had a five-hour interview with Tucker and, during that time, she had learned that Karla had begun using marijuana at the age of nine. By the time she was ten, she had become addicted to heroin. Except for one two-week period, Tucker had used hard drugs from that age until the day of the slayings.

The doctor described Tucker's state of mind on the day of the killings, saying that she hadn't slept for three days. She told the court that Tucker had been drinking, had used her usual narcotics and was injecting speed every two to three hours.

In answer to questions, the psychiatrist testified that she doubted that Tucker received any sexual gratification from the killings, as was recorded on the tape. Furthermore, she said, her interview with the defendant a month ago revealed that "Karla Tucker had never had a pleasant sexual experience in her life."

On Tuesday, April 24th, 1984, Karla Tucker went on the witness stand. She told the jury: "I don't see how anybody could ever be forgiven for something like I've done."

She said that if someone did to her what she did to the victims, it would not be justice enough. "Since the day Jerry Dean took a photo album of mine and stabbed and cut up the only photographs of my mother, I just never could forgive him," she went on.

The defendant then offered her version of the events leading up to the merciless hacking of the victims. "We went to Dean's apartment early in the morning. I used a key I'd taken from his wife's home. I followed Danny into the bedroom and the light was out. There was a little crack in the curtains, with some light coming through. I could see the silhouette of a body sitting up. At that point, I knew it was Jerry.

"I went to him, sat down on top of him, told him to shut up," Tucker continued. "He said, 'Karla, we can work it out. I didn't file charges'. He was referring to the fact that his wife and I had used his bank card to clean out his account.

"He grabbed my arms. We started wrestling. Danny came up and got between us. I saw the silhouette of Danny Garrett beating Jerry on the head with what appeared to be a hammer. I could see the outline of everything, like a shadow on the wall."

Karla then turned on the light and saw that Garrett had stopped hitting Dean with the hammer. "But then I heard a noise," she said. "It was a gurgling sound. It was coming from Jerry. Danny walked out of the room and I was standing there. I kept hearing the sound. All I wanted to do was stop it!

"I saw a pickaxe leaning up against the wall. I reached over and grabbed it. I swung it, hit him in the back with it." Although she hit him four or five times, the gurgling sound continued.

"He kept making that noise. When Danny walked in, I told him to make him stop that noise. Danny took the pickaxe, swung it several more times, hitting him in the back. Then he turned him over and hit him in the chest and the noise stopped," she added tearfully.

She then told how, after Danny left the room, she noticed that there was a person underneath some covers, lying against the wall, with her head under a pillow and her body shaking. "My mind, I don't know where it was at. I picked up the pickaxe again. I swung it, but it did not penetrate. I tried it again a second time. And when I did, the person came up from under the covers. It was female — and she grabbed the axe."

She told the court that when Garrett returned to the room, she left. But she came back later and saw Garrett striking the woman with the axe. "When I walked into the bedroom, the girl was sitting. The pickaxe was real deep in her left shoulder. She had her hands on the pickaxe. She said, 'Oh, God, it hurts! If you're going to kill me, please hurry up!' He hit her and put the pickaxe right there in her chest," Karla said.

She denied being sexually aroused with every stroke of the axe. She said she was bragging because she believed that she would fit better into Garrett's lifestyle that way.

The defendant said the killings were not real to her. She did not see the bodies. "I do not remember seeing any holes, or any blood." She also denied that she looked at Sheehan and smiled when she swung the axe.

On Wednesday, April 25th, the jury deliberated nearly three hours before returning the death penalty. At the time of writing, Karla Faye Tucker awaits her fate on Death Row.

Daniel Garrett went on trial for the murder of Debra Thornton before Judge A. D. Azios in early November. One of the first witnesses was Karla Tucker, marking one of the few times in the state's history that a witness was brought from Death Row to testify.

While Tucker was on the witness stand, she told the court that she loved the defendant very much. However, she said: "I testified once for me. I had to do that to more or less set myself free. Now I'm doing it because people deserve to know the truth."

The Texas prison inmate told the seven-man, five-woman jury that she did not really want to talk about her activities with Garrett, but that she was doing it because it was the right thing to do. She told how she and Garrett used to wear camouflage jackets, jeans and boots and crawl through ditches carrying guns, pretending they were soldiers stalking an enemy. According to Tucker, their slogan was: "Kill them all and let God sort them out!"

Tucker went on: "Danny said he was going to make me one of the best hit-women around. He said he could more or less train me. He could get the jobs. I could make the hits — and we could make lots of money.

"He talked of killing a lot of people, like in assassin work. It fascinated me. I wanted to hear what it was like and what he felt," she told the jury. After the killings in June, Tucker said, Garrett "bragged on me, like I'd passed some sort of test. He told me he was proud of me that I didn't turn and run."

The defence questioned Tucker about a conversation she'd had with an acquaintance before the arrest of Garrett and herself, as they looked at a newspaper story about the killings. In that conversation, Tucker now admitted, she'd told the woman that she did the slayings by herself.

On Tuesday, November 20th, the jury found Danny Garrett guilty of the capital murder of Debra Thornton. Then, during the punishment phase of the trial, prosecutors showed jurors a videotape made in the Dean apartment. It had been made shortly after the bodies were discovered on June 13th, 1983. The jury also viewed colour photographs of the bodies.

The prosecutor asked the jurors to practise swinging the axe with its three-foot handle to see how heavy it could become. "Then imagine over 40 holes in the two bodies," he said.

The defence produced relatives of the defendant to testify that he was a gentle, loving man. Another witness told how Garrett had saved his life when he was in a motorcycle accident that severed his leg.

The state wound up its case with testimony from Garrett's former psychologist, who said he had counselled Garrett in 1975. He said the defendant was a sociopath, knowing the difference between right and wrong, but "could not repress a need for gratification immediately, even if it meant actually breaking the law."

On Thursday, November 29th, the jury retired to deliberate the fate of Garrett. Texas law states that, in order to return a death sentence, a jury must determine that a person deliberately committed a murder and that he probably would become violent again and be a continuing threat to society.

In two and a half hours the verdict was returned by the jury — death by lethal injection. And now both Daniel Lynn Garrett and Karla Faye Tucker are in a Texas penitentiary, awaiting their fate on Death Row.

4

DEAREST STU,

Barbara Graham

"And don't forget — if I have the right to ask twelve guests to watch me sit in the cyanide seat, I don't want you of all people to be one of them."

Susan Hayward's portrayal of Barbara Graham in the Hollywood movie *I Want To Live* won the actress an Oscar. Barbara, of course, never knew.

In March 1953 Barbara Graham and three others broke into the home of elderly Mabel Monahan. The old lady was pistol-whipped and died from her injuries. Barbara and two of the others were arrested. In prison she was tricked into accepting a false alibi. The man she thought she could trust was a police officer posing as an underworld character. Barbara was found guilty and sentenced to die in the gas chamber at San Quentin.

During her agonizing time on Death Row Barbara was permitted to correspond with Stuart Palmer, a freelance writer. Palmer had reported the murder trial and worked closely with Barbara's attorney, Al Matthews.

Here are her heartrending letters from San Quentin's Death Row.

San Quentin Prison
January 19th, 1954
Dear Stuart Palmer,

Thank you for coming all the way from Los Angeles up to San Francisco just to see me. I guess I was really a sight, because I didn't know you were coming that day and the matron had just finished cutting my hair off short. Maybe it will look like something when I get a curl back in it? I'm not a real blonde, you know — any more than I'm a real you-know-what!

Thank you for the cigarette holder and the books on Cezanne and Goya. About all I do here is smoke and read and sleep. And think about how I managed to get myself into this mess. I could exercise, but as you know there really isn't any room for that in what the newspapers call my "suite" and especially not when I have two armed guards and a matron looking on.

Al Matthews, my attorney, says he is going to send me up a little TV set. That will be a real help. Maybe I'll see one of your old screenplays!

I'm sorry that I can't send you any pictures of my girlhood for your paper. Oh, I just thought. I might be able to get you a couple of snaps of me when I was about 16, but I'll have to send for them myself as I don't want the name of the people who have them to be in anyone's hands but mine. I'll write them tomorrow, but don't count on it.

From the beginning of this horrible mess I've tried to keep what family I have out of it. I don't want to drag them down with me. The only one I've wanted to hear from was my mother, and as I told you she washed her hands of me years ago.

No dice on the poetry. I'm sorry I told you I'd tried to write any. It isn't for publication. It's just that when you get alone in a place like this, you have to pour your heart out onto paper sometimes and the stuff ought to be torn up at once, like most amateur poetry. I hope this letter finds you happy and in the very best of health.

Sincerely,
Barbara Graham.

January 20th, 1954
Dear Stuart Palmer,

Received your letter. I'm worried about Mom [her mother-in-law, Mrs. Webb] and Baby Tommy. If Mom has moved, I don't know anything about it. I just hope that the money for the story about me in the magazine gets used for Tommy and isn't wasted.

If Hank [Barbara's husband Henry Graham] is using narcotics again, then that may be the answer. He writes that when he gets out of the jug he is coming up here so he can see me on visiting days. I hope so much he means it. But he's no letter writer, and he's not much of a promise keeper, either, but if he came, it would make all the difference in the world to me. I feel so terribly alone all the time.

I wish so much that Tommy could be sent away somewhere, where he's safe. I'll work it out, maybe. I've got some relatives up north who might take him for me. Mrs. Webb has to work and the kid is alone all afternoon there. He's only a baby!

No further news at this end. The grapevine doesn't shake. I'm glad to hear that you had a long talk with the chaplain, Father McAllister, while you were up here. he's a wonderful little man, but I can't talk to him much. I just can't. I think of all of those times I didn't go to Confession, and didn't go to Mass.

Yours sincerely,
Barbara Graham

January 25th, 1954

Dear Stuart Palmer,

Your letter arrived yesterday, and was I glad to hear from you! About the black eyes — two, not one — that you noticed in that old police mug photo you found somewhere in the newspaper files, taken when I was under suspicion of being in bad company or something or other. It was nothing dramatic. The cops never laid a hand on me.

You won't believe it, but here goes: I was driving down Broadway in heavy traffic one Saturday, listening to "Tales of Hoffman" on the car radio, and when I leaned over to turn up the sound a bit, the car in front of me stopped suddenly and I whacked their bumper and banged my own steering wheel with my face. Twenty minutes later I had two beauts. My eyes and nose were so sore that I couldn't put my glasses on for days. So, you see — no melodrama like writers are always looking for ...

I can't think of much of anything to say today — I haven't been to sleep since yesterday and I'm a little heavy-eyed. I can't sleep nights at all — not with the guards coming in and giving me the flashlight in the face every 15 minutes, in the daytime I read and drowse.

Everything gets that way when you're in a place like this — you get too concentrated on your own little self. Well, my face is hitting the keys, so will close for now. Oh, I finished the book on Goya's life; I really enjoyed it. Thanks a lot.

Sincerely yours,

Barbara.

January 28th, 1954

Dear Stuart Palmer,

Thanks for your good letter. Nothing new up here except that I got the bad news about the little TV set that Al Matthews was going to send me. Some reporter on a San Francisco newspaper heard about it and wrote a story about how I was living here in fantastic luxury in a three-room suite that cost the taxpayers thousands to build — all the comforts of home and so on. I shouldn't be surprised, after what most of the newspaper people did to me before and during the trial. They all had me painted "the ice-blonde witch," and stuff like that.

You saw my "three-room suite" — a partitioned hunk of the hospital corridor with an easy chair for the matron, a closet on one side for my few clothes and a table to write on, and the cell that's just got room for my cot and the John. Anyway, the warden now says it's not on, the TV. Of course I can't get out to exercise or go to the movies, being the only woman here. So I sit in a room without even a window.

Don't forget to send me the books. If you have any spares. I've never been much of a mystery fan, or any fiction, for that matter. I like biographies and stuff about art and music. So-called crime books are a laugh to anybody who's knocked up against some of the people I have in my cloudy past. Writers dream up underworld characters, as they call them, who just couldn't possibly exist.

I hear, via the grapevine, that Hank would like to have the money for my story in his name — I mean to share. Remember, it has to go into the bank in Tommy's name, care of Mrs. Webb. I have told Hank that is the way and there is no changing my mind, understand?

Hank doesn't write to me much and I'm afraid I was wrong when I told you that I was sure he'd learned his lesson and would strictly leave the hay and the junk alone from now on and be a real daddy to Tommy. Anyway, maybe he's not much, but he's all I have, and I'm still counting on his coming and getting a job near here as he faithfully promised.

Have been having daily sessions with the prison dentist. I sure hate it, but always feel better afterwards. He is doing wonderful work. I'll be a glamour-puss yet! Don't you think it's sorta funny, their putting in gold inlays and bridges and stuff, when they've already got some cyanide eggs marked with my initials?

Will close for now, hope this letter finds you happy and in the best of health. Sometime have one little Scotch-on-the-rocks for me, will you? Bye for now.

Yours,
Barbara

February 16th, 1954
Dear Stu Palmer,

I haven't forgotten you and I did receive your letter. I would have written sooner, but I have been sitting in the middle of my bed doing exactly nothing for two weeks now. My brain, such as it is, feels numb. No sleeping pills any more, either — maybe you read in the papers about some joker who tongued them and kept them until he had a fistful and could knock himself off in his cell?

So they're forbidden.

I'm sorry I couldn't have the last books you sent. I don't know why they sent them back. Maybe murder mysteries might contaminate the morals of the club? Anyway, I have the magazine with your novelette about Walt Disney's studio in it. I'll let you know frankly what I think. So far so good. But your heroine is too dam pure.

I have to disappoint you about the snapshots, but I guess nobody's kept any of me when I was a girl. Maybe they got disgusted and tore them all up. There's plenty of later ones in the newspaper files, mostly taken with the camera flash held upside down so I'm lightened from below and look like a witch or something.

Did any girl ever get a worse press than I did?

Thanks for the news about your children. Hug them close, as I wish I could hug Tommy.

Sincerely,

Barbara.

February 25th

Dear Stu,

There is some talk about my eventually going back to Corona, because of the expense in keeping one woman here in a man's prison. As you know, I was moved here because some people thought there might be an attack on my life in the other place, which is so much more open. That's a lot of nonsense. There are only two people who might like me out of the way — John True and Willie Upshaw — and I don't think either of them would try anything as long as I am in prison.

Sincerely,

Barbara.

Dearest Stu,

Your letter arrived today. As usual, I'm so glad to hear from you.

So you went up to the Ventura School for Girls and checked up on me and on my mother's record there! So

Helen Coad is assistant matron now — isn't she a large, pleasingly-plump woman with a sweet-tooth? Send her some candy for me, and tell her hello for me. I'm sorry that I'm not one of her graduates to be proud of.

When I came here to Quentin, there were four of us condemned people here in this wing of the old hospital. By the time you receive this there will be one, me. Another execution tomorrow. It's not publicly announced, of course, but everybody knows.

That's all for this time, Stu. Thanks for everything. Will write you more later, because a girl in this fix just has to have somebody to talk to now and then. Best to your family, and hold them close.

Always the same,
Barbara

March 14th, 1954

Dear Stu,

The cheque arrived OK. Even though it wasn't certified, it went through, and now I can pay for my own cigarettes and soap and such like that. Was thankful, because I was really broke. Was also thankful to realise that the bigger part went to Mrs. Webb, to help her in taking care of my Tommy.

If only Hank won't get his hands on it, and go on a spree! He hasn't written, or come up. I am strictly alone, sleeping my life away in the daytime and lying awake all night. I just don't want to do anything! Magee extended the time I could move out into the corridor and exercise, but how can you exercise in six feet of space with a matron and two guards watching you? I ask you. So I just sit.

This should take the prize for being the shortest letter on record, but more later. Write, huh? I gotta talk to somebody.

Sincerely,
Barbara Graham, or what's left of her.

March 18th, 1954
Dearest Stu,

Thought I had better answer your letter today, because I will probably feel worse tomorrow.

I had a tooth extracted yesterday. Really, I'm going to be the loveliest corpse! And don't forget — even if I have the right to ask twelve guests to watch me sit in the cyanide seat. I don't want you of all people to be one of them. I won't ask anybody, except my mother — who would really enjoy it. You may be on the warden's list, but don't come, please, even if he asks you. If I have to take it, I'll take it, but I wouldn't want a friend watching. Please.

I hear that you have been trying to use influence with the big people at Sacramento to get me the lie-detector test I've been screaming for. Maybe that means that at last you are coming around and beginning to believe that maybe I'm innocent! Or maybe you're just being objective again? But I never killed that old lady, and she was a Catholic and I'm a Catholic and I'd be glad to meet her in Purgatory, any time, and shake hands.

Barbara

P.S. I just read that District Attorney Roll has tried to nip the idea of a lie-detector test for me. Wonder why? Do you suppose they're afraid to have it?

April 14th, 1954
Dear Stu,

We are having a good rain. I can't see it through the walls, but I can hear it. Wish it would keep on for weeks. Sounds so good, but sorta lonesome, too. Lonesome! That's it, you can be lonesome, even with two guards and a matron watching you night and day, 24 hours.

Hank wrote that he is maybe bringing Tommy up here to see me Wednesday. I hope and pray that this time he remembers not to forget. But you know Hank!

Overlook this typing tonight. My nails are very long and I keep hitting the wrong keys. Am trying to figure out a way to trim them, but I can't have my manicure scissors or a file. They're forbidden, too. I guess I'll have to start biting my nails. So she's in a death cell and she's worried about fingernails! It's true, in a place like this everything gets out of focus and little things become foolishly important — like fingernails and who is going to witness my execution.

Wish this was all over with, one way or the other. The mills of the gods don't have to grind this slowly, do they? Well, I've run off enough at the mouth. So I'll bring this to an end. Hope all goes well with you.

Love,
Barbara.

May 18th, 1954

Dearest Stu,

At long last. No, I haven't died on the vine, at least I don't think so. I received all your letters, but I haven't been feeling well lately, and have let my writing all go to pot.

As you said when you were up here — I didn't believe you then — it's true, from what I hear, that there has been a reaction and that they aren't screaming for my blood as they did last summer and fall. But, on the other hand, what is the sense to living, if that life has to be spent in prison? And for something I didn't do, yet!

Once in a while I get the feeling that it might be nice to have my sentence commuted, but the feeling never lasts long. Not when I think of Tommy growing up without me and not having his love. I don't mind telling you that when I think of him not recognising me as his mother, hence no love from him, it tears the heart out of me. He was up to see me last week and I try to pretend to myself that he still remembers me. How I love him!

I told you when you were here that I had nothing to confess, and that if I ever had I'd tell you first. But I wish you'd break down and forget your objective viewpoint and say just once that you don't believe that I killed Mrs. Monahan.

I suddenly find myself out of words, so will bring this to

an end, with the hope that all is well with you and yours. Do write when you have the time.

Sincerely,
Barbara

June 4th, 1954
Dear Stu,

Received your letter today, and as usual I always find something in it that is humorous. My letter-answering is quite a chore now. No typewriter, and how I hate to write in longhand. The machine I had was a borrowed one and had to be returned. Needless to say, I miss it. No hints. Well, I don't have to worry about my fingernails, anyway.

I have some beautiful flowers here in my 6-by-8 cell. Roses, carnations, and Martha Washingtons. The roses are especially pretty — white, yellow, pink and red ones. I had a black one a few weeks ago. I got it just as it was opening, so I watched it most of the night. When I woke the next morning it was dead.

Been listening on my little radio to the ball game from the East. I am still pulling for my Dodgers! They played a terrific game the other day against the Phillies. Almost had me climbing the walls!

I read in the paper that three groups of people have formed committees on my behalf, one from San Francisco, one from Oakland, and the other from Los Angeles. It brought back my faith in the human race a little. But, believe me, after all, the truth only tends to hurt one instead of helping. Justice! I would have to give you my thoughts on the subject. They would be horrible, I only hope something happens to change my mind.

I want you to know that I appreciate everything you are doing for me. Al tells me that you have gone out as a private investigator — where's your Chicken Inspector's badge, bud? — and tried to get me a lie-detector test. If the co-operation at this end is not forthcoming, believe me, it's just that I don't have the information you seek.

To repeat myself — I want to know — why does

everybody seem to think that I am such a fountain of information? If pcoplc truly knew how little I know about any old capers or unsolved crimes, they'd be shocked. I know it sounds incredible that I've nothing to tell that I haven't told, but I haven't.

Well, my wrist is becoming limp, so will bring this to my usual abrupt ending. There just isn't any news from this end. Let me know what happens with the long-distance chess game. I enjoy your letters. Objective Observer. All you'll ever say is that you don't believe me "guilty as charged," but I like to think that you don't really believe me guilty at all — only you can't afford to stick your neck out and say so.

As always,
Barbara

June 6th, 1954
Dear Stu,

Your letter. As usual. I am glad to have it, though you kid me a lot and press me a lot in your quiet way. I will swear to my dying day — which may not be too far off — that Jack and Emmett were with me at the time Baxter Shorter or Shorter Baxter — I never can even get the name straight — was supposedly kidnapped and dumped down the drain. Whatever they may have done, they didn't do that one.

I realise how much, as a writer and newspaperman, you want to break that thing, but I honestly can't help you there. I'm not trying to defend Jack and Emmett. I have only myself to think of now. But there it is.

The news has just come. The State Legislature will not appropriate extra funds for four matrons to guard me, so I have to go back to Corona while we sweat out the appeals and all that stuff. They have different rules there, and probably you won't be permitted to come and see me or even to write to me. Anyway I'll send messages to you through Al, or through the relatives that are permitted. I probably won't be allowed to write to you — at least, not for a long time. Go and see Tommy and give him a hug for me.

Love,
Barbara

March 1st, 1955
Dear Stu,

I guess this is maybe the last letter I will ever be able to write to you, but I want to say how much I appreciate all your efforts in my behalf, and how much I wish that you really would say once out loud that you believe in my innocence.

I wasn't there! I didn't kill poor old Mrs. Monahan and I don't even know who did.

But the prospects are not good, and getting worse by the minute. I don't know how much longer Al Matthews can put up the dough for the cost of appeals and things — and they can only appeal on minor technicalities, anyway. Legal twists, that's all.

Meanwhile life goes on, but sluggish. I play my records over and over. I eat sometimes, without tasting anything, and I sleep and doze and sleep again, but at night I mostly don't sleep. This is a period in which I guess I'm supposed to review my whole life, like a drowning man is supposed to do. But I'm just too tired and too bored.

I don't eat enough and I don't exercise. I am just a clam that crawls back into its shell and stagnates. Just waiting. But I still want to go free, or get the business. I cannot look forward to most of my lifetime behind bars. You yourself say you can get itchy and nervous when you are in a prison for a few hours, even though you know you can get out any minute. How do you think I feel? As if you didn't know!

I'm beat, kid. I don't care what they do, only I want it over with. You asked me once if I could remember anybody. I mean any law officer, or matron, or stuff like that, who had ever in my long career taken time out to try to make friends with me and help me change directions. Not once. Really not one time. Nobody ever gave a damn, except the

Good Sisters, years ago, and I should have stayed with them — and of course Hank, and some of the boys on the other side of the fence, who were always quick with a $20 when a girl needed it.

But I'm so alone. Nobody is so alone as I am. This goes on and on and never stops. Jack Hardy and Al Matthews and Bill Strong have done their best and I guess they are still doing it, without a thin dime of pay. But, in the appeal to the Supreme Court, what have they got to say except the minor stuff about the prejudice of the press and all that? I'm not kidding myself — I'm not going to get a new trial.

And I don't think I could live through it, even if I got one.

Sharon and some others of my family come to see me quite regularly. Hank comes sometimes. They will tell you hello from me. I wish I could see you, and keep on getting your letters, even if you kid me sometimes.

I'm sorry to hear that your cocker got run over, but you still have your cats and your children and your home. Go and see Mam and Tommy sometime, and give him a big hug for me. I wish I could see him grow up. But I won't, so what's the use of wishing — of thinking. The best to you, always.

Love,
Barbara

On June 3rd, 1955, Barbara Graham was executed in the gas chamber at San Quentin. A witness recalled, "The cyanide fumes began filling the chamber and Barbara's head dropped to her chest. Most of the witnesses were certain she was dead and I was relieved that she had died quickly and easily after the long, nerve-shattering delay … But I was wrong.

"For, in a moment of horror that sent shivers down my spine, Barbara slowly lifted her head. From the strained, piteous look on her face, it was clear that she was holding her breath in a frantic attempt to cling to life just as long as she could.

"I watched with growing terror, until she could hold her

breath no longer. Then with what seemed to be a sigh of despair, the breath burst from her lungs and, a second later, she gulped in the lethal fumes that snuffed out her life."

The full incredible story of Barbara Graham's crime, trial, double-cross and execution is told in ON DEATH ROW by Mike James, published in paperback by True Crime Library. ISBN 1 874358 05 2

5
THE HAUNTED HOUSE MURDER

R. J. Gerrard

"Now I know why you brought me up here" ... Handyman Harry Wright's whispered last words to his killer.

There was a world championship bout in progress. Suddenly it ended. A coveted title had changed hands. There was a new heavyweight champion of the world — a young California-based boxer with immensely broad shoulders, broad nose, broad and easy smile ... The telephone rang. Bill Cadwell switched off his desk radio. Somebody wanted to know about the big fight? You called up the police for just about anything here in Otsego County. He reached for the phone.

"State Police. Trooper Cadwell," he said in his familiar monotone.

"Hello —" It was a woman's voice. It was husky and sounded somehow urgent. She wasn't phoning to ask about a prizefight. "This is Mrs. Coo. At Woodbine Inn. Have there been any accidents on the roads hereabouts?"

"Nothing reported to me," the trooper said. "Not here at Schenevus. Why?"

"It's my handyman — Harry Wright."

"I know Harry. What about him?"

"Harry's missing. That is," said the worried, husky voice, "he left here just after seven o'clock this evening to go see about a painting job at Johnson's. And he hasn't returned."

"You rang up Johnson's?"

"An hour ago. Harry never arrived there."

"O.K." said Cadwell. "I'll be right over."

The state trooper drove rapidly from his post in the small upstate New York community of Schenevus to the roadhouse called Woodbine Inn. This establishment was owned by Mrs. Eva Coo. Some 20 miles from the county seat, Cooperstown, it was on the Maryland-Oneonta highway and a short distance outside the Oneonta town limits.

As Cadwell drove up the inn blazed with light, but its regular business of providing entertainment and refreshments seemed to be at a standstill. The trooper found but three people in the roadhouse. Besides the proprietress there was a farmhand, Fred Palmer, and a young woman named Lottie James, who was identified as an "entertainer."

Mrs. Eva Coo was a big, blue-eyed, bleached-blonde, brassy type of individual. She was considered to be a bad influence in that part of the county. Both big Eva and her little inn enjoyed a shady reputation. Yet business out here at Woodbine Inn could be more than brisk on a Saturday night, and Eva herself did not lack for the protection of a wide and knowing acquaintance in that part of the Empire State.

Tonight, however, was Thursday — the soft and summery Thursday night of June 14th 1934. Except for Palmer, who said that he had dropped over for a bottle of beer and to listen to the fight, the inn was curiously bereft of patrons.

Mrs. Coo repeated what she had already told Cadwell over the phone. All she could add were a few quiet words which hinted that her slightly-built, none too able-bodied handyman might be off somewhere, drunk. Harry Wright, she remarked, was a hard drinker once he got started. Since he hadn't even arrived at Johnson's place — well, it sounded like poor Harry *had* got started.

"But don't be too rough with the little guy when you collar him," Eva urged.

"Why should I be rough with him?" Cadwell retorted.

As the state trooper drove away from the roadhouse he turned onto the highway in the direction of Oneonta. He drove slowly and spread the beam of his headlights so as to cover both sides of the road. Suddenly he slammed on his brakes, sprang out of the car, and crossed to the ditch beside the road. He stared into the long grass and sighed. There was Harry Wright. The state policeman had found him only a few hundred yards from the inn where he worked. But Harry wasn't drunk and passed out cold. *Harry was dead.*

Cadwell drove back to Mrs. Coo's. He found her in the kitchen, anxiously pacing the floor. And she had managed to communicate her anxieties to the James girl and Palmer.

"Looks like you bring news, Bill!" Lottie exclaimed. She was trying to sound her usual gay and flippant self, but her eyes were wide and worried.

Cadwell only nodded. He approached the more agitated Eva Coo. "I found him," he said. "Too late, though. Harry's dead. I've got to call Doc Winsor."

Dr. Earl C. Winsor drove over immediately from Schenevus. The headlights of the state trooper's and physician's cars combined to illuminate the somewhat grisly scene along the highway.

The body of Mrs. Coo's handyman, Harry Wright, lay where Cadwell had discovered it, on its back in a shallow ditch, about three yards from the concrete highway. There were bruises and smears of dried blood on the dead man's face.

"He must have been hit by a truck or a big car," Cadwell estimated.

"Another hit-and-run case," the doctor said bitterly.

Mrs. Coo knelt in the grass beside him, watching his deft work intently. Her face was pallid in spite of her heavy make-up, and in her effort to keep silent and not interrupt Dr. Winsor's examination, she bit her underlip grimly. She seemed close to tears.

A small, silent knot of onlookers, including the farmhand Palmer, and the entertainer, Lottie James, was grouped behind her.

At length, the doctor stood erect and squared his shoul

ders. "Appears to have died from a crushed chest," he said. "The ribs are crushed and, I believe, both shoulders fractured." The doctor was also able to say that Wright was not killed instantly.

Bill Cadwell put in: "Looking for him, I nearly missed him. The grass here is so high."

"Quite a number of drivers must have passed here and failed to see him," Dr. Winsor pointed out. "For, in my opinion, he has been dead nearly three hours."

It was now after 11.30 p.m. If the physician's preliminary findings were correct, then the fatal accident had occurred at early dusk, around 8.30, before it became very dark.

Winsor and the state trooper began closely scrutinising the surface of the highway, using their torches. They were looking for skid marks. But they found none.

"Whoever struck poor old Harry," one of the onlookers said, "didn't even bother to slow down."

"Harry wasn't so old," said Eva Coo. She spoke almost harshly, as if rebuking even a hint of disparagement concerning one who had been loyal to her and could no longer speak up for himself.

"Here's his cap!" Cadwell called. He was standing in the shallow ditch, some 20 yards from where the body lay.

The grey cloth cap was closely studied by everyone at the scene. "Never saw Harry wearing it," Palmer said.

"Did he have it on, Mrs. Coo, when he left your place tonight?" the trooper asked.

"He certainly did not. That's no cap of Harry's. He wore his same beat-up old felt hat," she volunteered.

"Then I'd better keep this," said Cadwell. "It could lead us to the hit-and-run driver."

"There's not a splinter of broken glass from headlamps to be seen anywhere," Dr. Winsor declared. He put away his torch. "It's the most baffling kind of hit-and-run case."

With the permission of the doctor, acting for the county medical examiner, an undertaker came and took away the body of the accident victim.

On returning to Woodbine Inn, Mrs. Coo was stolid and

unresponsive. She seemed entirely drained of her usual heartiness and energy. Fred Palmer and the others had gone to their homes. The proprietress of the roadhouse and her entertainer, Lottie James, were left alone. Eva began switching off lights. There would be no high jinks out there that night.

"Say, what about Ernie?" Lottie asked.

"I suppose we got to go look for him," Eva said after a sombre pause. "It's always the same. But I sure hope that nothing's happened to *him*."

Ernie Tatum was the one permanent — and unpaying — guest at Woodbine Inn. Eva was too fond of him, it appeared, to heave him out and Ernie was too obsessed with his craving for alcohol to find a job or to resume taking care of himself.

Gossip had it that Ernie had stopped by Eva's roadhouse one day to try to interest the owner in a new furnace. Ernie was then gainfully employed as a furnace salesman. Also he was debonair, attractive — and younger than his potential customer.

He hadn't been able to interest Eva in a new heating appliance for her rowdy roadhouse, but he had received an almost immediate invitation to warm the lady's receptive heart. Instead of selling a furnace, Ernie had bought himself a red-hot momma — or so said the ribald element that frequented the inn. And Ernie's irresponsible ways and frequent bouts of imbibing had soon become a byword.

On that early morning of June 15th, Eva and Lottie drove into Oneonta in the latter's sedan and dragged Ernie Tatum from the gutter into which he was tottering. All the way back to Woodbine Inn, the two women tried to rouse Ernie from his numbing alcoholic torpor and acquaint him with the tragic news about Harry Wright.

"Good ol' Harry! I spoke with 'im t'night, just 'fore he went off some place —" Ernie managed to mumble.

"He went off some place, all right," Lottie said, with her habitual nervous giggle. "Old Harry's dead. He tried to buck a trailer truck. So poor old Harry's dead as mackerel."

"Harry wasn't so old," Eva Coo contradicted stolidly. "Why does everybody keep calling him old? He was forty-eight."

"Did he tell you forty-eight?" Lottie giggled. "Just forty-eight, my foot!"

"Beans," Ernie mumbled gleefully. "A thousand on a plate! The way that dumbcluck of a cripple loved his baked beans! Good ol' Harry — he gets a square shake up in Heaven. They'll let 'im come back to eat beans in Boston."

"Just shut up!" Eva Coo thundered. "Haven't you any respect?"

She and her now-subdued entertainer put Ernie Tatum to bed with their customary firmness and dispatch. Then the two sat in the kitchen of the darkened roadhouse, sipping black coffee and vaguely debating the quick, uncertain twists and turns of life or fate.

During the afternoon an autopsy was performed upon the body of Harry Wright. Dr. Winsor and two associates came up with a rather baffling summary of their professional findings. As a result, the doctor drove to Cooperstown with Trooper Cadwell and there, at 5.30 p.m., conferred with State Police Sergeant John L. Cunningham and Owen Brady, undersheriff of Otsego County.

Nearly all of Wright's ribs, the post-mortem showed, had been fractured. Both his shoulder blades had suffered multiple fractures. A wound on his temple suggested that he had been struck by some heavy implement or object which was not a part of the motor vehicle that had crushed his thoracic cavity nearly to pulp.

"In my opinion," said Dr. Winsor, "the car that killed Wright passed over him not once, but twice."

"I still can't quite figure," Cadwell began, "why Harry was hit head-on by a truck or car on that side of the road. Shouldn't it have hit him from behind? Unless maybe the force of the first blow spun him around, so that he fell backward right in the car's path."

"Let's go over it again, from the beginning," Brady suggested.

Harry Wright, according to his employer Mrs. Coo, had left her place about 7 p.m. to go to Johnson's, to discuss a prospective job of painting. Harry's arrangement with the proprietress of Woodbine Inn permitted him to seek odd jobs around the rural locality whenever his services as painter and handyman were in no rush demand at the roadhouse. And Lottie James, with her nervous giggle, had mentioned the odd coincidence that Harry had just finished "his big paint job on the summer bungalows" adjoining the inn on Tuesday evening, only two days before his fatal accident.

Harry Wright had been alive for nearly an hour and a half after leaving the inn. Yet he had not reached his destination a walk of no more than 20 minutes, even to a man afflicted with a limp, as Harry was.

Harry had been found lying in the ditch on the eastbound side of the highway, the side on which traffic moved towards the inn from Oneonta. A local man, familiar with every yard of that area and a countryman all his life, Harry would have been sure to walk against motor traffic. On his way to Johnson's, which lay between Woodbine Inn and Oneonta, Harry would have automatically trudged along the eastbound side of the highway, in order to face approaching eastbound traffic. He would not, however, have taken almost 90 minutes to go less than a quarter of a mile.

"Could it be that he was struck by a westbound vehicle and knocked clear across the highway to the ditch on the eastbound side?" Brady speculated.

"Impact as heavy as that," said the physician, "would have surely produced leg or arm or pelvic fractures — possibly a series of them. Besides, Bill Cadwell and I combed over the highway for dozens of yards in both directions. There wasn't a tyre mark, a skid mark, or any spattering of blood. Also, he did not die instantly."

Had the victim, perhaps, been drinking and turned back towards home, forgetting both his Johnson errand and the ordinary precaution of taking to the safer side of the road?

"Wright wasn't drunk. We found only insignificant

traces of alcohol," Dr. Winsor said. "A shot of whisky or perhaps, a bottle of beer with his dinner."

"Bill, were you able to learn anything about the cap?" Sergeant Cunningham asked.

Cadwell said that so far he had shown the grey cloth cap to a number of shopkeepers in Oneonta, Maryland and Schenevus. He had been told that a salesman with a pretty cheap line of goods had come through the area about a year ago. He had been offering caps like this one. But it would be virtually impossible to trace the purchaser of a single cap.

In Oneonta, the largest of the three communities, there was a haberdasher with one of these same caps which he had been unable to sell. By comparing it with the grey cap found in the roadside ditch Cadwell discovered that a careful hand had snipped both the size and maker's labels from the cap near Harry Wright's corpse.

On Saturday morning, June 16th, Undersheriff Brady and Sergeant Cunningham referred the Wright case to Sheriff George Mitchell. The dim outline of an ingenious crime had begun to challenge the investigators. Possibly Harry Wright *hadn't* been struck in a hit-and-run accident, but by murderous design.

Wright had lived and worked around there all his life, and for the past three years at a disreputable roadhouse. He must have seen and heard any number of things. It was not improbable that he had made himself some enemies.

Originally his home had been in nearby Portlandville. He had lived there with his mother until her death three years earlier. He had then moved to Eva Coo's Woodbine Inn, earning his board and lodging as her handyman.

Since Harry wasn't robust, and was partially crippled, his handiness had many limitations. But Eva had seemed to find uses for him. She liked to freshen up her joint with an annual paint job, she said, in return for which she had granted the lonely and handicapped painter a home.

"Suppose you go to Portlandville and attend Harry Wright's burial service on Monday," Sheriff Mitchell suggested to Brady. "You might just pick up a bit of gossip over there — about who would want such an inoffensive little guy out of the way."

Brady found a pitifully small gathering of people at the cemetery, with the large Eva Coo in conspicuous attendance. She was escorted by an amazingly sobered-up and strained-looking Ernie Tatum.

Early that afternoon Brady reported to his chief, "Harry's name and birth year were already carved on the Wright family monument, together with those of his parents. Then I saw something else — a newly-cut numeral in Harry's birth year. So I looked up old MacGregor, the stonecutter. And what do you suppose he told me?"

Less than four weeks ago, on May 23rd, Brady reported, MacGregor had received an order to alter Harry's birth year from 1880 to 1885. The order had come to him, claimed the elderly Scot, from Woodbine Inn. Mrs. Coo, Harry's employer, had telephoned at Harry's request, saying that he wished to have a long-standing mistake set right. It had even been a joke in Harry's family, the lady explained. He was not 54, but 49, and not even that until next October. MacGregor had promptly complied. It had only meant changing an 0 to a 5. And Mrs. Coo herself had sent him the payment for his work.

"They tamper with a gravestone and in three weeks' time the poor guy's using it," the sheriff commented.

"The only answer seems to be insurance. Or else some kind of inheritance Harry was maybe due to get," Brady said.

"I'm thinking of insurance," Mitchell rejoined.

"It adds up," Brady said. "On May 23rd, Harry's made five years younger. Then, on June 14th, Harry's dead. How would a birth year on a gravestone matter, with Harry alive? You only had to ask him his age."

The sheriff nodded. "This could mean that somebody counted on Harry not staying alive."

"Well, on that score," Brady said, "I've got up a list. Besides H. Wright, deceased, and Eva herself, these four people are the most familiar with the sights and sounds at merry Woodbine: Martha Clift, known as the hostess; Lottie James, an entertainer; Olive Brooks, some kind of entertainer; and the star boarder, Ernie Tatum."

"O.K., we'll question 'em one at a time. Begin with Ernie," the sheriff said.

Meanwhile, Sergeant Cunningham and three of his troopers were following the original premise that Woodbine Inn's crippled handyman had been killed in a hit-and-run accident on the highway only a few hundred yards from the roadhouse. It was an enormous task to call at all the garages and filling stations in the wide area designated by Cunningham. But for many hours in a five-day period — Friday to Tuesday — the state officers worked at little else.

They kept asking people to think back. A none-too-agile man named Wright had been struck and killed on the Oneonta-Maryland road on Thursday about 8.30 p.m.

"Have you noticed any truck or car with damage that might have come from such a hit-and-run death? Or any driver on Thursday night who seemed in a state of nerves about something?"

This policy paid off, as it so often does when the investigative team is skilled, devoted and tireless. Early on Tuesday morning Trooper Cadwell questioned a mechanic who had worked on the late shift in an Oneonta garage on Thursday night.

"For whatever it may be worth," the mechanic drawled, "a gal was in here on Thursday night who seemed mighty flustered. She had rented for the evening our Willys-Knight, that heavy job over there. The ticket read that she was trying it out, and would maybe buy it, if she found she liked it."

"What time did you see her?" Cadwell asked.

"It'll be stamped on the ticket." He ducked into the office and came out with it. "She handed the car in 9.55 on June 14th. But she wasn't buying it, believe me. 'How'd she like the big bus?' I asked, just making conversation. She didn't make any back, paid what she owed and shot out of here, practically running. I looked the Willys over carefully, but she hadn't scraped it up none."

She had given the name of Martha Clift, an address on Main Street, Oneonta. She was a tall, nice-looking woman, maybe 26 or 27, and wore glasses with heavy black frames.

The state trooper checked this lead at once. Martha Clift, it developed, was currently employed as a hostess at Woodbine Inn. Martha had a driving licence, but didn't own a car.

Returning to the garage, Cadwell made a thorough examination of the Willys-Knight sedan. Then he sprang to the telephone and rang up Sergeant Cunningham.

"There are some small brownish splotches in the back, mostly just under the edge of the rear seat cushion. I've no equipment with me," Cadwell explained, "but I'm going to put the car on ice till you get here. The spots could be dried blood."

It was nearly noon when Cunningham telephoned Sheriff Mitchell to report Cadwell's find in Oneonta. Mitchell had his own find. At the moment he sat facing a taut, pallid and twitching Ernie Tatum.

"You look kind of peaked, Ernie," the sheriff was saying. "How about a good stiff jolt of black coffee?"

"No jolts, Sheriff. I'm on the wagon."

"Since when?"

"Not long. But you can't hang me for trying."

"We don't have hanging in this state, Ernie. Since when — on the wagon?"

"Does it matter?"

"It might. Would it be," Mitchell went on casually, "that Eva is making you stay sober now because she's afraid you'll talk if you get drunk?"

"What would I talk about?"

"The 'accident' that murdered poor old Harry Wright."

"He wasn't so old," Ernie Tatum began, as if parroting a stock phrase which had been remorselessly hammered into his booze-fogged brain.

"You're right. On his tombstone poor Harry's been getting younger every day," the sheriff said drily.

His words made Ernie shiver. "Guess I'll switch on you, Sheriff," he said, "and have that snort on the county. Coffee was all you offered, wasn't it?"

"Black coffee," said Mitchell.

When a deputy brought in the steaming container, Ernie swallowed the stimulant greedily.

"Now to business," the sheriff said. "I can hold you Ernie. As a murder suspect, or a killer's accessory, or as a material witness. Take my word, you'll find the first two don't rate with the last — a nice, co-operative material witness, resigned to telling the truth."

And so Ernie Tatum talked — at length. He swore that he knew nothing of the fatal mishap which had overtaken Harry Wright, who would have been 54 next October. He knew that Eva Coo had told the Portlandville stonecutter to change the year of Harry's birth. But he had never heard her discuss such a change with Harry, or the allegedly erroneous 1880.

His own relations with the handyman had been cordial. There had been a sort of common bond of helplessness and thrall in their respective existences at Woodbine Inn, said Ernie.

"Did you ever talk to Harry about his insurance?" the sheriff asked.

"I spoke to Eva about Harry's insurance."

"When?"

"On many occasions. I moved in with Eva last summer," the ex-furnace salesman reminded them blandly, "and almost right away she began telling me how Harry was nuts about insurance and wanted more policies. I took care of nearly all the correspondence, writing to various companies and signing his name."

"Naming yourself as beneficiary?" Undersheriff Brady put in.

"Are you kidding? Eva is Harry's sole beneficiary. She told me that he wanted it that way. That he knew he owed her everything."

The interrogators exchanged glances. Sheriff Mitchell

opened a new line of inquiry. "When," he asked, "was the last time you saw Harry Wright alive?"

Ernie said that around 6.30 p.m. last Thursday he had spoken briefly to Harry. They had each drunk a bottle of cold beer, and Eva's handyman had mentioned that he was going with her and one of the girls to dig up some shrubs. They'd be taking them on the sly, Harry had indicated.

"How did he indicate that?"

"Oh, Harry wasn't so dumb, Sheriff. He could seem dull and aggravating enough when he thought he was being put upon. But, last Thursday, I remember how he gave me a sort of wink when he said they were going up to the old Scott place on the mountain, to dig some shrubs Eva had been wanting for some time."

"Crumhorn Mountain? Was that where they went?"

"Wait," Ernie hastened to amend. "I don't know this of my own knowledge. But it's what Harry told me. I remember him saying, too, that Eva had promised they'd be back in plenty of time so he could hear Max Baer belt the ears off Primo Carnera down in New York City."

Ernie himself had dimly heard the radio commentary on the heavyweight championship fight in an Oneonta bar where he "was busy getting plastered". He was obliged to go over these statements again and again. And he swore that he was telling only the truth.

He averred repeatedly that he hadn't had even a minor part in any plot or conspiracy. He hadn't even suspected that there was a plot against Harry's life, despite the fact that he had been useful in signing Harry's name and otherwise helping Eva insure her handyman's life with a number of prominent companies.

"Why was it so important that Harry Wright be under 50 years of age?" Mitchell asked.

"Every policy I saw made Harry out younger than his actual age. We didn't dare insure him as a guy born in 1880. The premiums would have been too high, Eva said, and Harry couldn't afford to keep them up. Most of the policies were fairly small, requiring no medical examination. But they wouldn't have accepted Harry under those terms if we'd given his right age. Get it?"

"Sure, we get it!" Brady exclaimed. "And Harry's dying in a highway accident means that his beneficiary gets double indemnity!"

"On most of the policies that I've seen," Ernie conceded.

It was Sheriff Mitchell's turn to put through a call to Cunningham, whom he found in Oneonta. It seemed that the sergeant had already consulted his superiors in Albany by telephone, then sped to Oneonta and the garage where Trooper Cadwell stood guard, to examine the hired car, especially its rear seat cushion.

"The spots look like blood to me, all right," the sergeant informed the sheriff. "But whose? And human or animal? Quite a few people hire that big car in the course of a month, or since its last thorough cleaning. It will take our laboratory people some days to test for bloodstains. Even then, they may not be able to get us court evidence."

Mitchell then told Cunningham about Ernie Tatum's tip concerning Crumhorn Mountain and the Scott place.

An hour and a half later two fast cars, one carrying state officers, the other driven by Brady and bringing the sheriff and two deputies, converged upon the mountain which flanks the winding valley of the Susquehanna near its source in the Catskill foothills.

The investigators were now assuming that Harry Wright had met his fate far from the spot where his smashed and broken body had been found by Trooper Cadwell. And if Harry had been slain by stealthy design, the Scott place fitted nicely into any murderous pattern. The house was commonly reputed to be haunted.

The troopers and county officials had hardly begun their yard-by-yard study of the scene when another car came rumbling up the mountainside and stopped. Two women got out. Both were known to Mitchell and Brady. The one driving the car was Mrs. Ellen Fink, who had inherited the haunted house.

She greeted the officers and came immediately to the

point. Certain neighbours, she said, had been continually informing her that the Scott place was being systematically raided by thieves, looters, or just plain souvenir-hunters. That past Thursday, at about 8.15 p.m. it seemed, the owner of this abandoned and eerie property had been warned by phone that a big car was trespassing and two women apparently plundering the place. So, accompanied by her friend — the same who was with her this afternoon — and by a male relative, the owner had sped up the mountain to deal firmly with these presumed trespassers.

Mrs. Fink said that she had found the roadhouse owner, the notoriously tough-minded Mrs. Eva Coo, on her property, close to the deserted house. With her was a younger woman who wore glasses with heavy black frames, and who sat in silence at the wheel of a large, rather antiquated Willys-Knight sedan.

Mrs. Coo had appeared just to be idling about. But, contrary to her widespread reputation as a brassy-headed hussy and loudmouth, Eva had spoken gently, almost ingratiatingly, to Mrs. Fink and her companions. She assured them that not a thing had been taken unlawfully from the Scott place, insisted that they look in the sedan, front seat and back, to convince themselves that absolutely nothing of Mrs. Fink's was being carried away.

"It was getting on towards nine o'clock," the owner of the property concluded, "and we three tried to wait those women out. But they and their car didn't budge. So off we finally drove. Looking back, we eventually saw their car lights — they were starting to leave at last, and they followed our car down the mountainside."

Mrs. Fink confided to Mitchell privately that she had wondered and worried about the curious episode, particularly after reading in a local newspaper of the accidental death of Mrs. Coo's handyman.

Trooper Cadwell, acting independently of Sergeant Cunningham and the other officers, had come across some information which seemed hardly less vital as evidence for a murder indictment. Cadwell had dropped in to question further the farmhand, Fred Palmer, who by chance had been at Woodbine Inn on the Thursday night when Harry Wright's violent death was discovered.

Palmer worked for a Mrs. Wagner, who was Eva Coo's nearest neighbour. And Mrs. Wagner and her farmhand both had something which they felt they must tell the police, now that a crime more serious than a hit-and-run road accident was being investigated.

Early last Friday morning, Eva Coo had come to the farm to ask Mrs. Wagner and her hired hand to render her a service. "You see," she said, "I'm afraid there's going to be gossip. Some trouble, even. I mean, about poor Harry Wright's accident. I'd like both of you to be good enough to say, if anybody should ask you, that I was right there at the inn all last evening. I never went anywhere. Before Fred came over to hear the fight," Eva had coached a startled Mrs. Wagner, "you were there, remember, bringing some milk and cream and you used my telephone. O.K?"

Unaware at the time that it might entail perjury, both Palmer and his employer had agreed to Eva's proposal. But now, searchingly questioned by Cadwell, neither witness gave Eva Coo a moment's support for her crudely-improvised alibi.

The authorities were also hunting the car-hiring, bespectacled hostess at Eva's inn, Martha Clift. They couldn't find Martha all day Tuesday, but they did pick up the entertainer, Olive Brooks, with whom the Clift woman shared a small apartment on Main Street in Oneonta. And that other entertaining habitué of the inn, the shapely Lottie James, was also taken to Cooperstown for questioning.

From her the sheriff and Sergeant Cunningham got little save blank looks and agitated giggling. But from Olive Brooks came facts both pertinent and incredible. Olive proved to be a self-possessed person with nothing, either private or professional, that she cared to hide. She readily described how Eva Coo had got her to forge an entry in the old Wright family Bible, thereby confirming Eva's basic revision of the date of Harry's birth.

Obsessed by the need to shear five years off her handyman's age, before lopping off the rest of his life, Eva had told Olive: "Ernie can't do it, he's too drunk. Besides, darling, you write just childish enough to look exactly like the other handwriting on the flyleaf of that Good Book."

Olive also revealed that Eva, rather than being kind and motherly, had often been cruel, to Harry especially. "I've seen her knock him down and hurt him, many a time. Once I saw her flourishing a mallet, saying that she was saving it for Harry when her patience ran out. No, I don't know if it ran out last Thursday, Sheriff. I was entertaining an old friend, but not at Eva's dump."

Far-reaching investigation even dredged up the fact that Eva was pressed for funds that spring, that her taxes were overdue, not only on Woodbine Inn, but also on property in Oneonta which she owned. A banker in Portlandville confided to Sheriff Mitchell that Harry Wright had come into some $2,000 in savings accounts with his mother's death only three years ago. Under Eva's hospitable management, it had completely melted away. In addition, a small dwelling owned by Harry had burned down rather mysteriously. And Eva had promptly borrowed and used up the fire insurance money, likewise the cash that her crippled helper received when he sold the site on which the burned cottage had stood.

On Wednesday, June 20th, 1934 — six days after Harry Wright's death — Eva Coo was taken into custody. Martha Clift was also finally found and escorted to the county seat.

Obtaining a search warrant, state officers and deputies invaded Woodbine Inn. Eva, undergoing interrogation in Cooperstown, was angrily protesting her innocence, while fiercely complaining that the outrageous treatment being given to her, Ernie Tatum and the others, would cause her parrot and other pets to starve or the animals die of thirst.

The visiting officers fed and watered them, then began a probing and comprehensive search. They found the edited Bible. They found a stained and scarred mallet wrapped in a crushed and shabby felt hat. Ernie later identified this hat as Harry Wright's, the only one he owned. It was the hat that Harry had with him at 6.0 p.m. on Thursday, June 14th, when Ernie last saw him alive.

Determined detective work penetrated to Eva's special closet hiding-place and brought forth no fewer than 14 insurance policies. With Mrs. Eva Coo as beneficiary, these documents would have paid a total of nearly $10,000 on Harry Wright's life if he had died as the result of a genuine highway accident. Even without double indemnity, Eva had arranged to swap her handyman for an even handier amount of folding money.

Although the tests for blood on the hired car's rear seat cushion remained inconclusive, Martha Clift could be confronted with indisputable evidences of her participation in a brutal homicide. And she soon abandoned her defensive silence and told Mitchell, Brady and District Attorney Donald H. Grant a story of her part in the weird and vicious affair.

Martha admitted having known of Eva's sordid motives. She had heard Eva weigh and debate the feasibility of "getting rid of Harry in an accident." Martha admitted renting and driving the Willys-Knight on June 14th, with Harry and Eva as its passengers. But, she insisted, she had not actually helped in the crime, beyond being present on Crumhorn Mountain at 8.30 o'clock on that Thursday evening.

Eva, apprised of Martha's denial of major guilt, retaliated by swearing that she herself had only stood helplessly aside while Martha steered the heavy sedan not once, but twice, over Harry's prostrate form.

On Thursday, June 21st, three days after its interment, Wright's body was exhumed. For the purpose of reenacting the murder, it was taken at dusk up the winding dirt road to the haunted house on Crumhorn. At first, District Attorney Grant elected to play the part of the victim. Leaving the car, he walked down the driveway of the Scott place beside Eva, as she claimed that she and Harry had walked almost exactly a week ago. Martha Clift started the car and bore down upon them.

Afterwards, Eva took the wheel and brought the car back to the point where, she said, it had stood all the time that Mrs. Fink and the two others were up there. Eva and Martha both agreed that Harry Wright's recently-shattered remains lay under the murder car all the while that Eva graciously engaged the vigilant landowner and her companions in conversation, even insisting that Mrs. Fink and her two companions should make certain the sedan's interior contained no plunder.

To end the re-enactment, and score a "first" in the annals of the macabre, Harry Wright's poor, broken body, clad in a suit of borrowed clothes, was brought from the undertaker's vehicle and allowed to impersonate itself. That is, it was scrupulously placed in the various positions in which one or both of the accused women declared it had rested.

In spite of so much horror, both women stuck to their contradictory versions. Each, in fact, showed herself so strikingly insensitive to the ghastly Crumhorn operation that even case-hardened crime investigators were appalled.

On June 22nd Grant, who would prosecute her, had a crisp, decisive interview with Martha Clift. He had promised her a degree of immunity, since obviously she had stood to gain little or nothing from this savage crushing of a pathetic cripple's life. But if she were lying, she would lose her immunity, he warned her.

Martha came round and told what was eventually to be substantiated as the truth of the matter.

On June 14th, on their way to the haunted Scott place in the rented car, Eva Coo had made Harry Wright crouch down because she said they were going to steal Mrs. Fink's shrubs and Harry, the digger, mustn't let himself be seen. Eva was always the practical one. Hadn't she waited for this moment until her handyman-victim had finished painting her summer bungalows? Hadn't she trumped up an excuse to talk Harry out of his projected business negotiations at Johnson's?

And there was more. Eva had brought along her mallet. She had saved the grey cloth cap for this very emergency. A Woodbine Inn patron, obliged by an irate wife to flee in ill-clad haste, had neglected to take the cap and other articles of apparel with him. He had never called back for them. Eva had assured Martha that leaving the grey cap would add a touch of mystery and masculine participation to the accident scene near the inn with which they were to conclude their evening's outing.

In the Scott driveway, Eva had contrived to walk the limping Harry Wright directly into the path of the sedan. And Martha insisted that, once she had started and aimed the car, she grew too nervous to stop or slow down. Harry, however, had sensed the car coming at him, then whirled and seen his danger. He tried to dart aside to safety. But Eva had anticipated just such an impediment to her plot. She had brought the mallet.

Swinging it harshly, she struck Harry on the temple, knocking him right into the path of the car. It went over him.

Martha drove on, turned round behind the haunted house, and came back. Harry was hardier than Eva had expected. He wasn't dead. He had looked up into Eva's cruel face and whispered: "Now I know why you brought me up here!"

Eva had barked a peremptory command at Martha. Again the sedan rolled over the victim.

The two women, using an old blanket brought for that very purpose and later disposed of, had lifted the little handyman's corpse into the back of the Willys-Knight — but not until after long minutes of incredible, racking suspense, while Eva chatted with Mrs. Fink.

Subsequently, on approaching Woodbine Inn, the two had again used the blanket to lift Harry's body out and deposit it in the roadside ditch as evidence of an alleged accident, at the very point which Eva had selected in advance.

Eva and Martha were indicted separately on June 28th

by the Otsego County grand jury. Eva Coo was charged with first-degree homicide, and because of the callous, greedy motive and the base and brutal method of the crime, feeling ran high against her in the county and far beyond.

From her Cooperstown cell, she began issuing threats. She announced that she "had a lot on" prominent citizens who, unknown to their wives and families, had enjoyed the facilities of her roadhouse. But she retained eminent defence counsel also — Judge Everett B. Holmes and James J. Byard — and these gentlemen did not encourage their client's blackmailing.

Eva Coo was of Canadian birth, but she had come to live and work in Oneonta, dispensing, among other things, bootleg liquor before the 1933 Repeal. Then public resentment had induced her to move well outside the town limits, whereupon the shady Woodbine Inn had begun to flourish wickedly. It was said that Eva had been long since divorced by a Canadian husband, a trusted employee of the Canadian Pacific Railroad, and that he was now remarried.

Her trial began on August 13th, 1934, with Supreme Court Justice Riley H. Heath presiding. It was the first murder trial to be held in Cooperstown in 13 years.

District Attorney Grant prosecuted effectively. In all, 72 witnesses were heard. Defence counsel laboured manfully, but in vain. The jurors deliberated for only two hours on September 6th, and returned a guilty verdict. Judge Heath pronounced sentence at once: death in the electric chair.

Only minutes later, Martha Clift pleaded guilty to murder in the second degree and was given a sentence of 20 years to life. Since her release, the public has heard nothing more from her.

Eva Coo sat in the death house in Sing-Sing Prison, being distinguished by being assigned to the same cell which the notorious murderess, Ruth Snyder, had once occupied. Eva had stopped issuing threats. Her good humour and optimism now seemed all but invincible. To the end, she hoped to be spared the death penalty, but each of her appeals was denied.

On the evening of June 27th, 1935, one year and 13 days after the crushing death of Harry Wright, Eva Coo walked the last mile. Even when seated in the electric chair, she maintained her poise and aplomb. To the prison matrons who escorted her she called: "Goodbye, darlings!"

She had lived a tough life and she died a tough death. Those who saw Eva embracing her bitter fate spoke well of the cruel woman's courage at the end.

6

THE TEENAGED TORTURER

Benison Murray

"I'm lonely ... wanna take a ride?"
— The question that lured the victims to their deaths.

The last week of September 1982 ended the search. That was when the rugged Little River Canyon, in north-east Alabama, yielded up the abused body of 13-year-old Lisa Ann Millican.

The Georgia youngster had been dumped there and found only after a mysterious female voice called the police in both Georgia and Alabama about it. She never identified herself, however — simply gave directions as to where the dead child could be found.

The girl had disappeared from the Riverbend shopping centre in Rome, Georgia, while on leave from a facility for deprived and abused youngsters. She had been shot to death.

Then, two weeks later, Janice Morrow Chatman disappeared after she and her male companion were walking hand-in-hand down the street in Rome, when a young pregnant woman pulled up in a brown Dodge Charger with Tennessee licence plates. She asked if they wanted to take a ride — she was lonely, she said. The young couple were not alarmed — youth calls to youth. Besides, they had no pressing engagements. They accepted the offer.

Janice was not seen alive again ... But her male companion would later galvanise lawmen with his story and open an investigation into multiple murder.

North-east Georgia had been having a mini-epidemic of

murder. Macon and Albany each had their dead. Columbus had two female corpses. Monroe and Chattahoochee Counties had their own tally of one body apiece ... And now this.

The authorities did not think that there was one bad, mad killer. The sad thing was, there were no suspects at all. And later, when the horrific total was counted, it would be raised from eight to a possible 15 — and one body not even found yet ...

It was a typical Georgia evening, replete with the ceaseless creak of crickets, the rustle of sleepy birds going to roost. But the young man who crawled painfully from the underbush on to the rural road did not have his mind on these things. His whole self was concentrated on the seemingly impossible task of living long enough to tell police of his missing companion, Janice — and to get medical attention. He had been shot in the back.

Luckily, he managed to flag down a truck driver, who rushed him to hospital. There he told the police a frightening story.

He said that he and his common-law wife, 23-year-old Janice Chatman, had been picked up by a woman in a brown Dodge Charger. The new friend was young, red-haired and pregnant. The trio, he recounted, had driven around and been joined by the woman's husband in another car. Then, he said, the woman had marched him into the woods, shot him — and left him to die.

The police heard the fantastic tale with deep foreboding. If the man had been shot and left to die — where was Janice Chatman? What had happened to her?

Then, to confuse the issue and confound the authorities, the body of a man was found with his abandoned car near the Little River Canyon site, where the Millican girl's body had been found. So did any of the three cases have anything to do with each other — or was it simply a grisly coincidence?

The most Janice's 26-year-old companion could tell them was the make and model of car their deadly chauffeuse had driven, and that of her husband. He also thought the female voice on a police tape giving the location of the Millican girl's body might be that of his abductress.

Additionally, he explained that the woman had a CB handle of "Sundown" or "Sundance." And she had summoned her husband by the CB nickname of "Nightrider."

Hour after weary hour, detectives slogged through city streets, plodded rural roads, drove to schools and places of employment, questioning everyone. Rome police alone estimated since the probe began they had put in 1,000 overtime hours — with no end in sight. They felt that time had run out for Janice Chatman.

But if the days had seemed unending to those most interested, they at last came to an abrupt conclusion with huge headlines in local newspapers.

"Two Suspects in Custody!" one screamed. While below was: "Missing Woman's Body Found."

The couple in custody were described by police as "a pair of drifters and con-artists." One, Alvin Neeley, was 29 years old, a chubby, jovial-looking husband to Judith Neeley, his pregnant 18-year-old wife. They had both been arrested in connection with the death of Janice Chatman and the assault on her fiancé. The Neeley woman was also being charged in the Millican girl's death.

The pair were arrested in Murfreesboro, Tennessee, where they apparently ended a three-state spree of criminal activities. Among other things, they were accused of passing fraudulent money orders.

Janice Chatman's fully-clothed body was found 13 days after her abduction, lying face down in a creek in Chattooga County. According to police, both suspects had directed investigators to the spot where the young woman's body could be found. It was about 13 miles from where she and her companion had accepted the ride in the Dodge Charger. Janice had been shot in the back and chest.

The motive for the crime remained, for the moment, a mystery. But it was suspected that a local youth centre entered the picture when it was found that Judith Neeley had been a resident during 1980 after being arrested for armed robbery at the Riverbend shopping centre — the same mall from which the Millican girl vanished.

A fire-bombing had taken place at a youth centre employee's residence, with gunshots fired into yet another's house. Again, an unidentified female had called police to claim responsibility.

Where would it end? So far, there was revealed a potpourri of assorted evil. Altered money orders, armed robbery, abductions, fire-bombing and random shooting into dwellings, murder and — the last carrying the faint whiff of brimstone — rumours of sadism and torture.

Law agencies were scrambling to see just which charges could be brought against one or both of the Neeleys in the grocery list of crimes. And investigators now thought they could discern an apparent pattern in the manner in which potential victims were lured into the vehicle that would carry them to almost certain death.

The same ploy used to entice the couple could have been used with the Millican girl. It was an appealing call to the young: "I'm lonely — wanna take a ride?" It was especially apt to appeal to young rural people. After all, what else is there to do late at night in a sleepy Southern town but ride around in cars?

Police had by this time confiscated the Neeleys' vehicles — a red Granada and the brown Charger. Also confiscated were two .38-calibre and one .22-calibre pistols and two rifles. All would be subjected to ballistics tests.

Mourning for Janice, her family took some comfort that her suspected killers were behind bars. And her male companion was moved to comment: "I'm glad they got them before they do someone else any harm." He was by then at home, recovering from his gunshot wound.

"I had prepared myself for it [Janice's death]. The police prepared me for it," he said. "They told me that if they [the suspects] were the kind of people they thought, there was no way she was alive. But I did have hope."

Preliminary reports indicated that all three victims had been shot with a .38-calibre weapon. Lawmen waited on ballistics tests to determine whether it was one of the guns confiscated from the Neeley vehicles.

Awaiting trial, Alvin Neeley was in the custody of Sheriff Gary McConnell in the Chattooga County jail. Judith Neeley had been taken to the DeKalb County jail in Alabama, charged with the murder of Lisa Ann Millican. It was not yet known if she would be tried first in Alabama or in Georgia.

If the news up to this time had been sad, but expected, Sheriff McConnell told the media something that tallied with the rumours coming from Alabama and galvanised them and their readers.

"Torture, Sex, Grisly Slaying" were some of the local headlines as the information filtered out to the general public. And, as a result of intense questioning of Alvin Neeley, the sheriff was able to reveal that the suspects were implicated in at least seven other brutal killings — and perhaps as many as 15 — over a period of two years in a two-state area.

Under investigation was the murder of a woman in Macon, another in Monroe County, two in Muscogee County and the armed robbery and shooting of an Albany shop assistant.

The Monroe County woman had been found 18 months before, wrapped in a bedsheet in a desolate wooded area. Although her corpse was so badly decomposed that a determination of cause of death or identification was impossible, she was thought to be a runaway from the youth centre in Macon, Sheriff McConnell said.

The women from Muscogee and Chattahoochee Counties were both found tied to trees, bound with coat-hangers and strangled. The Macon woman was found in a burned house, also bound with coat-hangers and dead. The Albany shop assistant, pregnant when shot during the robbery, had not died, although she remained in a coma. She had been shot in the back of the head with a .22-calibre gun. Doctors reported that they had lost her unborn baby's heartbeat.

By this time, too, the authorities had the reports on the

ballistics tests — and they had paid off. For the bullets recovered from Janice Chatman's body had been linked by the state crime lab to the .38-calibre weapon recovered from one of the Neeley vehicles. It was, Sheriff McConnell said, also believed to be the gun used in the Millican girl's killing.

And the newly-released autopsy reports on the 13-year-old youngster found in DeKalb County, Alabama, presented information almost too ghastly to contemplate. For it revealed that the girl had not only been shot in the back of the head, but had been injected with Drano, a caustic drain-cleaner.

This torture prompted a new look at Janice Chatman. Fresh tests were to be conducted to determine whether she, too, had been injected with the caustic before she died.

Alvin Neeley, in the meantime, was indicating to the authorities that he had first-hand knowledge of the killings, but cannily stopping short of admitting actual responsibility for the deaths. During two days of questioning by law-enforcement officers, Neeley explained that he and his wife Judith were recruiters and enforcers for a prostitution ring, Sheriff McConnell revealed.

Neeley stated that they were trying to recruit females off the street to act as prostitutes, the sheriff claimed. He said that Neeley was "extremely knowledgeable" about the locations of the bodies of eight other victims — all murdered over a period of 18 months — and how each had died.

It seemed that Neeley would reveal new horrors each time he was questioned in the county jail. Now he admitted, he and his wife were linked with as many as eight — possibly 15 — tortured and murdered victims. And not only that, but both he and his wife had sexual experiences with the bound women before they were finally done to death.

Neeley explained that his wife would first pick a woman or girl from the street, then contact him on the CB. The couple would then take their prey to a remote area, or a motel room, where Neeley would bind and rape them. Judith Neeley would then commit sexual acts with the bound female after her husband left the scene.

Alvin Neeley, investigators said, recounted that Judith took "pleasure in killing the women." His wife liked killing, Neeley said, because "it gave her a feeling of authority".

When Neeley was arraigned before Judge Joseph E. Loggins, he totally dissociated himself from his wife. He claimed he didn't own either of the two vehicles confiscated at the time of their arrest — and that even the $1,200 in his pocket belonged to Judith Neeley.

He insisted that he wasn't present when the murders took place. But he pinpointed places on a map where the bodies of various victims had been found, telling what each had looked like and how they were killed.

Investigator Bobby Gilliland testified that eight of the bodies Neeley described had been found — "but he says there is another body in Alabama, which has not turned up". By this time, news of the Neeleys' arrest had reached their home towns in Tennessee. People who knew them seemed to divide into two camps — pro or con Judith and Alvin Neeley.

Some placed the blame on Alvin, insisting that Judith's troubles began when she met him. Others said that Alvin was "just a poor slob in love" — with the wrong kind of woman.

Records showed that when Judith was 16 the Neeleys had been arrested in Rome, Georgia, in October 1980, charged with armed robbery. This involved a gun, a woman and the Riverbend shopping centre — the same mall where the Millican girl was to disappear two years later.

Judith was sent to the youth rehabilitation centre in Rome by the juvenile court. While there she would give birth to twins.

Alvin Neeley was a Georgia youngster, whose family later moved to Tennessee. Married once before, he met and married Judith when she was 14 — legal in some Southern states — and he was 25. When Neeley was arrested for the mall robbery in 1980, Floyd County Sheriff Bill Hart had received four requests from various Georgia agencies that he be held in custody.

In Floyd County, Neeley had been charged with theft by conversion because he failed to deposit $1,896 in takings belonging to a filling station where he had worked for a week. He was sentenced on the lesser charge, and the armed robbery charge was dropped. So it was clear that the Neeleys were no strangers to a courtroom.

On October 23rd Judith Neeley was bound over to a grand jury in Fort Payne, Alabama, in the case of the death of Lisa Ann Millican, whose body had been found in Little River Canyon five days after she disappeared.

Charges against the Neeleys were now amplified to include forgery and theft. During the month of June, it was alleged, they had altered and cashed in six money orders, plus a U.S. Treasury cheque for $2,500.

Of particular interest to the officers was the manner in which Janice Chatman was murdered. Hers was the only killing with which Alvin Neeley and Judith Neeley would be charged jointly out of the deaths for which they were thought to be responsible. And the complaisant Neeley set out to give particulars of the last terrible moments of the unfortunate woman's life.

His story was frightening in its simplicity. After shooting her fiancé in the back, the pair took Janice to a Rome motel, where the trio spent the night. She was handcuffed to the bed — and both Neeleys had sex with her.

The next afternoon Alvin Neeley, followed in the other car by his wife with Janice, travelled down U.S. Highway 27, towards Tennessee.

Suddenly, Neeley said, his wife veered onto a side road and told him via CB she was going to take care of Janice Chatman in the same way as she had the woman's companion.

According to Neeley, he told her that he'd heard on his police scanner that the man had survived. Judith, he said, replied that the woman knew too much anyway.

To cap this grisly story, Neeley claimed that the Millican child had been kept for three days, with both Neeleys having sex with her before she was killed and dumped in Alabama.

With both Neeleys eventually indicted for murder in the Chatman case — and Judith alone in the Millican case — the trials were set for the spring of 1983. And DeKalb County in Alabama was first out of the chute, when Judith Neeley went to trial for the brutal and sadistic killing of the 13-year-old Millican girl.

Dressed in a flowered blouse, her hair curling about her shoulders, and smiling, she was accompanied to court by her lawyer. She looked slender again, her baby having been born while she was in jail and custody given by the judge to her grandmother.

With the jury finally chosen and seated in the courtroom of Judge Randall Cole, the State proceeded to present 24 witnesses and introduce more than 50 exhibits. A forensic pathologist from Huntsville told the court that the Millican girl had died from a gunshot wound in the back. "Death," he said, "was almost instantaneous." And Judith Neeley wept as the bloodstained blouse of the young victim was held up for the jury's inspection.

Her lawyer had asked that the statement made by her and given to an FBI agent be thrown out, but Judge Cole ruled that it could be introduced as evidence. So, FBI Agent Bill Burns, of Rome, Georgia, was able to take the witness stand for a marathon four hours' testimony. At one point in his recital Judith Neeley was led in tears from the courtroom.

When she returned, Agent Burns said: "It was my conclusion that she enjoyed torturing people and killing them — and she did so."

Judith Neeley, still sobbing uncontrollably in the courtroom, was found guilty and sentenced to death in Alabama's electric chair for the September 1982 murder of 13-year-old Lisa Ann Millican.

Just 20 minutes after the sentence was read out, the young woman was led by deputy sheriffs to a waiting patrol car and taken to Julia Tutwiler women's prison, near

Montgomery, Alabama.

Judith Ann Neeley is still on Alabama's Death Row. Her husband, however, escaped the death penalty and is serving two life sentences.

7

KISS AND KILL

D. L. Champion

"Don't do this to me. Think of my baby." — Anna Hahn's final plea as she was being led towards the electric chair.

Her name was Anna Felser. Her eyes were blue and cold as a limpid Alpine lake. Her hair was blonde and her figure, at least to a masculine eye, was noteworthy.

In 1919, when she was 19 years old, she still lived in the little town of Füssen where she was born. Füssen is a neat, prim settlement on the Bavarian border with Austria.

Füssen, in those distant days before the world had heard of Adolf Hitler, was a quiet place. It contained a single fleshpot in the form of a beer garden where the burghers consumed great quantities of beer and sausages and taxed their lungs singing melancholy *Lieder*.

None of these minor vices was designed to appeal to a young and attractive girl. Anna Felser's life was as dull as a text book, as uneventful as a blank page. She lived in vague discontent and dreamed of riches and romance with a gay and handsome sweetheart, a Prince of Pilsen.

These actually arrived in Füssen one day — in the person of Dr. Kurt Schmidt, a medical man from Vienna. He was spending his holiday at the lake of Ammer See, a few miles from Füssen.

Schmidt was a worldly individual — tall, blond, extremely handsome. He was in his middle 30s, and he dressed well. His voice was a deep, resonant baritone, which he used effectively in his romantic episodes. These were inevitable and casual, forgotten as swiftly as they began, especially if the lady's intentions became too serious.

On a Sunday afternoon in May, Anna Felser packed a substantial lunch and took a bus to the Ammer See. There she met Kurt Schmidt. He impressed her. He was suave, debonair, not at all like the rustic swains who had paid her court. She impressed him too, for entirely different and quite obvious reasons.

They saw a great deal of each other. The doctor assured Anna that he loved her and she implicitly believed him. For her part Anna Felser declared that she adored him and would do anything and everything in the world for him.

What followed proved to be the happiest week in Anna Felser's life. Never before had she lived so joyously. And never again would she do so. She was in love. She was ecstatic. The drabness of Füssen was already no more than a vague grey memory to her.

But shortly afterwards it became a harder and grimmer reality than it ever had been before.

In June, the doctor returned to Vienna. He left Anna Felser with fervent kisses and promises to send for her as soon as he had settled certain personal affairs. Anna waved at the train until it disappeared over the eastern horizon. Then she went home to await the magic letter which would take her from Füssen for ever.

It never came. At first Anna was inclined to blame the inefficiency of the post office. But her dozen letters and two imploring telegrams to the doctor in Vienna remained unanswered.

The truth of the matter was obvious. It was also unpleasant, and Anna Felser was reluctant to accept it. She put through a telephone call to the doctor's Vienna office.

Dr. Schmidt did not mince words. He made it crystal clear that nothing he had said to Anna Felser had been sworn before a notary, that a man could not be held to promises made in moments of passion, and that as far as he was concerned the affair at Ammer See had never happened.

Within a week Anna Felser had more or less pulled her emotional self together. She was endowed with a vast amount of hard, common sense. There was no point in permitting the episode with Schmidt to ruin her life. She would, she resolved, obliterate him from her memory. She would completely forget him.

Two months later she learned that this would be far more difficult than she had expected. The doctor had left an absolutely unforgettable memento behind him. Anna Felser was pregnant.

Now to be pregnant while unmarried is embarrassing anywhere. To be in that condition in a small town is intolerable. Anna Felser was treated as a pariah. The honest burghers called her by a name which sounds even more harsh in German than it does in English.

After the birth of her child, whom she christened Oscar, Anna Felser decided that she could no longer live in Füssen. She wrote a pleading letter to her uncle, Max Doeschel, who lived in Cincinnati, Ohio, imploring him to send her enough money to get her to the United States. Three weeks later, she received an international money order for $236.

Anna Felser bought a steamship ticket, left little Oscar with her parents, and set out for America and the Middle West. Before she did so, she swore a solemn oath. Never again would any living man betray her.

Cincinnati, Ohio, is known as the Rhineland of America. For every German living in the town of Füssen, there are 25 in Cincinnati. The men, for the most part, are frugal, industrious artisans. Their wives are immaculate housekeepers, competent cooks.

Max Doeschel, Anna Felser's uncle, was a 74-year-old retired carpenter who lived at 3540 Evanston Avenue. He was a widower, in need of a housekeeper. This need, he believed, would be filled by the presence of his young niece.

In that he was mistaken. Anna Felser was a casual cleaner and an indifferent cook. Moreover, her heart was by no means in her work. Cincinnati had infinitely more to offer a young girl than Füssen. Anna took far more interest in the motion picture theatres and dance halls than she did in undertaking the management of her old uncle's home.

Max Doeschel disapproved of her attitude and her conduct. He made this fact clear in loud, guttural German. The argument continued for some time. It resulted in Anna packing her bags and taking her departure.

She lived for a short while in a furnished room on Walnut Street. Then she moved in with another German couple. These were Karl Osswald and his wife, who was Max Doeschel's sister. They lived at 1400 Sycamore Street, and there Anna Felser apparently found a home more congenial than the one she had left.

Anna had lived at the Sycamore Street address for less than a month when Mrs. Karl Osswald died suddenly. After the funeral Osswald asked Anna to stay on as his housekeeper.

Unlike Max Doeschel, Osswald did not object to Anna's casual cleaning methods. He did not complain of her inadequate culinary technique. There was a reason for this. Osswald made it quite clear one night.

"You are a beautiful woman," he said. "I want you to marry me."

These were the words which Anna Felser had wanted above all else to hear at Ammer See. Now she was strangely indifferent to them. Nevertheless, she did not turn Osswald down. She agreed, after some conversation, to marry him. But not immediately.

She had a reason for this. It was in her mind to return to Füssen, pick up her son and bring him back to Cincinnati. This would require cash. Anna had none. But there was no good reason why a girl couldn't borrow from her fiancé.

Not that it was easy. Karl Osswald was not a prodigal man. He had saved his money, dollar bill by dollar bill. He was accustomed to spending it the same way. However, Anna Felser was a blue-eyed blonde, and physically as attractive as a magnet.

Anna cajoled, wheedled and pleaded with Osswald for a

substantial sum of money to finance her trip to Germany. At last, Karl Osswald reluctantly yielded. But on one point he was adamant. He would not *give* her the money. He would lend it to her, without interest. That, he considered, was extremely generous.

In July, 1930 Osswald handed Anna Felser some $2,000 in bonds, which she promptly cashed. While she was arranging for her passage, she met Philip Hahn. Hahn was young, moderately handsome and, he disclosed to her, he now had a fairly good salary as a telegraph operator.

Hahn took Anna out on several occasions. On one of these, he told her that he loved her beyond life itself. Anna, recalling the Ammer See episode, was wary.

"If you love me," she said, "why don't you marry me?"

Philip Hahn thought this over. He found no good argument against it. They were married in October. Shortly after that, Anna sailed for Germany.

She returned with her son Oscar, to find Philip Hahn and two lawsuits awaiting her. Max Doeschel was suing to recover the $236 he had originally advanced to her to come to the United States. Karl Osswald, furious at her marriage to Hahn, was demanding the return of his $2,000.

Anna Hahn was indignant. "What are those old fools bothering me for?" she asked her husband. "They have plenty of money. They never spend what they have, anyway. I think they've got a lot of nerve. Besides, they're related to me."

"But, after all," Hahn replied reasonably, "you owe them the money. They expect to get paid."

"Well, they won't. At least, they won't get all of it. I'm entitled to some of it, for having lived with them, putting up with their senile nonsense."

Anna Hahn settled the suits out of court with a payment of 50 cents in the dollar.

Early in 1931, Anna and her husband opened a combination bakery, delicatessen and restaurant on the corner of Bates and Colerain Avenues. It was a legitimate and profitable enterprise. It was not the last profitable enterprise in which Anna Hahn was to engage. It was, however, the last legitimate one.

In the bakery Anna Hahn became acquainted with Ernest Koch. Koch, a retired teamster, lived alone in a rococo mansion on Colerain Avenue, a few blocks away from the Hahn establishment. He was an old man, in ill health. Anna's beauty and youthful vitality attracted him. He spent a great deal of time sipping coffee at the marble-topped table in the restaurant. Anna, aware that he was wealthy, treated him with something more than cordiality.

At the same time Anna became interested in racing. A casual customer had given her a tip about a horse running at the Coney Island race track. Anna bet two dollars on it and collected 18 more when it won. It was easy money, and it made her thoughtful.

She realised that she had been lucky to win. She realised that if she played constantly she would not win in the long run. She deduced that only the bookmaker did that. Her conclusion was simple and inevitable. She would make the book.

She did so, setting up a small book in the back room of the bakery. Her front-room customers became her back-room clients. Within a few months, she was doing very well. Then an opportunity arose which would enable her to do even better, she decided.

She spoke of it one night to her husband. "Phil," she said, "old man Koch wants me to move into his house and be a sort of practical nurse to him."

Philip Hahn thought this idea extremely out of order and he said so.

"I don't know," Anna argued. "He said he'd pay me well and remember me in his will. He must have a lot of money and he has no relatives in this country."

"So what? He might live for another twenty years," Philip countered.

If at that moment Anna considered accelerating the demise of Ernest Koch, she did not mention it to her husband. She said instead: "I really think I should take the offer. There might be a lot of money in it, eventually."

Philip Hahn firmly put down his conjugal foot. "No," he said flatly. "I never should have let you start that bookmaking business. You've enough to do in the shop, and taking care of me and Oscar. I certainly won't permit your going to live in Koch's house."

Anna Hahn gazed at her husband absently. "You know," she said thoughtfully, "we ought to do something about those rats in the basement."

Philip agreed.

"I'll attend to it tomorrow," Anna said. She added: "I'll get some croton oil for Oscar, too. The boy needs a purgative."

On the next day, Anna attended to it. She contrived to meet a friend, Rudolph Gertner, a youthful employee of a Cincinnati drugstore. Rudolph Gertner was a more or less casual acquaintance of Anna, but that wasn't his fault. He was quite willing for the acquaintanceship to develop into something warmer and more intimate. Anna, fully aware of this desire, exploited it.

Anna made a date with Gertner for that evening and during its course she was more cordial to him than usual. Before they parted her reason became apparent.

"Rudy," she said, "I want you to do me a favour. I want you to get me some stuff from the drugstore where you work."

"Sure, Anna. Be glad to. Anything at all."

"First, I want some croton oil. A quart or two, maybe."

"A quart or two? What for?"

"Oscar needs a purgative."

Gertner pointed out that two quarts of croton oil were enough to purge a battalion of Prussian Guards. Nevertheless, after some discussion, he agreed to procure the powerful laxative.

"There's one more thing," said Anna. "I need some arsenic. Our cellar's infested with rats."

"Sure. But you'll have to sign for arsenic. That's the law."

But Anna Hahn, for reasons of her own, had no wish to record her signature in the drugstore's poison book.

"But you'll have to," Gertner argued. "It's the law."

"Isn't there some sort of law about you going out with married women? Isn't there some sort of law about you making love to them? If you can break a law for yourself, you can break one for me," Anna argued.

By the time Gertner had kissed Anna goodnight for the third time, he had agreed to bring her both the arsenic and the croton oil on the following day. There would be no need for her to sign her name in the book, he agreed.

During the next few weeks, oddly enough, the rats in the cellar of the Hahn establishment flourished. Philip Hahn, however, did not. He became violently ill.

His case baffled his doctor, who prescribed various pills which brought about no improvement. Hahn vomited constantly and within a month he developed a partial paralysis.

His mother insisted that he be moved to a sanitorium for medical treatment. Anna was left alone with little Oscar to run the business. But in a little while there wasn't very much business to run.

Anna Hahn was so avid for money that she made an error which few bookmakers ever make. She began to bet her book profits with other bookmakers. She became a player as well as a layer. She bet as much as $50 a day and she lost heavily.

Within six months of Philip Hahn's departure to the hospital Anna had given up the book, sold the bakery and moved into Ernest Koch's elegant house on Colerain Avenue.

In Cincinnati's Germantown there existed two schools of thought regarding Anna's living with the elderly bachelor. The first held that she was a brazen, mercenary hussy who cared more for a potential inheritance than for her good name. The second argued that she was a kindly, Christian soul who devoted herself unselfishly to nursing old man Koch through his declining days.

In any event, Ernest Koch died on May 6th, 1933. And when the will was opened the birds began to sing — at least for Anna Hahn. She was bequeathed the $12,000 Colerain Avenue house, along with its grounds and its furnishings.

Old man Koch was hardly cold in his coffin before certain officious members of the school which held Anna Hahn an avaricious wanton made a number of anonymous telephone calls to Cincinnati's Detective Bureau. The purport of each call was the same. Ernest Koch had been poisoned — obviously by Anna Hahn.

As a result, a court order was obtained and the remains of Ernest Koch exhumed and removed to a laboratory. An autopsy was performed by the Hamilton County coroner.

The doctor's report absolved Anna Hahn and confounded her enemies. Koch, the coroner stated, had died of cancer of the throat.

But Anna's troubles were not yet over. Koch was survived by several relatives back in Germany. When they heard of his death they engaged a lawyer. He argued that Anna had exercised duress on the dying man, influencing him unlawfully, to change his will in her favour.

Anna finally offered the relatives a settlement of $4,000, which was accepted. Miraculously, it didn't cost Anna a penny.

It just happened that during the week when the $4,000 was due to be paid to Koch's relatives, two fires broke out in the Colerain Avenue house. The damage, Anna Hahn notified the insurance company, totalled exactly $4,002.

The insurance company added up the fact of the will settlement and the amount for which they were liable and figured it all came to arson. There was, however, no evidence to this effect and the insurance claim was duly paid.

Now that Anna Hahn had successfully nursed Ernest Koch into his grave and ended up with a $12,000 property, she decided to make a career of catering to ill and elderly people. Not only could she thus draw a salary, she could also, if her patients possessed decent instincts, receive favourable mention in their wills.

Early in 1936 Anna Hahn was introduced to a Hungarian woman, Julia Krecskay, in the Blade Café on Elmwood Place. Mrs. Krecskay was only 48 years old, but she was in ill health. Nevertheless, she believed that she could hold a government job and eventually became eligible for a pension.

At this point Anna's nostrils twitched slightly. She smelled money. She assured Mrs. Krecskay that a government job could easily be obtained through the good offices of Anna Hahn herself. Anna, it seemed, had connections in Washington, eager to perform any service for her. Naturally, it would cost a dollar or two.

Mrs. Krecskay found this reasonable enough. "How many dollars?" she asked.

Anna thought a hundred might do for a starter. Mrs. Krecskay gratefully wrote out a cheque.

During the next four weeks no offer of a government job came to Mrs. Krecskay from Washington. And Anna Hahn's connections apparently had some very bad days at Bowie race track. They needed more of Mrs. Krecskay's money. Mrs. Krecksay trustingly handed over another $400 to Anna.

Then Mrs. Krecskay suddenly became ill. She took to her bed in the boarding-house where she lived. Anna Hahn immediately volunteered her services as a nurse. Mrs. Krecskay, properly grateful, accepted.

By this time, Mrs. Krecskay and Anna had become good friends. The Hungarian woman had no relatives in the United States. But she had money. Anna was quite willing to be her heir if, perish the thought, Mrs. Krecskay should die.

In spite of Anna's tender ministrations Mrs. Krecskay did not improve. On the contrary, she grew steadily worse. That she did not die was probably due to the sharp eyes of Walter Koenig.

Koenig, a lodger in the house where Mrs. Krecksay lived, was more or less friendly with the woman. While visiting her one afternoon, he observed that blisters formed on her lips whenever her saliva touched them. This struck Koenig as odd. Later that day he spoke to a doctor about it.

The doctor stated that it sounded as if Mrs. Krecskay was suffering from poisoning. He suggested that Koenig have her sent to a hospital.

Over Anna Hahn's angry protestation Koenig arranged for the sick woman to be removed to Cincinnati's Good Samaritan Hospital. When Koenig visited her there she told him of her payments to Anna for the job she desired in Washington.

Koenig, by no means as trusting as Mrs. Krecskay, called on Anna Hahn. He came to the point at once. "It's my opinion," he said, "that you've tried to poison Julia Krecskay."

Anna's blue eyes flashed in anger and indignation. A moment later, they blurred with tears. "How can you say that? Julia's like a sister to me. How could I do anything to harm her?" she choked out.

"You swindled her out of five hundred dollars," Koenig stated.

"I did not! All that money went to people in Washington to get her a government job."

"I think you're lying," Koenig said. "I want that money back for her."

Asking Anna Hahn for money was like asking Cyclops for an eye. At this stage in her career Anna Hahn loved money more than she had loved the dashing Dr. Schmidt back in Ammer See.

"If you don't return the money," Koenig threatened, "I'm going to the police."

This, to Anna Hahn, was a convincing argument. Perhaps there were already incidents in her career which would not comfortably bear official scrutiny. Anna delved deep into her bosom of her dress and produced a crumpled wad of banknotes. She counted out $500.

Koenig took the money and returned it to Julia Krecskay.

He also informed the police of the transaction. Detectives visited the hospital and urged Mrs. Krecskay to sign a complaint against Anna Hahn.

The sick woman refused. "Anna is my good friend," she insisted. "You people don't understand her beautiful character."

Mrs. Krecskay recovered her health, which was unusual for a patient who had been attended by Anna Hahn.

Anna's next financial venture involved a retired railwayman, Albert Palmer. He was 72 years old, in ill health, and lived alone. He possessed a gullible nature and a bank account. These facts made him eligible for Anna's attentions.

In spite of his age and infirmities, Albert Palmer still had an eye for a pretty girl and Anna Hahn was still attractive. He began making love to his nurse. Exactly how Anna reacted emotionally to his overtures is not a matter of record. However, since her goal was a financial one, she indulged the old man to some extent, at least.

But Albert Palmer was a long time dying. Anna Hahn became impatient for his will to be opened. One bright morning, after she had fed him two eggs and three kisses for breakfast, she unfolded a sad story.

"Albert," she said, "I'm in a little trouble. My son Oscar's been sick. I've just paid the taxes on my house and a lot of other expenses have eaten up my cash. I need some money."

Palmer was a credulous man and he was extremely fond of Anna Hahn. But he was also a frugal man. He merely said: "Don't worry, Anna. I'm sure things will be all right."

But Anna was not interested in optimistic philosophy. She wanted something more tangible. Mobilising her shrewd wits and her not inconsiderable physical charms, she went to work on Albert Palmer.

Eventually, he capitulated, but not completely. He agreed to lend Anna Hahn $2,000, but he insisted that she give him a note for the money.

Anna, who for reasons of her own firmly believed that

Palmer would be far out of this world when the note became due, agreed. She signed the note and Palmer gave her the cash.

Albert Palmer died on March 27th, 1937. His will left nothing to Anna Hahn. On the other hand she had no intention of returning the $2,000, so she was at least that much ahead. Besides, she had just met George Heis, who was also aged, moneyed and ill. He was well fitted to take the place of the deceased Albert Palmer.

Heis was less close, financially, than his predecessor Palmer, had been. He recognised Anna Hahn immediately — and incorrectly — as a kind, honest, Christian soul. He was happy, he said, to lend her $1,200. He asked for neither a receipt nor a note.

Anna insisted that for his health's sake Heis live on a diet of beer and spinach. Following this advice, Heis consumed gallons of beer which eventually made him sicker than he had been before. Anna assured him that the spinach would counteract the ill effects of the beer.

So George Heis consumed vast amounts of spinach. The vegetable proved no panacea at all. Heis became partially paralysed. He suffered such pain that he completely lost faith in Anna's remedies. He accused her flatly of trying to poison him and ordered her from the house.

Anna left. On the way out, in order to cut her losses, she picked up $140 in cash and $75 worth of jewellery.

In April 1937 Jacob Wagner, who lived at 1805 Race Street in Cincinnati, confided to his friend, Fritz Grafemeyer, that he was contemplating marriage. Since Wagner, a retired labourer, was in his late 70s and suffering from diabetes, Grafemeyer registered surprise.

"She's a wonderful girl," Wagner said. "A blonde. Young, too. And she loves me."

Grafemeyer regarded his friend cynically. "If she's young and beautiful," he remarked, "it must be the dough you have in the bank she loves. Not an old fogey like you."

"You don't know what you're talking about," Wagner

declared. "She's got more money than I have. She's a rich widow."

Grafemeyer remained unconvinced. After he had been introduced to Anna Hahn, who by then was staying in Wagner's home, he was more sceptical than ever.

"Jake," he said to Wagner, "you're getting senile. That girl's too young for you. She's after your money. I don't believe she's got a nickel of her own."

"No? I'll prove it to you. I'll get her to show you her bankbook," Wagner said.

On the following evening, a smiling Anna Hahn met Wagner and Grafemeyer in a local beer garden. She opened her handbag and said to Grafemeyer: "I understand you wanted to look at my bankbook. Well, here it is."

It was a book issued by the savings department of the Cincinnati Trust Company. It showed quite clearly that the balance in Anna Hahn's name was $16,003. Fritz Grafemeyer was impressed.

He shouldn't have been. Anna Hahn's balance at the moment was precisely $3. Anna, a handy girl with a pen, had written the figures 1,600 in front of the 3.

Naturally, Fritz Grafemeyer could not know this. Now that his suspicions were allayed he was happy that his friend had found romance, though he still thought it odd that a girl as young as Anna should be attracted to old Jake Wagner.

It seemed that Jacob Wagner did not thrive on love. He frequented the beer gardens less often. He appeared to lose his vitality. At last, he took to his bed. Anna Hahn remained at his side and nursed him diligently.

On June 2nd Jacob Wagner died. On the same day, Anna Hahn presented herself at Wagner's bank, asserted that she was his niece and wished to draw out $1,000 from his account. On the following day she visited the Probate Court, again posing as Wagner's niece, and requested that the dead man's room be searched for a will.

Charles Dothauer, a court deputy, accompanied her back to Wagner's apartment and conducted the search for the will. Hardly to Anna Hahn's surprise, he found one. It was scrawled in pencil on a dirty sheet of writing paper. Complete with spelling errors, it read:

"I hereby make my last will and testament. I am of sound mind and no influence. I have money in the Fifth Third Bank. I want my funeral expenses paid and all my bills. The rest I want to go to my relative, Mrs. Anna Hahn, 2970 Colerain Avenue. I want Mrs. Hahn to be the executor of estate. I don't want any flowers and I don't want to be laid out."

The will was unwitnessed and it was dated January 10th, which was some three months before Jacob Wagner ever met Anna Hahn. That interesting fact was unknown to the Probate Court at the time, but the will was refused for probate because there were no witnesses to Wagner's signature.

Anna Hahn had not done very well this time.

At this point in her career Anna made the acquaintance of Mrs. Olive Koehler and George Gsellman. Mrs. Koehler, who lived with her sister at 104 West Elder Street, was an invalid who had been ordered to hospital by her doctor. However, Mrs. Koehler preferred to remain in her own home. She decided that if she hired a nurse she could obtain as much care at home as she would receive in a hospital. She hired Anna Hahn.

George Gsellman, a 67-year-old retired carpenter, lived alone in a shabby room at 1717 Elm Street. Anna Hahn met in a beer garden, listened with interest to his story of loneliness and listened with even greater interest to the tale of how he had saved enough money to enable him to retire.

George Gsellman evidently felt the same way about Anna Hahn as had the deceased Jacob Wagner. Gsellman informed his best friend, August Schultz, that a lovely young woman was madly in love with him. Gsellman showed Schultz several photographs of Anna.

While Anna Hahn was alternately flirting with and nursing Gsellman, she was also taking care of Olive Koehler. Since Mrs. Koehler lived with her sister, and since she had numerous relatives in Cincinnati, it seems reasonable to assume that Anna Hahn's high hopes of inheriting Olive Koehler's money slowly diminished.

That fact might account for the cash and jewels which vanished from the Koehler home. The total value of the stolen articles was something in excess of $180. Both Mrs. Koehler and her sister were inclined to lay the blame on some decorators who had recently been working in the house.

Anna Hahn, of course, concurred in that opinion. She even went further. "I have a friend," she announced, "who has underworld connections. I'm sure he could get the money and jewels back for you."

Mrs. Koehler suggested that they call in the police. Anna Hahn scoffed at the idea. The police, she maintained, were inefficient, if not downright crooked. It was pointless to enlist their services. On the other hand, her friend with underworld connections was trustworthy and reliable. There was no doubt of his ability to find the missing items. Naturally, there would be a small fee involved.

Mrs. Koehler obligingly handed Anna Hahn $80 to give to the friend with the underworld connections. Oddly enough, he never returned the stolen goods. Even more oddly, Anna Hahn did not come back to the Koehler house.

She was quite busy now with George Gsellman. Somehow she induced him to sign his money over to her.

"Although," as he later remarked to August Schultz, "all I ever got for it was a couple of kisses."

One afternoon late in June, Anna Hahn had an appointment to meet Gsellman in a downtown beer garden. She arrived first. She became bored with waiting and decided to do some shopping. She fished an old streetcar transfer ticket from her purse. On the back of it she scrawled a note to Gsellman and left it with the bartender.

The note read: "Go home. I'll come there."

She didn't bother to sign it. Nevertheless, that note was destined to haunt her. It was to reappear one day in a tense and crowded courtroom. The apparently worthless streetcar transfer was to become a grim ticket, good for one admission to a prison death cell.

It wasn't exactly coincidence that George Gsellman's health had been failing gradually since the time he met Anna Hahn. On July 1st, 1937 he was stricken so badly that he could not leave his home. Anna remained with him all day, save for a short period when she went to his bank to cash a cheque for $100.

On July 6th George Gsellman died. The death certificate stated that the cause of his death was heart disease. One person, at least, knew better.

By this time Anna Hahn was well known in the German section of Cincinnati. Originally, there had been two schools of opinion as to her motives. Now the two schools were rapidly merging into one.

Those who had stoutly held that Anna Hahn was a true angel of mercy were beginning to wonder. There was no doubt at all that she ministered to the old and infirm, but the mortality rate among them was impressive. She was known to have ministered to eight people, including her husband. Five of them were dead. One, her husband, was still in a hospital. George Heis was spending his declining days in a wheelchair. Only Julia Krecskay had recovered.

But there was still at least one man left in Cincinnati who was apparently unaware of Anna's lethal record. He was George Obendoerfer, a retired cobbler, 67 years old. He was a widower of long standing, and his bank balance reflected a comfortable five figures. Perhaps George Obendoerfer did not regard money as one of the three most important things in life, but he certainly would have been hard put to name the other two.

He had lived all his life in cheap and shabby boarding houses. He had dined on kraut and wurst in inexpensive restaurants. His clothes were not fashionable, but they were durable.

Financially, George was no one's sucker. He did not invest in stocks or shares. All his cash was stashed away in the vaults of the Clifton Heights Building and Loan Association in Cincinnati. He was not interested in large dividends or a quick turnover. If you wanted to sell the Brooklyn Bridge, an oil well or the Cincinnati Reds' ball park, you could not sell them to George Obendoerfer.

The last man in the world, you would think, to fall for Anna Hahn would be George Obendoerfer.

When they first met, Anna Hahn realised shrewdly that Obendoerfer's suspicions would be aroused if she attempted to borrow money from him. Anna, therefore, decided to pose as a wealthy woman. She told Obendoerfer that while she was short of actual cash, she owned vast real estate interests in Colorado.

Shortly after this Obendoerfer confided to Harry Fuhs, a friend for many years, that he was having a love affair with Anna Hahn. "We're going out West together," Obendoerfer said. "Anna has a big farm out there and we're going to live on it. She has another place, too, and there's an offer of $5,000 for it. We're going to sell it."

While preparations were being made for the trip George Obendoerfer became ill. Perhaps this did not surprise Anna Hahn. In any event, she insisted that the trip take place exactly as planned.

Obendoerfer was so ill that Anna had to help him onto the Chicago train. Accompanying them was Anna's young son, Oscar.

Ill as Obendoerfer was, he flatly refused to go to a hotel in Chicago. He insisted that it was a waste of money. He spent the night in a Madison Street flophouse, where the charge was only 25 cents. Anna Hahn and her son took quarters at a Loop hotel and paid $8 for accommodation.

They arrived in Denver on July 23rd, 1937. Anna registered for them at the Oxford Hotel. Obendoerfer, now too weak to protest, immediately went to bed. He ordered, the room clerk recalled later, several pitchers of ice water.

Two days later the hotel manager suggested that Anna call in a doctor to examine Obendoerfer. Anna haughtily refused and moved her menage to another hotel, the Midland.

Then there began a clash of wills. Anna told Obendoerfer

that she needed some cash to pay off a few paltry mortgages on her lands in order to sell them. Obendoerfer wasn't, however, putting in a dime until he had actually seen the real estate. And he was far too ill to do so at the moment.

Anna Hahn took matters into her own hands. She went to the Denver National Bank, announced that she was the wife of George Obendoerfer, that she wished $1,000 transferred to the Denver bank from the Building and Loan Association in Cincinnati. She produced Obendoerfer's passbook and a note apparently written by him.

The Denver bank told her to write direct to the manager of the Cincinnati firm. She wrote the following letter:

Dear sir:

"Inclosed, you will find Mr. Obendoerfer's passbook. I adviced him to the Denver Nat. Bank, they will take care of him. I am leaving for Newcastle tomorrow to take care of my own business matters then I will return to Cinc. by Saturday or Sunday. Mr. Obendoerfer is going to stay in Colo. With his sister-in-law or whatever relation she is to him. He also has quite a number of friends here from the old country and he'll enjoy life more than he ever did before.

"He was thinking of buying a little chicken farm. He has one in mind if he can get the right price for it he'll take. Mr. Obendoerfer want the Building and Loan to send him a cheque for $1,000 and send it to the Denver National Bank where he is going to deposit the money. He would like to have it as soon as possible in case he would find a nice place so he could take it right away. As soon as I return to Cinc. I'll stop in and see you about some property."

This letter was signed, for reasons never established, "*Anna Felser*".

Harry Becker, the manager of the Building and Loan Association, regarded this ungrammatical epistle with a sceptical eye. He did not forward the $1,000.

In the meantime the wife of the Midland Hotel manager, Mrs. Rose Turner, became concerned over the suffering of George Obendoerfer. In her opinion, he should be sent to hospital, she told Anna. But Anna disagreed with her.

Mrs. Turner came into the room one day while Anna was doctoring the old man. She observed that Anna was giving him a copious draught of croton oil.

Mrs. Turner gasped: "Croton oil! That's too harsh and powerful. You shouldn't give him that. You should send him to a hospital."

"I'm the best judge of what he needs," Anna snapped. "I'll treat him my own way."

"If you do, you'll kill him," Mrs. Turner protested. She threatened Anna. "If you don't call a doctor for him, or send him to hospital, I'm going to call the police."

"In that case," Anna said, "we'll move."

But before doing so, Anna entered Mrs. Turner's apartment and made off with $300 worth of rings. Perhaps she was motivated by anger at Mrs. Turner, or perhaps just keeping her hand in.

Obendoerfer, young Oscar and Anna Hahn then set out for Colorado Springs. Obendoerfer collapsed as he stepped from the train to the platform of the railroad station. A policeman summoned an ambulance and Obendoerfer was taken to the Bethel Hospital, despite Anna's strenuous objections.

On August 1st, George Obendoerfer died. The hospital authorities, believing that Anna Hahn was his wife, broke the news to her gently.

Shedding no tears, she disavowed him. "Why tell me?" she asked. "I only met him on the train. He means nothing to me."

She packed her bags and began, with Oscar, a leisurely trip back to Cincinnati. Her eyes were just as blue as they had been when she was a girl in Füssen. Perhaps they were not as keen. She failed completely to see the net which was tightening slowly around her.

When Mrs. Turner missed her rings, she was quite sure who had taken them. She notified the Denver Police. Within a few hours, a detective found the missing jewels in a pawnshop, where they had been pledged for $7.50 by a woman who called herself Marie Fisher. The pawnbroker's description of her, however, was a description of Anna Hahn.

It was a simple matter to trace the journey of Anna, Obendoerfer and Oscar to Colorado Springs. Inspector I. B. Bruce of that police department began to look into the death of George Obendoerfer at the Bethel Hospital. As a matter of routine he sent a posthumous photograph of the dead man to the Cincinnati authorities, asking for information.

Cincinnati was more interested than Inspector Bruce might have supposed. Less than 24 hours prior to the receipt of his inquiry, Fritz Grafemeyer had told a friend, Patrolman John Carroll, that Jacob Wagner had died under peculiar circumstances, after having become engaged to his nurse, Anna Hahn, the angel of mercy.

Carroll had passed this information along to Detectives William Rathman and Frank Kammer. These officers made a preliminary investigation, the results of which they considered important enough to communicate to their superior, Captain of Detectives Fred Hayes, and Prosecutor Dudley Outcalt.

A more intensive investigation revealed that Anna Hahn had been connected with several other people who had died suddenly. The prosecutor ordered that her affairs be thoroughly examined.

Olive Koehler, who had been taken to a hospital shortly after giving Anna Hahn $80 for her friend with the underworld connections, was interrogated by the police. She had only kind words for Anna.

Her sister, Mrs. Mary Arnold, took a different and more jaundiced view of the matter. "I never trusted that woman," she declared. "I know she stole those things from our house. She pocketed the $80 my sister gave her and she constantly fed her poisoned ice cream."

Checking on the death of Jacob Wagner, the detectives soon discovered that the "will," purporting to have been written by him, was dated three months before he met Anna Hahn. Apparently, through some psychic means he had bequeathed his cash to her.

Following leads picked up in the German section of the city, Detectives Stanley Grause and Philip Brewster called on George Heis. They found a gaunt, emaciated man, his paralysed legs stretched out like dead sticks on the bed. Brought to headquarters, Heis squirmed in his wheelchair and denounced Anna Hahn.

"She's a poisoner!" he shouted. "I lent her money and she fed me poisoned beer and spinach, so she wouldn't have to pay me back. I'd be dead today, if I hadn't ordered Anna Hahn to get out of my house."

Detectives Michael McShane and William Wobbs traced Julia Krecskay, and learned the story of the Washington connections and the subsequent poisoning of the ailing woman.

Assistant Prosecutor Frank Gusweiler discovered that Anna Hahn had also attended Albert Palmer before he died. From the executor of Palmer's estate, he obtained Anna's unpaid note in the amount of $2,000 and several letters which contained, alternately, requests for money and erotic promises.

Detective Rathman, pursuing a tip, interviewed August Schultz. Schultz had never met Anna Hahn, but he had been shown a photograph of her by George Gsellman. Moreover, he had always believed that suspicious circumstances surrounded the death of his friend.

All this was not merely enough, it was far too much for Prosecutor Outcalt. He obtained a court order for the exhumation of the bodies of Jacob Wagner and George Gsellman.

In the meantime, an autopsy had been performed on the corpse of George Obendoerfer in Colorado Springs. Dr. Francis McConnell, a Denver pathologist, examined the vital organs of the dead ex-cobbler. He announced that he had found definite traces of arsenic in the viscera.

Upon receipt of this news Detectives William Sweeney, John Bugganer and Frank Kammer were dispatched to the Colerain Avenue house with orders to arrest Anna Hahn.

Anna remained unruffled. "There's no use arguing with you," she said. "I can explain everything."

She attempted to do so to Prosecutor Outcalt and Cincinnati Chief of Police Harold Weatherly. Obendoerfer, she swore, she had met on the train to Chicago. She had never known him in Cincinnati. Gsellman she had never known at all, she declared. August Schultz was obviously trying to frame her.

"Why," they asked, "should he do that?"

Anna Hahn smirked. "A lot of men get angry with me when I reject their advances. This Schultz seems to be taking it harder than most."

Palmer, she maintained, was a good friend who had lent her money, never asking for its return. The note was a mere matter of form. Jacob Wagner she also put in this category.

She denied either poisoning Olive Koehler or stealing from her home.

"And Julia Krecskay," she said, "would never say a word against me."

That was true enough. Julia Krecskay held to her belief in the Angel of Mercy until the day she died.

George Heis was the most difficult for Anna to explain away. He was alive, articulate and bitter. He insisted that Anna Hahn had poisoned his beer and his spinach and that she owed him a large sum of money, Outcalt informed her.

"Delusions," said Anna. "The man suffers from delusions. I happen to know something about psychiatry."

Anna Hahn was remanded to a cell. A squad of detectives was sent to the Colerain Avenue house to search it. They found a bottle of croton oil and another bottle half-filled with a white powder which proved to be arsenic.

It was young Oscar who unwittingly branded his mother a liar in the matter of George Obendoerfer. "Sure," he said to Prosecutor Outcalt, "I knew Mr. Obendoerfer a long time. We went with him. I went to Union Station with my mother when she bought the tickets for the three of us."

On the following day autopsies were performed on the bodies of Jacob Wagner and George Gsellman. The results, announced by Coroner Frank Cappock, were negative.

"There is no obvious indication of murder," the coroner reported. "However, we are turning the vital organs of the two men over to the County Chemist, Dr. Otto P. Behrer."

Within 12 hours Dr. Behrer made public the fact that there were definite traces of arsenic in the viscera of the dead men. "There is very little of it, though," the doctor said. "It is my belief that Anna Hahn poisoned her victims with arsenic. Then, when they had reached the point of death, she dosed them heavily with croton oil. This would have a strong purgative effect, ridding the body of most of the remaining arsenic."

In the meantime, detectives had looked carefully through the effects of George Gsellman. They had come upon a crumpled streetcar transfer upon which was written: "*Go home. I'll come there.*"

Since the message was unsigned, the police handed it over to the handwriting experts, along with samples of Anna Hahn's writing.

The verdict was unanimous. Anna Hahn had, beyond all doubt, written the message on the transfer. That fact definitely established that she had been lying when she said that she had never known George Gsellman. And the bartender, reading the newspaper story of the transfer, recalled the blonde who had left it with him. He accurately described Anna Hahn.

Olive Koehler, now dying in the hospital, at last became convinced that her faith in Anna Hahn was misplaced. She came to the belated conclusion that it had been Anna who stole the cash and jewellery from her home. She signed a complaint of grand larceny.

Anna Hahn heard this news from Prosecutor Outcalt. She took it lightly. "She can't prove anything," Anna said. "I'll never go to jail for that."

"You probably won't," Outcalt agreed. "You'll never even go to trial for it."

"You mean you have no case?"

"I mean, I don't need a case on the larceny charge," the prosecutor said. "I have a strong first-degree murder case. It is my opinion that you have killed no less than half a dozen people. I think I can prove you murdered Gsellman and Jacob Wagner. But if, through some miracle, you should be acquitted, Colorado wants you for killing George Obendoerfer."

On August 17th, 1937 Anna Hahn was indicted by a Hamilton County grand jury on two murder charges. She had, the grand jury charged, committed malicious and premeditated murder, unlawfully, purposely, and by means of poison.

In October, a month before Anna Hahn was brought to trial, Olive Koehler died in the hospital.

In November, Anna Hahn faced a jury of 11 women and one man. The prosecution alleged that she had gained between $50,000 and $70,000 by her "nursing".

For her part, Anna looked at the jury with clear blue eyes and said: "I'm as innocent as a new-born babe. I have absolutely nothing to fear."

Six days later, the jury returned a verdict of guilty, with no recommendation for mercy. Judge Charles S. Bell sentenced Anna to die in the electric chair.

Until then, no woman had ever suffered capital punishment in the state of Ohio. Anna Hahn's attorneys fought desperately to save their client from being the first woman to be executed.

For nine months they struggled through the state courts all the way up to the United States Supreme Court. All their appeals were denied.

On June 20th, 1938, Anna Hahn was taken from her cell in the State Penitentiary at Columbus and led to the bare, grim room which holds but a single article of furniture.

When she saw the chair she screamed, "Don't do this to me! Think of my baby!"

She struggled as she was strapped in the chair — the chair which marked the end of her long and lethal trail from Füssen, Germany.

It is a matter of medical record that Anna Hahn died far less painfully, but much more quickly, than any of her unfortunate victims.

8

DEATH OF A MARTINET

R. J. Gerrard

"Her eyes were cold with hate. She raised the axe again." — William Place's statement from his hospital bed.

At the back of the house the smell seemed to be getting worse. You couldn't mistake the odour of carbolic acid, Hilda Jans thought. Hilda, the housemaid, was a plump young blonde, and as a rule enormously diligent. But now, trying to do the breakfast dishes, she paused to wipe her eyes, just as her employer, Mrs. Martha Place, bustled into the kitchen, lean, tall, erect and accusing.

"Good gracious!" Mrs. Place fumed. "How can you be so slow, Hilda? You know how much has to be done around here today."

"Don't you smell it, ma'am?" the maid asked.

"Smell what?" Mrs. Place looked annoyed. "You know how I dislike foolish excuses. If you're behind with your work — well then, you are, that's all."

"But that carbolic smell —" Hilda turned from the sink to gesture with soap-dripping hands, as if the foul reek was eddying around them.

"Why, yes," said Martha Place, slowly. "I do notice something, now that you mention it. But it's hardly carbolic, Hilda. It's not an acid smell. More likely a gas leak."

"Carbolic," Hilda persisted. "I even went and looked down the cellar. Thought maybe something had tipped over, ma'am. I'm sure it's right here in the house, somewhere."

Martha Place stared. Her lips formed a thin line, her cold

grey eyes swept over Hilda, over the nicely-kept kitchen. When she smiled, her smile was patronising. "In this house? Don't be absurd. Whatever it is, must come from the Weldons' next door. That woman is simply crazy about germs and bacteria, disinfecting everything."

Hilda nodded, relieved. "So she is. I didn't think of that," she said.

Mrs. Place's smile grew even more metallic. "Well, you won't have to think about these neighbours much longer," she told the girl. "Dry your hands and listen to me. There are certain things you have to do right away."

Hilda Jans turned from the sink to give her mistress her whole attention. And what she heard astonished her. Mrs. Place was explaining that she and Mr. Place had decided to move away from Brooklyn. In fact, they were going to leave Hancock Street immediately.

"Am I to go with you?" Hilda asked. And when Mrs. Place emphatically shook her head, the maid sniffed, and said bluntly, "Then you're firing me? I don't give satisfaction, is that it?"

Martha Place answered curtly, as one with much to do and not nearly time enough in which to do it. Yet she didn't sound disagreeable. "I've no fault to find with you, Hilda," she said. "This decision of ours was a sudden one. And Mr. Place and I are pressed for time.

"What about Miss Ida? She hardly ate any breakfast."

Mrs. Place said, "Oh, her." Ida was her stepdaughter, a girl of 17. Mrs. Place said that Ida was just whimsical and moody. Hilda needn't give her another thought.

It was now about 9.30 on the bleak and dreary morning of February 7th 1898. What Mrs. Place wished particularly to impress upon Hilda Jans was that she would be dealt with fairly. And it was a pleasant surprise to Hilda to learn that she was to receive one month's wages in lieu of notice.

What was more, said Mrs. Place, the maid could earn herself a bonus by getting her clothes and other possessions packed, her trunk closed, roped up and out of the Places' comfortable dwelling here at 598 Hancock Street before 5 p.m. that day. Mr. Place himself had insisted on this, said Mrs. Place. In order to expedite their own packing and prompt departure, he wanted Hilda packed off, bag and baggage, that Monday afternoon before he returned from Manhattan.

Hilda couldn't quite understand the importance of her own hurried leave-taking. But she understood a month's wages, and an extra $5, and she assured Martha Place that she would do as she was told. It transpired that her mistress had a number of things she wanted Hilda to do for her. First, she asked Hilda to go in haste to the Brooklyn Savings Bank. Mrs. Place had left her bankbook there on February 2nd, to be balanced as of January 31st. Now she wanted it.

This errand Hilda did, managing to combine it with another, whereby she arranged for an expressman for the Stuyvesant Heights district to call for her trunk between 4.30 and 5 o'clock.

By the time Hilda returned, her mind busy with her personal problems, Mrs. Place had another urgent errand. Hilda was directed to hurry off to the annex boat at the foot of Fulton Street and see the baggage-master about a trunk which her employer was shipping. Hilda was to tell the baggage-master that he must make sure Mrs. Place's trunk was picked up in time to be put aboard the 3.45 train for New Brunswick, New Jersey.

"What about Miss Ida?" Hilda inquired.

"Well, what about her?"

"Won't she be wanting her lunch?"

Mrs. Place nodded absently. "She's up in her room packing. She'll moon over everything, I expect. Probably take all day. But when my stepdaughter says she's hungry, Hilda, I'll see to it. So get on with you."

Hilda was busy every minute, dumping her possessions helter-skelter into her big oval-top trunk. Once Mrs. Place called her to go out and mail five letters which she said she had just dashed off. Again, about 3.15 p.m., when the doorbell rang, Mrs. Place told her that it was only a man calling to sell something and she had no time for him. Hilda obediently allowed the bell to ring and didn't answer it.

By 4.45 that afternoon, Hilda Jans was dressed in her best. The expressman she had engaged was already at the front door. Hilda gave him the address. She had made sure of her wages and bonus, and had a $10 bill and two $5 bills pinned to her corset.

Rather rattled by all this rush and urgency, yet touched by sentiment, Hilda went along the upstairs hall on tiptoe. Mrs. Place might scold her if she seemed to defer her going or to delay Miss Ida's preparations. However, she rapped gently on the door of Ida's bedroom. She got no answer. Hesitating a moment, she tried the door. She found it locked.

"Hilda!" Mrs. Place shrilled. "Don't you want to pay your expressman now?"

"No, ma'am. I'm to pay him when he delivers it," the maid called down.

Abandoning her idea of saying a cheerful goodbye to the girl, Hilda took hurried leave of the only member of the family available. Mrs. Place agreed to convey her farewells to Mr. Place and Ida.

Hilda left the house, believing she was through with 598 Hancock Street for ever. She had earned her modest, unexpected bonus with minutes to spare. It was only 4.50 p.m. Not until that moment was the maid reminded of something she had meant to mention to Mrs. Place — that smell of carbolic again. She was certain that the odour had been pungent and offensive as she stood rapping and trying the knob at the door of Miss Ida's bedroom. It most certainly wasn't coming from the Weldons' house.

At 6.15 that wintry evening, William W. Place, an insurance adjuster, who had travelled by way of the Brooklyn Bridge from his New York office on lower Broadway at Pine Street, used his latchkey to let himself into No. 598. He had been surprised as he approached to see no lights on in the house and once inside the front door he called out: "Martha! Are you home, Martha?"

He closed the door and called again: "Ida, my dear!" And

then, as an after-thought, and louder, in order to carry to the kitchen, he called: “Hilda!”

Surprised and puzzled by the unaccustomed silence, William Place turned on the light in the front hallway at the foot of the stairs. He began to walk slowly through the hallway, towards the rear of the house.

At 6.32 p.m. Patrolman Harvey McCauley was walking his beat and, at that moment, traversing the 600-block of Hancock Street. Suddenly, in the light from the street lamp at the next corner, he saw a tall, lean and agitated man hurrying towards him. The man, disregarding the biting cold of night on the windswept Brooklyn street, wore neither hat nor overcoat.

Coming up to McCauley, he halted, waving his arms. “Come with me, Officer,” he urged.

“Come where? What is it?”

“It’s the house next to ours — I’m Norris Weldon — 596 Hancock,” the man panted. “There’s somebody hurt — screaming — in 598. Please, hurry!”

In spite of a deep-seated professional resistance to over-excited householders, McCauley hurried, for Weldon, agile and muscular, had seized one of his gloved hands and was virtually dragging him.

“All right, I’ll come,” the patrolman agreed. “Leggo my hand. Take it easy, mister. What’d you hear?”

“Awful cries and moans,” said Weldon. “Somebody was screaming, ‘Murder!’ My wife and sister heard it, too.”

When the pair bounded up the brownstone steps of No. 598, they found the storm door slightly ajar, but the inside front door was locked. McCauley pressed hard on the doorbell, asking Weldon who lived here. And as Norris Weldon, still gulping for breath, gave the information, the two men facing the locked door heard a sound.

It was a piteous moan: “Help! Martha — murder — help me —” The sobbing outcry trailed off in a kind of bubbling gasp.

McCauley was no longer sceptical, or reluctant. “Come on!” he barked at Weldon. “We bust in!”

The two men lunged at the locked door. It gave with a crash and flew inward. Because of their momentum, the two men all but trod on the form of William Place. He lay barely two yards inside his own front door. Blood smeared his face, gushing from deep head wounds.

McCauley knelt beside him. "Bad," he said. "He's only just alive." The officer stared up at the ashen face of Norris Weldon. "You know where that new call box is?"

"Next corner, isn't it?"

"That's right. Know how to work it?"

"No."

"Then get the druggist there to help you. I've showed him how, in case of emergencies. Just tell 'em the address and get an ambulance here from St. Mary's, fast."

Weldon ran like a man 15 years his junior. He not only managed to send the police signal to the Ralph Avenue Station, but also got the druggist to telephone directly to the hospital.

In the dimly-lit front hallway of the Place residence, McCauley was doing his best to attend to the injuries of the unconscious William Place. At the same time he kept sniffing and glancing up the stairs. There was a strange smell that he couldn't identify. Nor could he be sure that the injured man's assailant wasn't still lurking in the house. As a precaution, McCauley eased the gun in his holster.

Because of the double alarm which Weldon and the druggist had transmitted, two ambulances from St. Mary's Hospital clanged to a halt by the kerb. Immediately afterward Captain Ennis, commander of the Ralph Avenue Precinct, arrived at the house, accompanied by Detectives Becker and Mitchell.

Two young doctors, Gormully and Fitzsimmons, had come with the ambulance. They examined William Place, and nodded approval of McCauley's efforts to check the flow of blood. "I'll take him," Dr. Gormully told his colleague.

Captain Ennis and his men were searching the house. The smell which had penetrated to the patrolman turned out to come from a heavy concentration of illuminating gas. The upper hall was choked with it.

The officers traced it to a front bedroom and opened the door. Ennis and the detectives threw open the windows. There was too much gas to risk striking a light and in the dark Detective Becker stumbled over something. It turned out to be the prostrate form of a woman.

As soon as the inrush of icy night air made it safe to put a match to a gas jet, they glanced around the bedroom. Two other gas jets, on the wall on either side of the heavy walnut dresser, had been bent down to an angle of 45 degrees. Both were wide open and pouring gas into the room. The way they had been bent made it impossible to shut them off entirely.

"Pass the word to one of those ambulance surgeons," Ennis ordered. "He's needed up here."

The woman on the floor was unconscious. She was fully clothed, and wrapped in a down quilt evidently snatched from the big double bed, which was in tumbled disarray. Her head had been thrust inside a white pillowslip, adding a peculiar gruesomeness to the scene.

As Becker pulled off the pillowslip and he and Mitchell lifted this second insensible victim onto the bed, Dr. Fitzsimmons hurried into the room. "Gas poisoning," he diagnosed hastily. "Better take her to the hospital, too. We'll soon bring her round."

Norris Weldon had identified the victim with the savage head wounds as William W. Place, owner of the house. And now the shocked neighbour identified the gas victim as Martha Place, William's wife.

Because of the arriving ambulance, a large crowd of onlookers had poured out of surrounding residences. Ennis had stationed policemen to hold back this throng, but now a well-dressed young man broke through the blue-coated cordon. He rushed up to Dr. Fitzsimmons as he, his driver and Patrolman McCauley came down the front steps with the stretcher bearing Mrs. Place to the waiting ambulance.

The young man stared frantically at the blanket-covered

figure. "Is it Ida?" he cried.

"Who's Ida?" the doctor asked.

"Miss Ida Place — my sweetheart. She lives here."

"Then this is probably Ida's mother," McCauley said.

"Mrs. Place? She's Ida's stepmother," the young man corrected him. "Where's Ida? Haven't you seen her?"

"Not me," McCauley said. "You better go in there and tell your troubles to the captain."

The young man raced up the steps. He met Captain Ennis and the two detectives in the front hall. "Sir, can you tell me where I can find Ida Place?" he asked the precinct commander.

"Who are you?" Ennis asked.

His name, the young man said, was Edward Scheidecker. He gave his address, in this same Stuyvesant Heights section of Brooklyn. He described himself as Ida's best beau, with every expectation of becoming her husband just as soon as they were both old enough. He already had the consent of Ida's father, he explained.

"Calm down, son," Ennis said kindly. "We haven't seen your girl. Besides Mr. and Mrs. Place and Ida, who else lives in this house?"

Edward told them that there was only one other person — the Places' maid, Hilda Jans.

"That's odd," said Ennis. He and his subordinates had searched the house with thoroughness, on the assumption that a single assailant had tried to asphyxiate Mrs. Place, had been detected by her husband on his return from business, and had attacked Mr. Place as he made for the front door to try to call for help.

The officers had seen no signs of a servant, or of breaking in, ransacking, or robbery. Nor had they come across the weapon which had given William Place his fearful head wounds. The maid appeared to be strangely missing. Detective Mitchell said that he had looked into the small room, second-floor rear, normally occupied by the servant in a dwelling of this style. He had found the window raised a few inches, the closet clean and entirely empty. Also empty were the bureau drawers.

"Hilda was here yesterday," Edward Scheidecker asserted. "She let me in when I called on Ida, as I do every Sunday afternoon. If Hilda had been going to leave, I think Ida would have told me about it."

"Tell me this, son," Ennis said suddenly. "Do you know of any reason why Ida would be away from home at this hour?"

Edward replied: "No, sir, I don't."

"Wouldn't she have mentioned it to you yesterday, if she planned to be out?"

"I'm sure she would have, sir. But —"

"But what?"

"Ida never goes away on visits."

"Any special reason?" Ennis asked. When the other seemed to fumble for an answer, he said sternly: "Come now, you'd better tell me everything you know."

"Ida doesn't go out, I guess, because her stepmother makes such a fuss about it."

"She and her stepmother have had arguments?" At Edward's unhappy nod, Ennis turned to Becker and Mitchell. "What did you find in the daughter's room?"

"We never found it. No sign of any daughter, Captain. But," Becker continued,"there's a door a little way along the hall from the room we take to be the servant's room. It's locked. I planned to go back and try to get in there, after we'd explored everything else. I took it to be a locked storeroom."

Ennis asked Edward: "You know which is Ida's bedroom?"

"I've never been in it," the youth answered stiffly. "But I know where it is. If it's locked," he said, "then maybe ..." He pushed past the officers and started to dash upstairs.

"Wait," said the captain. Then he and the two detectives, Patrolman McCauley and the youth pounded up the stairs and stood before the only locked door on the bedroom floor. Ennis knocked on the door.

McCauley sniffed. "There's that smell, sir. I told you

about noticing it in the hall below, before I smelled the gas."

"If you ask me, it's carbolic," Mitchell said.

McCauley was down on his knees, sniffing at the crack under the door. "That's it! Carbolic acid!" he exclaimed.

Becker got out a bunch of skeleton keys and was trying the lock. "Forget that," Ennis snapped. "Break the door down."

They forced the door and entered. Even before Mitchell lighted a Welsbach burner, light from the gas bracket in the hallway revealed that a violent struggle had taken place in this room.

The officers, taller than Edward, stood between him and the bed. Edward stood on tiptoe. "It's Ida!" he cried. "Oh, no!"

"Keep back, son. Stay out in the hall." Ennis growled.

The neatly-shod feet and shapely legs of a girl were protruding from under the mattress on the furiously disordered bed. Becker and McCauley lifted the mattress. They thrust the bedding and pillows to one side. The 17-year-old girl, lying on her back, was dead. She had obviously been lying beneath the mattress for many hours. The biting reek of carbolic acid was almost intolerable. And what the acid had been intended to do, and had done, was gruesomely plain.

Ida's face, eyes, lips and mouth had been seared and blistered with the carbolic. There were other signs of violence, dim marks not made by the acid, on her slender throat and on one temple. But there wasn't a single spot of blood on the bed, its furnishings, or anywhere else in the room. If the acid had not caused her death, then the daughter of William Place had been smothered or strangled.

Ennis told McCauley to stand guard outside the bedroom door and permit no intrusion until the arrival of the coroner. Becker and Mitchell were careful to add no disarrangement of their own to the confusion and disorder. They used their handkerchiefs when pulling open dresser and bureau drawers, or opening the door of Ida's neatly-kept clothes closet, in their search for the bottle or container which had held the carbolic acid.

If they could learn where it came from, they might be able to identify the purchaser and user. No ordinary household solution of the stuff had been used, that seemed certain. A devastating concentrate known to chemists as phenol had been hurled into Ida's young face. But nowhere in the house could the detectives find a bottle.

Notified by Captain Ennis, Coroner Delap soon arrived at 598 Hancock Street, accompanied by the noted pathologist Dr. Alvin C. Henderson. They made an examination of the girl's body and ascribed her death to asphyxiation.

"In spite of the terrible acid burns," said Dr. Henderson, "I believe an autopsy will prove that Ida Place was strangled to death."

Coroner Delap gave permission for removal of the body. Before convening a coroner's jury, he and Dr. Henderson made a careful study of the front bedroom, with the bent gas jets. They attempted to discern the path followed by the hacked and bludgeoned William Place to the blood-drenched spot just inside the front door where Patrolman McCauley and the neighbour, Weldon, had discovered him.

From St. Mary's Hospital there now came word that both Mr. and Mrs. Place might survive. Mrs. Place, they said, was partly conscious, but incoherent. She kept calling for her husband. "Willie? Where are you, Willie? Why don't you come here to be with me?"

William Place, a slight, precisely groomed man of 47, was still unconscious. But his strong constitution seemed visibly to resist death.

Detectives Mitchell and Becker questioned Norris Weldon, his family, and other neighbours, and learned a good deal about the Places. When the daughter, Ida Place, was only 11 her mother, a charming and devoted woman, had died. The distraught widower, seeking to keep his home intact, had engaged Mrs. Martha Savercool as housekeeper. Martha, who hailed from New Jersey, was a capable, aggressive woman. She was fond of relating how she had succeeded as a dressmaker after her own untimely widowhood.

William Place was both a prosperous and a lonely man. Less than a year after his wife's death, and only three months after Martha Savercool came to live under his roof, he decided to marry again. So Martha, from housekeeper and a kind of upper servant, who showered attention upon little Ida and the bereaved William, became overnight a stepmother, a cherished bride and the mistress of the house.

Ida, the neighbours revealed, had never appeared to accept Martha as her second mother. And William's relatives, residing in Brooklyn, had firmly, even rudely, declined to accept her. After a year of this second marriage it was apparent to the neighbours that the William Places were a long way past their honeymoon.

Bitter and increasingly numerous arguments rocked the dwelling and echoes of them seeped inevitably into nearby houses. The Places' rows and recriminations became a familiar part of the local scene. Once, at least, they had attained the scandalous proportions of a case taken to court.

As for this very day, said the Weldons and other neighbours, Mr. Place had been observed making his customary Monday morning departure. But nobody in the 500-block could recall having seen Ida Place after 8.20 a.m. At that hour the daughter had appeared at the front door with her father and they had been seen exchanging affectionate farewells.

Then, during the afternoon, two different expressmen had called at the Place residence and each had carted away a trunk. The first expressman was seen by Mrs. Weldon shortly after 12.30 p.m. The second had come later, around 4.30. The first express wagon was one serving the baggage department at the foot of Fulton Street. The second bore the name of Broderick.

Mrs. Weldon and others had surmised that Hilda Jans was taking leave of the turbulent family. This was confirmed when, soon after Broderick drove away, the blonde maid emerged, clad in her Sunday best. Looking neither hurried nor troubled, Hilda had disappeared into the gathering winter twilight.

Early the next morning, February 8th, Detective Becker went over to Fulton Street and soon traced a trunk which on the previous day, on the orders of Mrs. Martha Place, had been transported from her Hancock Street home. It was on record that Mrs. Place had sent the baggage-master an urgent message concerning this trunk. She had wished to have it shipped to New Brunswick, New Jersey, insisting that it be put aboard a certain train — the 3.45 out of the Pennsylvania Railroad Station in Jersey City. And this had been done.

Finding a local expressman named Broderick was more difficult. Many expressmen had their own small businesses in Brooklyn at that time, and several of them were named Broderick. But the determined Becker and Mitchell eventually found the right Broderick. From him they learned that a trunk belonging to Miss Hilda Jans had been conveyed, late the preceding afternoon, from the house on Hancock Street to No. 1118 Prospect Place.

The detectives hurried to interview Hilda Jans. They found her friendly, puzzled, frank and co-operative. And they heard from her more about the friction in the Place household.

Step by step, Hilda related her experiences of the previous day, saying that she had been paid a month's wages and a $5 bonus to pack her things and be away from the house within seven and a half hours after hearing that she was to go. Hilda mentioned that she had been bothered in the kitchen by the smell of carbolic acid.

Had she seen or heard anything unusual before smelling the carbolic? No, said the maid. It turned out that she had been sent into the back yard at No. 598, right after the family finished eating breakfast and Mr. Place left for Manhattan. Mrs. Place had wanted certain things hung out to dry, saying that she had read in the *Eagle* that they were in for a new siege of snow.

"Then you came back indoors and began to do the breakfast dishes? How soon after that did you smell the carbolic?" Becker asked.

"Why, I guess, almost right away."

"What time was it? Think carefully, please."

Hilda said she was certain that it had been about 9.15. The reason she was so sure was because of that surprising conversation with Mrs. Place about their hurried departure from No. 598. It had been 9.30 by then. Her errands — first to the Brooklyn Trust Company to get Mrs. Place's bank-book and next to see the expressman, Broderick, about picking up her own trunk before 5 p.m. — had followed in rapid order. While going and coming on her various errands, she had seen no sign of Mrs. Place ever providing Ida with any lunch, Hilda told Detective Mitchell.

More questions by Mitchell and Becker brought Hilda Jans around to her most startling recollection. She had wanted to say goodbye to Miss Ida — such a sweet kid, and always in trouble with her stepmother. But Ida's bedroom door had been locked, and Hilda's rap hadn't been answered. The maid had thought that Ida might be packing, or perhaps catching a little nap. It was only some time afterwards, said Hilda, that she realised when she stood at Hilda's door she had smelled the carbolic again.

From Coroner Delap came an announcement of the results of Dr. Henderson's autopsy. The murdered girl, it was reported, had sustained a heavy blow on the left temple just at the hairline. But the actual cause of death was asphyxiation. It was Dr. Henderson's belief that the girl had been strangled some time between 8 and 10 a.m. on February 7th, and that she had been dead not less than 10 hours when her body was discovered by Captain Ennis and his men.

Henderson's report added something which sent shivers of horror through newspaper readers in Brooklyn and all over America. Ida Place, the physician stated, had been seared and blinded by the acid while still alive, still conscious.

Later that Tuesday morning Ennis sent a number of men to resume by daylight a thorough search of the house and yard at No.598 and the neighbouring yards. The acid container and the weapon used in the attack on William Place were still missing. But one of the officers found a bloodstained axe sunk in a sloping pile of unmelted snow in Norris Weldon's side yard.

Recalling that the window in the servant's room vacated by Hilda Jans had been found raised a little, the police were able to plot a line leading to Weldon's side yard. Apparently the axe, wet with the blood of William Place, had been hurled from the window of the maid's room. As it was then after nightfall, no one at home in the Weldon household had chanced to see the weapon describing its grisly arc.

Captain Ennis also sent Detective-Sergeant Bardon to scrutinise the records of the Gates Avenue Police Court. And Bardon learned that a year ago William Place had been so outraged by his wife's threats of violence, coupled with her intolerant treatment of her then 16-year-old stepdaughter, that he had obtained a warrant for her to appear before a magistrate.

The magistrate had held the belief that all domestic relations were plagued with a certain amount of turbulence and reckless talk. He had declined to entertain William's charges against his wife and succeeded in effecting what he felt to be a socially desirable reconciliation. But from this family quarrel, so hopefully resolved in court, there had come no happiness. Instead, it seemed, there had come murder and attempted murder.

Shortly after noon on that Tuesday, William Place regained consciousness for a few moments. He accused his wife of having attempted to kill him. He begged that his daughter be given police protection "from that fiend incarnate". He was still too close to death to be told the truth about Ida.

William Place was a patient on the top floor of the hospital, while Martha was a patient on the floor below. A police stenographer sat at William's bedside, a police matron waited beside Martha. The stenographer, who had been waiting for William to speak, took down every word of his whispered but explicit accusation — whereupon the matron was reinforced by a uniformed officer, who posted himself at the door of Martha's room. Mrs. Place was now a candidate for a first-degree homicide indictment.

Doctors at the hospital were somewhat puzzled by the woman's condition. The duration of her exposure to the gas from two open jets in the closed room was uncertain. She was acting like one who had barely escaped self-destruction. And on learning of William Place's accusation, the doctors agreed that Martha was acting a role. She had, perhaps, attempted suicide by turning on the gas, in the belief that she had killed both her stepdaughter and her husband. But the helpless bewilderment in which she now enfolded herself was entirely feigned and defensive.

By the afternoon of Thursday, February 10th, 1898 her husband's condition had so far improved that he was allowed to talk to Assistant District Attorney McGuire, Captain Ennis and other police officials.

"We had been getting on badly for many months," William Place told them. "Last Saturday I had one more bitter argument with my wife, about the usual things — how I indulged my daughter, and Ida's shameless ingratitude in showing Martha neither affection nor respect.

"Added to this, there was a dispute over money. Martha had run up some extravagant bills. I knew she hoarded money, had her own considerable bank account. I told her: 'No more allowance for you this week. Your allowance money is going to help pay those bills.'

"That only made her more furious. The argument began again on Sunday and she resumed it before breakfast on Monday. My wife threatened me. And not for the first time."

"What did she say?" McGuire asked.

"She stormed: 'I want my money! If you don't give it to me, I'll make it cost you ten times more!' "

William Place explained that he had worried about this all day and returned home to Hancock Street with a sense of foreboding, not only because of Martha's venomous attitude but for his daughter, at home and at her mercy.

Startled to see no light in the house, he had let himself in and called the names of his wife, then his daughter and the servant. He put on the front hall light and went towards the rear, expecting to find Hilda Jans busy in the kitchen. But the rear of the house was dark and deserted also.

"I walked back through the hallway towards the front door. I was frantic about Ida. Then I heard a step. I turned — someone was creeping down the stairs. It was Martha. She had a terrible look. I called to her.

" 'Why isn't Ida at home?' I asked. 'Why hasn't Hilda got dinner ready?' She came rushing down the stairs. I saw too late that she carried an axe. I wanted to escape, to warn my daughter not to enter the house. But as I tried to reach the front door, Martha struck me with the axe. Her eyes were cold with hate. She raised the axe again. After that, I only knew agony and a kind of delirium."

"You must get some sleep now, Mr. Place," the nurse said.

The man with the bandaged skull wounds and fracture closed his eyes. But after a moment he opened them. "A charge of attempted murder is really not so serious, is it?" he inquired.

"It may be very serious," McGuire evaded.

"It was good of you to try to spare me," William Place murmured. Then he asked hoarsely: "You mean there *is* to be a murder charge against my wife?"

McGuire and Captain Ennis exchanged glances. The captain nodded. "There will have to be a murder charge, Mr. Place," he said grimly.

"So Martha had to try to kill me because she had already struck down my child!" Place groaned, choking back a sob. "Even in my delirium, I feared that."

"You must try to rest quietly, Mr. Place," McGuire said. "We'll be needing you later, I'm afraid."

Place said: "If she has killed Ida, nothing you can do to punish Martha will punish her enough."

On being charged with murder, Martha Place denied everything. She was removed from the hospital to a cell in the Raymond Street Jail. Interrogated again on that February 10th, Martha then admitted that she had struck her husband with the axe. "But only after he struck me," she insisted. As for harming her stepdaughter, why, all she had done was throw a dose of salts which Ida had refused to swallow in the impertinent girl's face.

Detectives Becker and Mitchell then escorted Martha Place to the morgue. First they showed her the acid-burned dress and other garments taken from Ida's body. But Martha refused to admit that her "dose of salts" had been carbolic acid.

When the detectives compelled her to look at Ida's ravaged young face, Martha, still unemotionally, conceded that what she had thrown might not have been salts, but an acid of some sort. Yet nothing strong enough to blind or kill her sly and antagonistic stepdaughter, she insisted.

A Brooklyn grand jury thought otherwise. Martha was indicted for first-degree homicide and for attempted homicide. Since William's sturdy constitution had pulled him through, his wife did not have to come into Brooklyn County Court to face two murder charges.

Ida Place had perished horribly on Monday, February 7th, 1898. On Tuesday, July 5th, 1898, Martha Place came to stand before the bar of justice. The accused woman was clad entirely in black, her dress a richly brocaded silk. In one elegantly black-gloved hand she held a large palm-leaf fan, which she waved gracefully throughout each broiling summer day of her trial.

As a native of New Jersey, she had insisted that one of her counsel be the New Jersey lawyer, Howard McSherry. The other was a noted attorney of Brooklyn, Robert J. Van Iderstine. Assistant District Attorney McGuire appeared for the prosecution, with Judge Hurd presiding.

As he had available such witnesses as William Place,

Hilda Jans, the neighbours, and the expressmen, McGuire undertook to establish clear premeditation. Martha Place, he declared, had only waited on that dread Monday morning for her husband to leave for his Manhattan office, and then found an excuse to send Hilda, her maid, into the back yard out of earshot. Martha had the carbolic acid ready. She went up to Ida's room, struck the girl on the temple, knocking her onto the bed. After Martha hurled the acid she then strangled Ida, making sure of the murder by leaving the victim to smother beneath the mattress and bedclothes.

Martha, the prosecutor went on, after locking the door left the dead girl lying there all day, going about her own activities, displaying no signs of grief or remorse. She had hurriedly got rid of Hilda. She had packed and shipped a trunk, recovered her bankbook, shown in every move that she planned an ingenious disappearance after ambushing and killing her husband, the devoted father of the dead girl in the locked bedroom.

Martha's feeble attempt at suicide was dismissed by McGuire as the sudden, frenzied reaction of a calculating murderess. She had meant to kill William, like Ida, by stealth and she had panicked when she realised that her husband's cries of "Help!" and "Murder!" had surely been heard by their near neighbours.

In the courtroom while on trial Martha Place never varied her bland and indifferent attitude, thereby making a most unfavourable impression on everyone. She took the witness stand in her own defence and testified for an hour. She admitted the axe attack upon her husband, but declared that she had been under intense provocation. She admitted hurling acid at Ida, but, again pleading extreme provocation, denied either premeditation or desiring to disfigure or kill her stepdaughter. Under cross-examination, she steadfastly refused to divulge where she had obtained the acid, or how long she had kept it hidden in their Hancock Street residence.

William Place was a star witness for the State, yet his

testimony was hardly more damaging than the detailed analysis of Ida's fatal injuries presented by Dr. Alvin Henderson. Martha's attorneys made no attempt to allege insanity, simply offering a general denial. This the hard-headed Brooklyn jury contemplated for three and a quarter hours before returning a verdict of guilty, with no recommendation for mercy.

Martha's comment at this moment was unique. "Really, this is remarkable," she said, and wrinkled her hitherto placid brow. The verdict, while hardly remarkable, was binding upon the court. And on June 12th Judge Hurd, in a grave voice, pronounced the mandatory death sentence.

No woman had been executed for murder in New York State for a number of years, and the last of these executions had been a hanging. Now, however, the electric chair was established by law, and male killers had already been executed by this means. But as soon as the condemned Martha Place was taken from Raymond Street to the prison at Sing Sing, a great outcry rose, disputing the right of the State to electrocute a woman.

Governor Black declined to pass comment on the merits of this contention. Nor did he grant the appeal for clemency urged upon him by Martha's attorneys. In November came the state election and the new governor was that dynamic New Yorker, the hero of San Juan Hill in the recent 100-day war with Spain. Theodore Roosevelt moved into the governor's mansion in Albany early in 1899 and soon characteristically came to grips with the issue of Martha's pending electrocution.

On March 15th the celebrated T.R. wrote: "The only case of capital punishment which has occurred since the beginning of my term as Governor was for wife murder, and I refused to consider the appeals then made to me after I became convinced that the man had really done the deed and was sane.

"In that case, a woman was killed by a man; in this case, a woman was killed by another woman. The law makes no distinction as to sex in such a crime. This murder was one of peculiar deliberation and atrocity. I decline to interfere with the course of the law."

Five days later, on March 20th, 1899, the execution took place. Exactly 58 weeks prior to that very morning, young Ida Place had felt blistering acid sear her eyes and mouth.

Martha Place, the first condemned woman ever to sit in the lethal chair, entered the death chamber in Sing Sing at 10.57, arrayed in flowing black, with a white silk ribbon around her throat and her hair so coiffed that it did not expose where her head had been shaved for the electrode.

At 11.01, she felt her electric shock, and, whatever the intrinsic horror of this new invention, it surely accorded Martha a more merciful end than that which she visited upon a 17-year-old girl in Hancock Street.

9

BAD DAY IN THE BAYOU

D. L. Champion

"Hello, Sheriff, I've been expecting you. I should have done what I intended to do — shot myself."
— The words of James Le Boeuf's murderer.

The waters of the Bayou Teche run black and deep beneath a canopy of huge trees silently strangling in the grip of grey Spanish moss. The stream, dark as sin, unruffled as a mirror, moves as sluggishly as the alligators which infest it, flows imperceptibly into the Atchafalaya River, and on to the Gulf of Mexico.

In 1926 Morgan City, in St. Mary's Parish, Louisiana, was a somnolent community, slow-moving, humid and eminently respectable. It is situated on the swampy edge of Lake Palourde, which is part of the bayou itself.

The inhabitants of Morgan City were quiet folk, solid and contented. They attended to their various businesses competently, yet without frenzied bustle. They had no intention of wearing themselves out amassing fortunes they couldn't take with them.

They loved their wives, respected their parents, sent their children to school and attended church regularly. If they were addicted to the major vices, it was not apparent to the naked eye. If they drank — it was the Prohibition Era — they did so discreetly.

Their immediate neighbours, the dwellers in the bayou, possessed almost none of the virtues of the denizens of Morgan City. The Bayou Teche was populated by trappers, alligator hunters, fishermen, moonshiners and those whose occupation was not at once apparent — not even to

Sheriff Charles L. Pecot, who checked up on them from time to time.

The people of the bayou were rough, tough, with little respect for the law and none whatever for the 18th Amendment — the Prohibition Law. They were heavy drinkers and crack shots. They had quick tempers and profane tongues, and their opinion of the Morgan City folk was equalled only by Morgan City's opinion of them. All were colourful, hard-bitten characters. Two of them were unique.

James Beadle was a fisherman, a trapper and an alligator-hunter, who sometimes engaged his prey with his bare hands. He was 45 years old, with a wiry body and a complexion the colour of leather.

He lived in a shack at the black water's edge, drank prodigious quantities of corn whisky and was a crack shot. He was also quick to resent an insult. Although he owned few worldly goods, his sense of possession was that of a parsimonious magpie.

At the other end of the bayou, six miles from the unpainted shanty occupied by James Beadle, lived the witch. Of course, Emmy Mae Hawks wasn't a genuine witch. However, among the bayou people, she had that reputation.

Externally, she didn't resemble a witch. She was neither old or grizzled. She wasn't ugly and her customary method of transportation was a dug-out canoe, not a broom. She was in her early 30s. Her hair was red, her features regular. Her temper was violent, and when she was in its grip her vocabulary was as shocking as her voice was loud.

Three years before she had married a trapper almost twice her age who reputedly had several thousand dollars hoarded in his cabin. It was also alleged that old Ephraim Hawks wasn't quite all there.

Six months after marrying Emmy Mae, he wasn't there at all.

He was found, one dank winter morning, on the bank of the Atchafalaya River with a huge hole in his head, a shotgun grasped firmly in his right hand. Two deputy sheriffs called upon the widow and informed her that she was under arrest for murder.

Emma Mae announced her opinion of sheriffs' deputies in ear-splitting, obscene language. She was taken off nevertheless to the parish jail in Franklin, where she swore that her elderly husband had been brooding and had doubtless taken his own life. The coroner was compelled to admit that such was possible, so Emmy Mae was released.

She returned to the bayou, where she resumed her life of loneliness. She drank heavily and permitted nobody to come near her cabin, save a few thirsty cronies. One of these was James Beadle. She never worked, but she always appeared to have enough cash to pay her bills. Perhaps she had come upon the hidden fortune her husband was reputed to have accumulated.

She was still reasonably attractive to look at. Her body was slim, her figure good. Her face could have been called pretty, although there was a certain hardness about it.

She had few friends among the bayou people and none at all in Morgan City. The Morgan City folk considered her eccentric and left her alone, as they did all the bayou people.

Then, in December, 1926, Ada Le Boeuf began to suffer a series of sick headaches, a development destined to unsettle the even lives of both the Morgan City and the bayou folks.

Ada's husband, James Le Boeuf, descended from the French Acadians exiled to Louisiana two centuries before, was perhaps the most successful man in Morgan City. He was superintendent of the Morgan City Light and Power Company, a utility which owned subsidiary establishments all across the state.

Le Boeuf, a handsome, powerful man accustomed to authority, had married Ada 25 years before. They had five attractive children of various ages. Ada was now approaching 50, a chronological fact not at all visible to the naked eye. She was extremely good-looking, tall and of graceful bearing. Her eyes were dark and her lips full. She spoke softly, with a caressing Southern drawl.

The married life of the Le Boeufs had been as uneventful and serene as a summer day. They were the social leaders of Morgan City. No breath of scandal had ever touched them.

It was a week before Christmas when Ada Le Beouf suffered her first attack of migraine. It struck as she sat at the breakfast table with her husband. It was almost 9 a.m. as he gulped his coffee with one eye on the ormolu clock which ticked away on the mantelpiece.

Ada uttered a little gasp, blinked her eyes and put her hands to her temples.

Jim Le Boeuf put down his cup. "What's the matter, honey?"

"A headache. I've suddenly got a terrible sick headache. It hurts very badly."

Jim Le Boeuf expressed sympathy. He offered to stay home from the office and minister to his wife.

This suggestion she emphatically turned down. "I don't need you. I'll call Tom Dreher. He'll give me something to stop it," she said.

Dr. Thomas E. Dreher, a medical graduate of Tulane University, had come to Morgan City to set up his practice more than 20 years before. He had married, raised two girls and a boy and had prospered. Both the doctor and his wife, prominent in local society, were intimate friends of the Le Boeufs.

Jim Le Boeuf rose from the table. "Sure," he said. "Tom'll give you some pills to stop it. I'll call him as soon as I get to the office."

Ada Le Boeuf, her head still in her hands, uttered a faint groan which her husband took to be an expression of mingled pain and assent.

He said: "Goodbye, then. And I hope you'll feel better."

As he strode from the house Ada Le Boeuf lifted her head. Perhaps her head still ached, but there was a smile on her red lips.

That evening Le Boeuf was pleased to find that his wife's headache had vanished.

"Tom Dreher gave me a prescription," she said, "and it worked like magic. I've felt fine all day."

But, as the week went by, it became evident that the cure was not permanent, Ada Le Boeuf underwent several painful attacks of migraine. Sometimes they occurred when her husband wasn't at home — either during the day, when he was at the office, or at night on occasions when he was out of town on power-company business.

This was something which James Le Boeuf never noticed. It later became apparent that someone else did.

Now, Jim Le Boeuf was fond not only of his wife and children. He was also fond of the dark waters of the bayou. As a child he had played on the swampy banks of Lake Palourde, and the black, mysterious water exercised a strong fascination for him.

Whenever it was possible, he ignored his car and travelled by pirogue. A pirogue, the principal means of transport for the bayou folk, is a heavy affair, shaped like an elongated, symmetrical leaf and hewn from the trunk of a single tree. It is extremely difficult to manoeuvre, even when handled by an expert. Jim Le Boeuf liked nothing better than to set out through the bayou in a hired pirogue.

Spring comes early in the Bayou Teche country. And so, on a February afternoon when the air was still, the sun warm and the butterflies trying their fragile wings, Jim Le Boeuf strode along the shore of Lake Palourde. He followed a narrow trail among the thick tree trunks until he came to James Beadle's shanty.

Le Boeuf had often hired one of Beadle's pirogues for a trip through the darkness of the bayou. Now he knocked at the door of the shack, expecting to do so again. But there was no answer. Beadle apparently wasn't at home.

Le Boeuf walked down to the shore, where two of Beadle's pirogues were moored, their paddles shipped. He shoved one of them into the still water and hopped in. After all, he was a regular customer. He could pay Beadle for the boat's hire when he returned. It never occurred to him that there was anything irregular in his action.

Le Boeuf paddled lazily through the ebony stream. Spanish moss brushed against his face. An indolent alligator stirred in the mud and yawned toothily. Wild orchids grew between the huge tree boles at the waters edge.

Two hours later, Le Boeuf returned to Beadle's shanty. He sprang from the pirogue and pulled the boat onto the shore. He turned and faced the shack. "Jim!" he yelled. "Jim Beadle, are you there?"

Jim Beadle was there. The door of the cabin opened and Beadle emerged. He was carrying a shotgun, its black muzzle aimed at Le Boeuf's heart.

"Put that gun down," said Le Boeuf. "It might go off."

"It will go off," Beadle said loudly, "unless you can give a damned good reason why you took my pirogue without permission."

Le Boeuf stared at Beadle in surprise. "Why, you weren't here, Jim. So I just took it. I figured I'd pay you for its use when I got back. What's wrong with that? Tell me what I owe you for it."

Beadle came closer. He did not lower the gun. Le Boeuf could see that the trapper's eyes were bloodshot, his face unshaven. There was a powerful, sour odour of bad whisky on his breath, but he held the shotgun steadily enough.

"If anyone touches my property without permission," Beadle said, "I'll kill them."

"You're drunk," Le Boeuf said. "Put down that gun. I'm willing to pay you. I've done no harm."

Beadle squinted along the gun barrel. He said: "It ain't a matter of doing harm. It's a matter of respecting property. Just because you're careless with yours, you can't make free with mine."

"You're talking like a fool. And what do you mean by saying I'm careless with my property?"

"I'm talking about your wife," Beadle retorted. "If you're careless about her doings, I don't expect you'd be careful whose pirogue you take. I'll let it go this time. But touch my stuff again and I swear I'll kill you. Now, get off my land."

"Wait a minute. What do you mean about my wife?"

But Jim Beadle had dropped that subject. "Get," he said again. "Get off my land while you're still alive."

Le Boeuf turned and walked along the dark trail which led away from the bayou. By the time he arrived home he was a most disturbed man. It was upsetting enough to engage in inane argument with a drunk, and infinitely more so to spend 10 minutes staring at the wrong end of a shotgun. But it was Beadle's cryptic remark about Ada which worried Le Boeuf most of all.

Le Boeuf's first inclination was to dismiss the matter from his mind. If Beadle had intended to hint that Ada had been unfaithful to her marriage vows — well, that was unthinkable. Even if the utterly impossible had somehow happened, how would an ignorant swamp rat like Beadle know it?

Le Boeuf made no mention of the affair to his wife. The following morning he told his colleagues at the power company of his run-in with Beadle and the trapper's threat to kill him. He did not repeat Beadle's remark concerning Ada.

Even so, he did not forget it — but not for lack of trying. It gnawed at his mind. Finally, he paid a visit to Philomena Brown. Mrs. Brown was a woman who had known Ada Le Boeuf almost all her life. They were intimate friends.

Le Boeuf put his problem in Philomena Brown's lap. He told her of the clash with Beadle and on this occasion he omitted no detail. "It's probably nonsense," he said, "but I can't get Beadle's remark out of my mind. I'm really worried. Is there anything you can tell me?"

Mrs. Brown looked grave. "Jim," she said. "I've heard some gossip about Ada lately. But, of course, it's a lie. And I've been doing my best to put a stop to it."

"But who's the man?" Le Boeuf asked.

"There isn't a man, naturally. It's only malicious small-town gossip. Some of these women are saying that Tom Dreher is visiting your house too often."

La Boeuf was stunned. "But Ada's been having migraine

headaches," he said. "Tom's treating her. Besides, he's the best friend I have in all Morgan City."

Mrs. Brown nodded. "I know, but you can't stop gossip. It's vicious and wicked."

Le Boeuf paced the floor thoughtfully. "Look," he said at last, "I don't want to talk to Ada about this, but I think she should know. Will you mention it? Ask her to be discreet. Warn her of what's being said."

This Philomena Brown agreed to do.

Ada Le Boeuf took the matter lightly, saying: "Of course. Tom's been here when Jim was away. He's been treating my headaches. Both Tom and I have grown children. This gossip is the silliest thing I've ever heard. I'm just going to ignore it completely."

Mrs. Brown duly reported this conversation to Jim Le Boeuf. Le Boeuf, considering that the matter was now out in the open, spoke of it to Ada.

"You know," he said, "these headaches of yours seem quite serious. I think I'll get a specialist up from New Orleans. If he can cure you, Tom Dreher won't have to make so many calls. Maybe we can stop gossip and headache at the same time."

Ada Le Boeuf did not consider this a good idea. "It's migraine," she said. "Tom says it can't be cured. Only relieved. He gives me these prescriptions and comes here personally to give me a hypodermic when it's very bad. You could hardly have a man come up from New Orleans each time I need a shot."

That argument appeared to be reasonable. James Le Boeuf shrugged. "All right," he said, "we'll forget it. The people who really matter in town will recognise the malicious talk for what it is. We'll forget the whole thing."

Unfortunately, it wouldn't stay forgotten.

A month went by. Jim Le Boeuf attended to his business. Mrs. Le Boeuf suffered from headaches. And Dr. Dreher attended her. Morgan City was serene, as always. Then one hot morning Le Boeuf received a telephone call in his office. Mrs. Thomas Dreher was on the other end of the wire.

"Jim," she said urgently, "can you come over to Tom's office right away?"

It was inconvenient, but the woman sounded distressed. Le Boeuf left his desk and drove to the doctor's office.

Dr. Dreher was sitting at his desk, an expression of grave concern on his face. Mrs. Dreher was standing by the window, holding a sheet of yellow paper in her hand. As she turned to greet Le Boeuf he noticed that she had been crying.

She said: "Jim, read this!" She thrust the sheet of paper into his hand. It was lined paper which had been torn from a pad. The handwriting was a childish scrawl. The message was unsigned.

It read: "Two nights ago there was a lady and a man in that empty shack in the bayou again. One of them was Ada Le Boeuf. One of them was your husband. What kind of treatment is he giving her out there?"

A startled Mrs. Dreher demanded: "Again? You mean this has happened before?"

"Nothing has happened," Dr. Dreher said patiently. "I've told you that before."

"Tom's right," Le Boeuf agreed. "Don't get yourself upset. Nothing has happened except this gossip. We've got to stop it."

Mrs. Dreher said miserably: "So there's nothing in it, Jim? You're sure?"

"Of course not," Le Boeuf declared. "If there were, do you think I'd be taking it so calmly? If it was true, I swear I'd kill Tom, even though he's my best friend."

Mrs. Dreher smiled at that. "The letter upset me so," she sighed. "I suppose I was silly. Of course, it can't be true."

Dreher cleared his throat. "Jim, I think you'd better get a doctor in from Franklin to look after Ada. I don't want you folks upset. I don't want my wife upset. And I can't afford this sort of thing. It's bad for my practice and I've a family to support. I won't visit Ada any more."

Both Le Boeuf and Mrs. Dreher thought this a foolish course to take. They argued that, as a physician, Dreher was obliged to go where he was called. It was absurd that he should lose a patient and that Mrs. Le Boeuf lose a good doctor, just because of these malicious rumours.

At last Dreher permitted himself to be persuaded. Painful as the lying tongues were, it was agreed to ignore them.

Another two months went by. If more scandalous tales concerning the doctor and Mrs. Le Boeuf were being told, they did not reach the ears of the principals. At least, not until the middle of June, when James Le Boeuf once again called upon Philomena Brown.

He came directly to the point. "Philomena," he said, "an employee of mine at the power company told me today that she'd heard something she thought I should know. She's been told that Ada and Tom Dreher were seen bathing together in the bayou near Emmy Mae Hawks's cabin. According to this tale, they hadn't bothered to put on bathing suits."

"You still don't believe it, do you, Jim?" Mrs. Brown asked.

Le Boeuf turned an agonised face to her. "No, I don't believe it. But it's driving me crazy. Suppose everyone in town calls you a thief. You may know you're not, but the gossip could upset you just as much as if it were true."

Mrs. Brown nodded sympathetically. "What do you want me to do?"

"I'd like you to run down the source of this rumour. Let's find out who started it. Then we'll know whom to deal with."

Mrs. Brown pointed out that the source of any rumour is often difficult to find. Nevertheless, she agreed to try.

On the following day, before she could take any further action in the matter, she was visited by Ada Le Boeuf. What Ada had to say amazed her.

"Philomena," Ada said, "I'm worried about Jim. More than that, I'm worried about our marriage. I just heard that Jim was swimming naked with that woman they call a witch — that Emmy Mae Hawks."

Mrs. Brown blinked. Then she laughed. "Ada," she said, "this just proves that one should never listen to gossip. Jim heard the very same tale, but in his case the principals were you and Tom Dreher. Now you hear it and the people involved are Jim and Emmy Mae Hawks. The whole story's obviously untrue."

But Ada Le Boeuf wasn't so sure. She refused to tell Mrs. Brown where she had heard her version of the nude swimming tale. "But," she said, "I understand the wife of a frog-hunter who lives near the Hawks' cabin actually saw them. I wish you would go into the bayou and ask her about it. Her name, I'm told, is Mrs. Ork Ardon."

"All right," Philomena Brown agreed. "I'll kill this rumour once and for all. I'll talk to Mrs. Ardon this afternoon."

Mrs. Brown went down to the shore to Lake Palourde, and walked along the same trail that Le Boeuf had followed on the day of his quarrel with Jim Beadle. She came to Beadle's cabin and rented a pirogue from him.

She paddled slowly through the dark waters towards the cabin occupied by Emmy Mae Hawks. Half a mile from that cabin, on the other side of the bayou, stood the wooden shanty occupied by the frog-hunter, Ork Ardon.

Mrs. Brown beached her pirogue directly in front of the Ardon cabin and walked up to the open door. She was greeted with marked hostility.

Mrs. Ardon, an ancient crone with wispy grey hair, a yellow skin and a protruding jaw, eyed Philomena Brown and said accusingly: "You're from Morgan City, ain't you? We don't want you folks in the bayou."

Mrs. Brown amiably stated her business. She impressed upon Mrs. Ardon that she meant no harm. She merely wished to save innocent people from the result of vicious scandal. She was certain that Mrs. Ardon had not seen anyone bathing naked in the bayou, she said. But she had come to make sure.

Mrs. Ardon looked at Mrs. Brown and her expression was not one of geniality. "I ain't going to get mixed up in these affairs," she said. "But I ain't going to tell no lies, neither. Sure, I seen a couple carrying on out there in the water. One was that red-headed witch woman. The man was Jim Le Boeuf. They was carrying on, with no clothes on at all. Why don't all you Morgan City folk keep away from the bayou? We're respectable people here."

Mrs. Brown was surprised and shocked. She questioned Mrs. Ardon closely, but the woman did not change her story. She had seen two nude bathers with her own eyes and there could be no mistake about it, she insisted.

Baffled, Mrs. Brown returned to the pirogue. She paddled slowly home, her brow wrinkled in thought. The gossip, if it really was gossip, was now quite out of hand. Originally only Ada and the doctor had been involved. Now it apparently also involved Jim Le Boeuf and the red-headed swamp woman.

Yet it was Le Boeuf who had first come to Philomena Brown asking her to check on the nude bathing story. Was it possible that he was guilty of infidelity and was covering up by asking Mrs. Brown to investigate? Was it possible that he was behind all the talk of his wife's affair with the doctor?

After several hours' thought Mrs. Brown removed herself from the entire affair. She kept to herself what Mrs. Ardon had told her and notified Jim and Ada Le Boeuf that she didn't want to have anything further to do with the scandalous rumours. Gossip, she said with finality, can do no one any good.

That was true. Murder can do no one any good, either. And, although Philomena Brown was unaware of it, a murder plot was being hatched at that moment in St. Mary's Parish. A plot as dark and treacherous as the waters of the Bayou Teche.

On Wednesday, June 29th, 1927 Alcide Mayon, a youth who lived in the bayou, walked idly along the shore of Lake Palourde. He came upon a gnarled cypress tree whose ancient branches stretched out over the water. The tree was dying, and Spanish moss draped it like a shroud.

Mayon leaned against its trunk and lit a cigarette. Then

he noticed something black and solid resting in a crotch between two branches. He pushed aside the Spanish moss and investigated. He found three railroad angle irons. An angle iron is a rolled iron bar with an L-shaped cross section, used in rail construction work.

Alcide Mayon had seen angle irons, but never in the branches of a dying cypress tree. He looked at them for a puzzled moment. Then, because he was still in his teens, the notion occurred to him that an angle iron tossed into the lake would make a splendid and resounding splash.

He lifted one of the irons from its resting-place and hurled it into the water. The splash quite came up to his expectations. Mayon finished his cigarette and walked away.

On the face of things he had merely tossed an angle iron into the water. Unwittingly, though, he had done much more. He had become the instrument by which a black crime would come to light eight days later.

On July 1st, Jim and Ada Le Boeuf decided to visit her brother, whose home was on the other side of Lake Palourde. The Le Boeufs borrowed a pirogue and made the journey by water.

In the course of the evening Le Boeuf remarked to his brother-in-law that on the following day he was due to take a business trip to Franklin, then on to New Orleans. Shortly before midnight the Le Boeufs said their goodbyes, climbed into the pirogue and began to paddle towards Morgan City.

It was a dark, moonless night. A whippoorwill sang eerily from a cypress limb, a water moccasin swam silently, tracing a slender wake in the water. The atmosphere was black and evil, a fitting background for the horror about to occur …

But the following morning was bright and hot and if evil had stalked the bayou on the previous evening Morgan City was completely unaware of it. Business went on as usual. Jim Le Boeuf was away, a common enough occurrence, although this time there were whispers that he had left to get a divorce. Ada Le Boeuf was stricken with migraine, also quite usual. And Dr. Dreher attended her, which was again normal procedure.

On July 6th Alcide Mayon, along with Paul and Norbert Didier, set out on Lake Palourde in a motor-boat for an evening of frog-hunting. Recently, due to floods, there had been extremely high water in the bayou and the lake. Now, however, the flood had abated and the waters were receding.

Paul Didier stood in the bow of the boat, a torch in his hand. His brother, Norbert, was at the tiller. Alcide Mayon leaned over the side of the boat. He too held a torch, which he used to illumine the black water while he looked for frogs.

Suddenly he saw something dark, moving slowly through the water ahead on the port side of the motor-boat. "Hey!" he yelled to Norbert. "There's a guy swimming up there!"

Paul Didier blinked. "You're crazy! Who'd be swimming in the bayou at this time of night?"

Paul Didier leaned forward in the bow, holding his torch at arm's length. He uttered a startled cry. "Reverse the motor!" he yelled to his brother.

The propeller bit deep into the water. The boat slowed down. Paul bent over the bow and stretched out his hand. "Alcide's right," he said in an awed tone. "There's someone swimming, all right. Only it's a corpse."

The trio leaned white faces towards the black water. A man's body swayed gently on the surface. Strands of heavy wire attached to his feet and hands apparently anchored him to the muddy bottom. His middle floated on the surface.

"Let's get out of here," Mayon said. "We'd better call the cops."

Paul Didier opened the throttle and the boat plunged towards a jetty. Norbert put through the telephone call. The boys waited at the landing until the Morgan City Chief of Police Louis R. Blakeman, arrived with Dr. C. M. Horton, the coroner.

They all climbed into the motor-boat and sped back to

the point where the corpse had been seen. The heavy wire which bound the dead man was too strong to be broken and Blakeman had brought no tools with him for that purpose.

Arduously the five men tugged at it, eventually dragging up a heavy angle iron to which it was attached. One angle iron had anchored the corpse's hands, the other his feet.

Dr. Horton examined the dead man by torchlight. He had obviously been killed by two blasts from a double-barrelled shotgun. Half his left shoulder had been torn away. The features were bloated and completely unrecognisable and there were three deep knife slashes across the dead man's belly. There were no identifying marks on the sodden clothing, no identifying items in the pockets.

It was almost dawn when the body was carried to Morgan City, where Dr. Horton proceeded to perform an autopsy. Sheriff Charles L. Pecot was summoned from Franklin and took charge of the investigation.

Alcide Mayon told the sheriff that a week previously he had found three angle irons, similar to those which had anchored the corpse, in a tree at the side of the lake. He mentioned the fact that he had thrown one of them into the water.

"I guess," he added, "that the other two were tied to the body to hold it down."

Sheriff Pecot agreed. "It indicates premeditated murder," he said. "Someone put those angle irons in the tree, against the night he intended to use them. Three angle irons would have held that body on the bottom of the lake forever. Two weren't quite enough. If you hadn't tossed an angle iron into the water, we might have never known that a murder had been committed."

Dr. Horton reported that the slashes on the stomach of the dead man had apparently been made in order that gases could escape, thus reducing the buoyancy of the body. Obviously, it had been the killer's intention to make certain that his victim would not float to the surface.

Sheriff Pecot realised that his investigation would not get off the ground until the dead man had been identified. To that end, he called upon Ada Le Boeuf.

"Mrs. Le Boeuf," he said, "I understand your husband has been out of town for about a week."

Ada Le Boeuf said that was true.

"Has he communicated with you at all, either by telephone or letter?"

"No. But then he rarely does, unless there's some emergency. Why?"

"I don't want to alarm you, Mrs. Le Boeuf. But it has occurred to me that the body found in the lake may be that of your husband."

Ada Le Boeuf didn't seem alarmed. She seemed amused. She exclaimed: "That's impossible! Who would want to kill him?"

The sheriff couldn't answer that. Nevertheless, he persisted. "Can you tell me what your husband was wearing when he left home?"

"He wore a brown suit and a pair of black shoes, a white shirt and a spotted bow tie," Ada said.

The sheriff frowned. The dead man had worn tan shoes, a pair of grey trousers and a plaid shirt.

Pecot returned to local police headquarters. There he talked again to Dr Horton, who assured him that the body had been in the water for six or eight days.

In reply to Pecot's question, Horton agreed that in general the body resembled that of Jim Le Boeuf. "But," he added, "that doesn't mean much. There are a hundred men in this parish built like Jim Le Boeuf."

So, 48 hours after the discovery of the swimming corpse, it was still unidentified. And on that day, July 8th, Ada Le Boeuf paid a visit to the family confidante, Philomena Brown.

"Philomena," she said, "I have something to tell you. The sheriff seems to think that the body they found in the lake is Jim's. I know it isn't. He's run away with that woman."

"What woman?"

"That redhead. The witch who lives in the bayou."

To Mrs. Brown, who recalled the story of the Ardon woman, this didn't seem surprising.

"I thought you told the sheriff that he was away on a business trip," Mrs. Brown said.

"I want to tell you what happened on that last night I saw Jim," Ada Le Boeuf went on. "We started back from my brother's house in the pirogue. During the trip we began to quarrel."

Jim, it appeared, had grown increasingly angry as they bickered. He swung the pirogue around and headed back to shore. There he ordered his wife out of the boat, remarking that he knew someone who would treat him more lovingly than she did. Then he paddled out into the bayou again.

Mrs. Le Boeuf had taken a pirogue belonging to her brother and gone home alone. She had not heard from her husband since. She was sure that he had run off with the red-headed witch, she said.

"Are you sure," Mrs. Brown asked, "that the dead man isn't Jim?"

"Positive."

"Have you seen the body?"

"No. Why should I? I'm certain it isn't Jim."

This struck Mrs. Brown as peculiar. A man was dead and Jim Le Boeuf was missing. It seemed reasonable that an anxious wife would at least view the corpse, in order to make certain it was not her husband. Yet Ada Le Boeuf seemed quite unconcerned.

Meanwhile, Sheriff Pecot had not been idle. He too thought Mrs. Le Boeuf's attitude curious. He was by no means convinced that the swimming corpse was not Jim Le Boeuf. He called in Le Boeuf's dentist to settle the matter.

The dentist examined the upper plate found in the dead man's mouth, compared it with his charts, and stated flatly that this was indeed the body of James Le Boeuf.

The news was promptly communicated to Ada Le Boeuf. She received it calmly. "The dentist is mistaken," she said. "My husband is alive. I know it."

The funeral was held that afternoon. Ada Le Boeuf attended, but she did not weep. She stoutly maintained that the man they buried was not her husband.

When Mrs. Philomena Brown heard of the body's identification, she decided that she must see the sheriff. She must tell him of the stories she had heard about both Jim and his wife. Reluctantly, for the Le Boeufs had been lifelong friends, she sought out Sheriff Pecot.

She told him all the gossip she had heard since the inception of the affair. She told him of Mrs. Ardon's report of the nude bathing party.

Pecot listened intently. He said: "I'll talk to Mrs. Ardon today. I'm going out to the bayou, anyway. I'd already heard that Jim Beadle threatened Le Boeuf during an argument over the pirogue. I'll also talk to Mae Hawks."

"Ada Le Boeuf says that Jim's run off with the Hawks woman," Mrs. Brown pointed out.

"It'll be easy enough to find that out," Pecot said. He thanked Mrs. Brown for the information and, an hour or so later, set off for the bayou, accompanied by Police Chief Blakeman.

Jim Beadle, whom they saw first, was sullen and uncommunicative. "Ain't seen Jim Le Boeuf for over a month," he said. "And now he's dead, I ain't crying about it. I never liked him much anyway."

"Maybe," Pecot suggested, "you disliked him enough to kill him. I hear that on one occasion you threatened him."

"I was drunk that night. And lately I've been too busy hunting 'gators to kill anyone. I sure didn't kill Jim Le Boeuf," Beadle declared.

"Can you prove it?" Blakeman asked.

"I don't have to prove it. It's up to you to prove I did."

It was an unsatisfactory interview. However, in the circumstances the officers didn't pursue the matter. There was no direct evidence against Beadle, save the fact that he'd quarrelled with Le Boeuf over the use of a pirogue some five months earlier.

Blakeman and Pecot climbed back into their boat and

paddled through the bayou. As they approached Emmy Mae Hawks's cabin they saw smoke rising from the chimney.

"Apparently, she's home," the sheriff commented. "In spite of what folks said."

Blakeman nodded. "I expected she would be. It's a cinch she hasn't run off with Le Boeuf. He's in his grave."

They beached the boat, walked up from the shore and knocked on the door of the cabin.

Emmy Mae Hawks opened the door. She was wearing a tattered pair of blue jeans, a man's shirt and heavy work boots. In spite of her garb, she was not unattractive. Her hair was flaming red, her lips full and her eyes sparkling. Her manner, however, was hostile.

"What do you want?" she demanded.

"Hello, Emmy Mae," Blakeman said. "We just want to ask you a few questions."

"I got no use for the law since you guys tried to frame me for killing my husband," she stated. "What do you want now? Are you trying to pin Jim Le Boeuf's murder on me, too?"

"Not pin it on you," Pecot said. "We'd just like to ask you what you know about it."

"I know nothing about it. I don't even know Le Boeuf, except by sight."

"No?" Pecot said. "Then how was it that you were swimming with him in the bayou? I understand you weren't wearing any swimsuits, either."

The redhead's eyes narrowed. She took a deep breath and said: "Cops are real dumb. They'll believe any lie they're told."

"A lie?" Pecot asked. "You mean Mrs. Ardon lied about it?"

"Sure she did. She saw Ada Le Boeuf and Doc Dreher swimming together."

"Then why did she tell Mrs. Brown that it was Jim Le Boeuf and you?"

"Because Jim Beadle made her. Either he gave her

money or he scared her into changing her story. First she said she saw Mrs. Le Boeuf and the doctor. When Jim Beadle heard about it, he said he was going to make her change her story. And he did too."

The sheriff and Blakeman exchanged glances. Blakeman said quietly: "We'll run along now and talk to Mrs. Ardon. Maybe we'll be back to see you later."

Mrs. Ardon, when they got there, was drunk and defiant. She made it clear immediately that she shared Emmy Mae's opinion of policemen. At first she flatly refused to answer questions.

Pecot said: "Do you know you could go to jail for slander? If your story of Le Boeuf and Emmy Mae swimming together is a malicious lie, you can go to prison."

"Who'd testify against me? Emmy Mae won't, and Jim Le Boeuf's dead," the woman countered.

"Mrs. Le Boeuf could prosecute you."

This statement sent Mrs. Ardon into paroxysms of bitter mirth. "Her? Fat chance! She wouldn't dare!"

Blakeman pounced on that. "Why not?" he asked sharply.

It took a solid hour to obtain the answer to that question. The officers conducted a ruthless interrogation, interspersed with warnings that Mrs. Ardon could still be charged with slander.

At last, somewhat more sober, she told the truth. "All right," she said, "I really did see Ada Le Boeuf and Doc swimming in the nude. I told some folks about it. Then Jim Beadle came and gave me 20 dollars to say it was Jim Le Boeuf and the witch woman, Emmy Mae Hawks."

"Why," Pecot asked, "should Jim Beadle do that?"

Mrs. Ardon shrugged her thin shoulders. "How do I know? He gave me the cash and I did as he asked. That's all I know. I can't tell you any more than that."

"It's enough," Pecot said. "Let's go."

Back in Blakeman's office Pecot sighed thoughtfully. He said: "Tell me, Louis, why should Jim Beadle give a damn who was swimming in the bayou?"

"He shouldn't."

The sheriff nodded. "As I see it, there are only two people who could possibly care."

"Right. Ada Le Boeuf and Doc Dreher. They're the only people who could gain by having Mrs. Ardon change her story."

"As I understand it," Pecot said, "Doc Dreher treated Ada constantly for headaches. I take it he prescribed various remedies."

"So Ada has said. Why?"

"There's something I'm going to check. But in the meantime let's talk to Mrs. Le Boeuf."

There were at that time three drugstores in Morgan City. After the sheriff had visited each of them, Blakeman went to bring in Mrs. Le Boeuf.

Ada Le Boeuf was nervous, but she still insisted that the man who had been buried was not her husband.

The sheriff dismissed this argument with a wave of his hand. "Mrs. Le Boeuf," he said, "you are aware that there has been a great deal of local gossip about yourself and Dr. Dreher?"

"Of course. But it's all nonsense. He was merely attending me for my headaches."

"And he gave you prescriptions?"

"Naturally."

"And you had them made up here in town?"

"Certainly. And they helped me."

Pecot drew a deep breath. "Mrs. Le Boeuf," he said, "you're lying. Within the past year, you've had only one prescription made up in Morgan City, and that was for your daughter who had the 'flu. So it seems to me that Dr. Dreher was visiting you for some other purpose than medical treatment."

Ada Le Boeuf lost her calm. She began to weep uncontrollably. Finally she said: "What do you want to know?"

"I want to know how your husband died."

There was a long silence. At last, Ada Le Boeuf spoke in a voice which occasionally broke.

"We had left my brother's and were almost home when

we saw another boat with two men in it. One man yelled out, 'Is that you, Jim?' The other man fired two shots. I heard my husband cry out. Then he fell into the bottom of the pirogue. I came home and said nothing about it."

"Why not?"

"Because I was afraid the gossips would say that Tom Dreher had something to do with the murder."

"And wasn't Dr. Dreher one of the men in that boat?"

"No — I mean it was too dark to see who they were."

"Was Jim Beadle in that boat?"

"I don't think so."

"Did you ever ask Beadle to give money to a woman named Ardon?"

Ada Le Boeuf shook her head. She was finished talking for the day.

Pecot addressed Blakeman. "Hold her on an open charge, while I go over to Doc Dreher's office."

Dr. Thomas Dreher was pacing his office floor. His face was pale and there were black circles beneath his eyes. As the sheriff entered he looked up, and it immediately became clear that Pecot was not the first to tax him with the murder of James Le Boeuf. His conscience had already done so.

Dreher said: "Hello, Sheriff. I've been expecting you. I should have done what I intended to do — shot myself."

"You killed Le Boeuf?"

"Virtually, yes. Actually, no. I was there when it happened, and I planned it. Jim Beadle fired the two shots."

Dreher was placed under arrest and escorted to Chief Blakeman's office by the sheriff. There the doctor made his confession.

"I was afraid Jim Le Boeuf would kill me when he found out abut Ada and me," he stated. "I spoke about it to Jim Beadle. He's an old friend of mine. We've hunted and fished together for years. Beadle offered to get rid of Le Boeuf for me."

On July 1st, Dreher disclosed, Ada had sent him a note, telling him that now was the time to act. She said that she and Le Boeuf would be on the lake late that night. She advised Dreher and Beadle to intercept them.

"We met Le Boeuf's pirogue," the doctor said. "Jim Beadle fired two shots at him. You can find the gun at my home. Beadle took nothing for the job. He liked me and he disliked Le Boeuf."

Ada Le Boeuf, confronted with the doctor's story, changed hers. But it still didn't match up with Dreher's.

Ada claimed that Dreher had called out in the night, "Is that you, Jim?" And her husband had answered, "Yes. I see you've got that rat Beadle with you." Whereupon Le Boeuf had fired two shots at Dreher's pirogue, Ada said. Two answering shots were then fired and Le Boeuf dropped dead. Ada Le Boeuf swore that she did not know who had fired the shots which slew her husband.

Jim Beadle, when he was brought in, made no confession at all. Neither did he say he was innocent. He glared at the sheriff and Blakeman and kept his mouth shut. The trio were taken to the parish seat at Franklin and charged with the murder of James Le Boeuf.

The sheriff was fully convinced of their guilt. He was also quite convinced that Ada Le Boeuf had arranged for Beadle to give the 20 dollars to Mrs. Ardon to change her story. Ada had obviously hoped that by starting gossip about her husband she could still the rumours about herself.

The women of the state of Louisiana apparently did not feel Ada's guilt as strongly as did the sheriff. Petitions poured in from every corner of the state, demanding that Ada be freed. This occurred even before she was actually brought to trial.

The trial began in Franklin on July 25th, 1927, before Judge James D. Simon. The trio were tried together. On the fourth day Ada Le Boeuf collapsed on the witness stand, necessitating an adjournment. On the sixth day, as Jim Beadle listened to Dreher's testimony that the alligator-hunter had fired the lethal shots, he apparently decided that the time had come to say something in his own defence.

He formally demanded a separate lawyer. The request was granted by Judge Simon.

When this was done Jim Beadle made his own confession. It differed from those of Ada Le Boeuf and Dr. Dreher.

Beadle claimed that after he and Dreher had set out in the pirogue the doctor had said: "Jim, I'm going to kill that damned Le Boeuf."

"Don't do that, Doc," Beadle had replied.

"Yes," Dreher had said. "I'm going to do it — and if you open your mouth about it, I'm going to kill you, too."

When they met Le Boeuf out on the lake, Beadle swore, Dreher had lifted his shotgun and fired twice. Dreher had then said: "I've got some angle irons hidden in that cypress. We'll use them to weight down the body."

After the corpse had been attached to the angle irons Dreher had slit the stomach open, announcing that it would then be impossible for the corpse to float.

On August 8th the jury found the trio guilty of first-degree murder. Two days later Beadle was sentenced to life imprisonment at the state penitentiary at Baton Rouge. Two days after that, Ada Le Boeuf and Dr. Dreher were sentenced to be hanged.

Until then no woman had ever been executed in the state of Louisiana. A tremendous legal battle ensued to try to save Ada Le Boeuf from the gallows. Her appeal went all the way up to the U.S. Supreme Court, where it was referred back to the Louisiana State Supreme Court which had originally denied it.

Her lawyers then addressed themselves to the State Board of Pardons. The Board of Pardons voted two to one to grant clemency to Ada Le Boeuf. Governor Huey Long, a man who knew quite a little about murder himself, remarked that the board's action looked like "a mockery against decency and order in the State of Louisiana".

However, Ada's lawyers managed to draw out the legal proceedings for more than a year and a half. On Friday, February 1st, 1929, Ada Le Boeuf and Thomas Dreher were hanged in a double execution in the parish jail in Franklin.

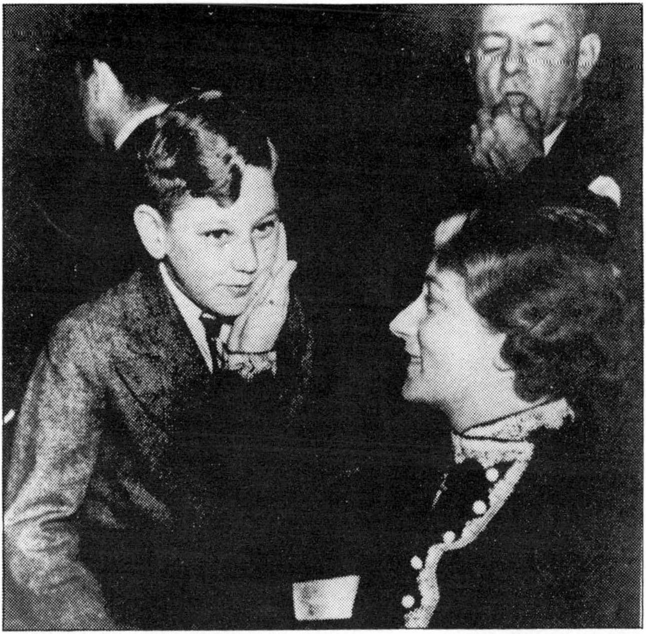

Anna Hahn with her son Oscar after the trial. As she was led to the electric chair she screamed: "Don't do this to me! Think of my baby!"

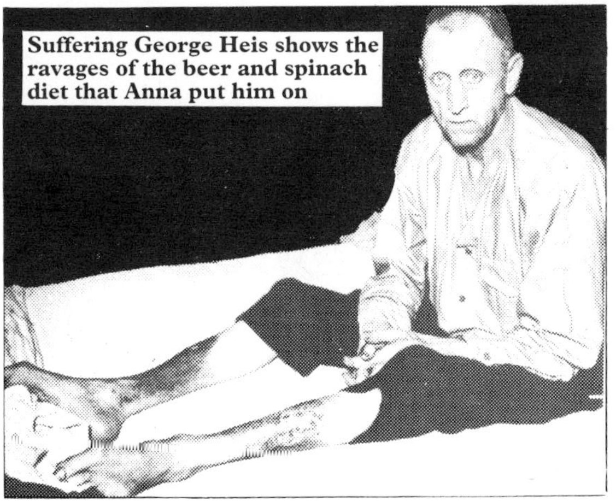

Suffering George Heis shows the ravages of the beer and spinach diet that Anna put him on

A contemporary sketch shows the history making walk to the death chamber when Martha Place (top) became the first woman to be executed in the electric chair

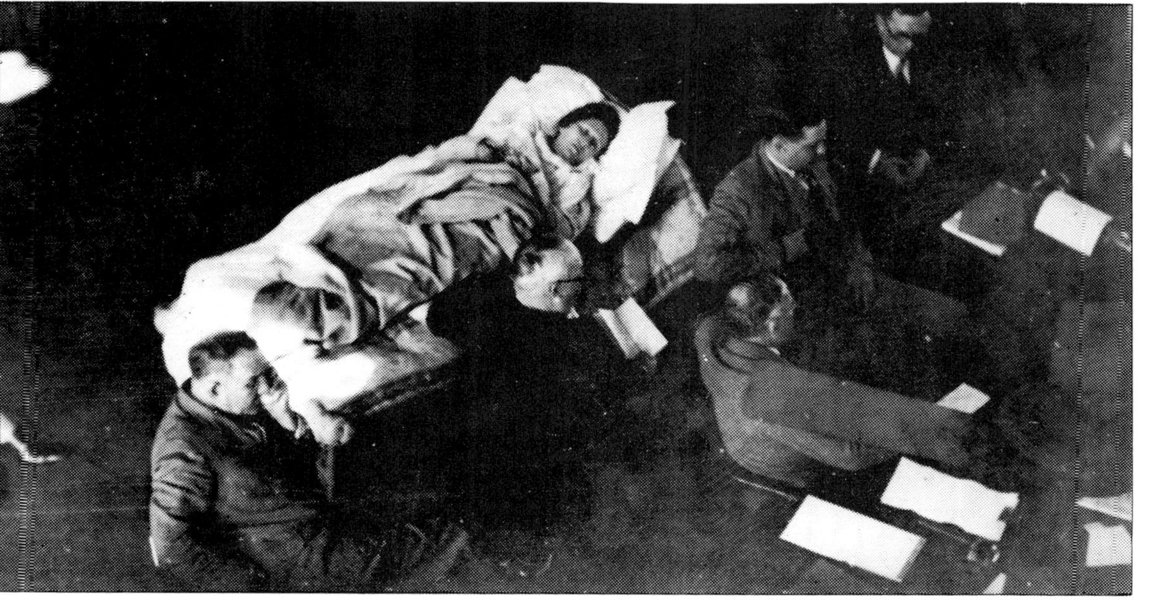

Ada Le Boeuf after she collapsed while giving evidence at her murder trial

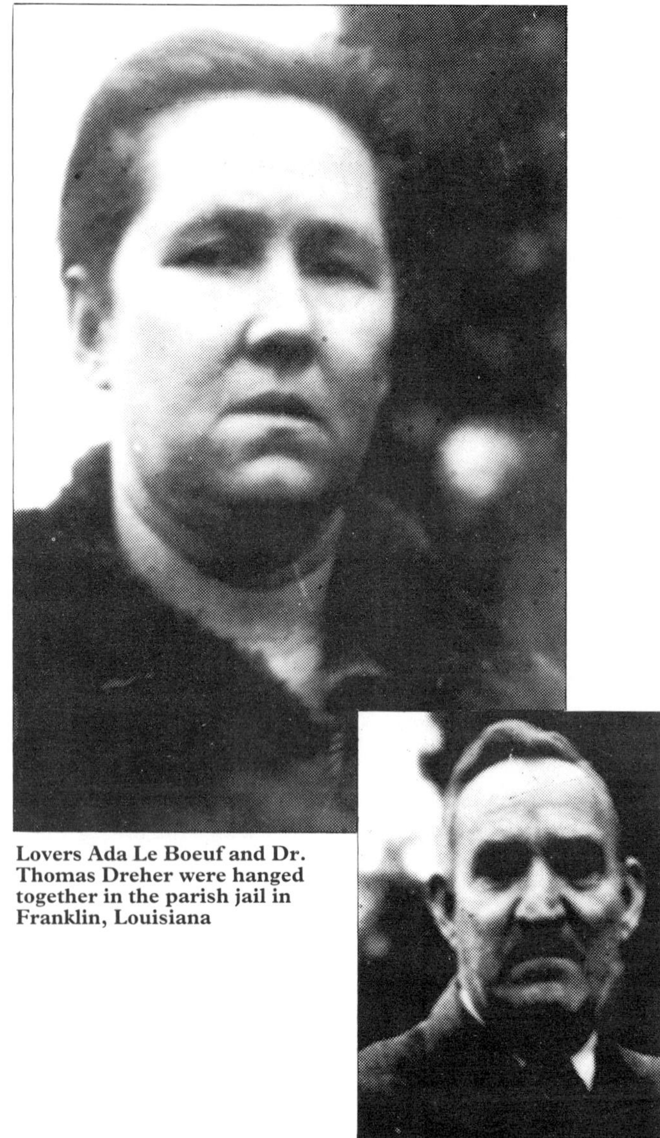

Lovers Ada Le Boeuf and Dr. Thomas Dreher were hanged together in the parish jail in Franklin, Louisiana

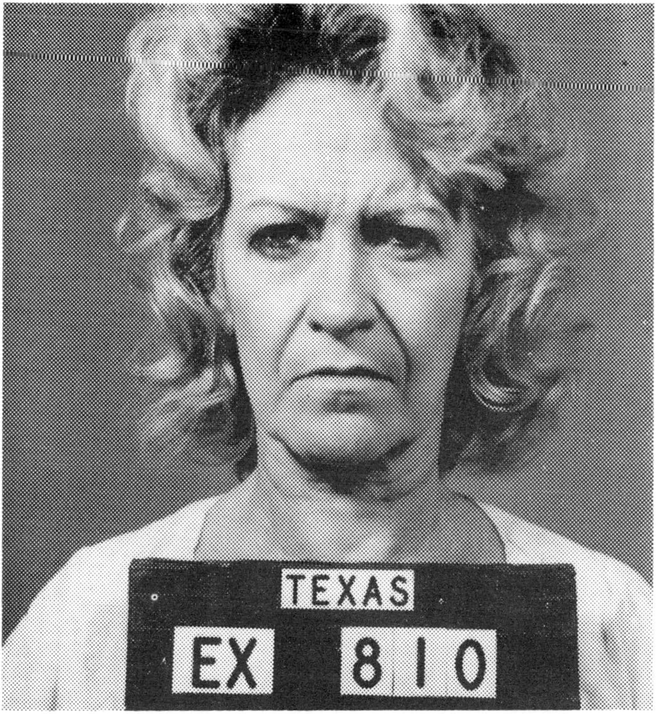

Betty Lou Beets (above) resides on Death Row at Gatesville, Texas. Below, police search the wishing well that Jimmy Don Beets had built. He didn't know he was digging his own grave

Police unearth the decomposed remains of Betty Lou Beets' former husband, Doyle Wayne Barker

Betty Lou Beets is escorted into court. Her husbands had a habit of disappearing in suspicious circumstances, police thought, then they discovered she was the killer

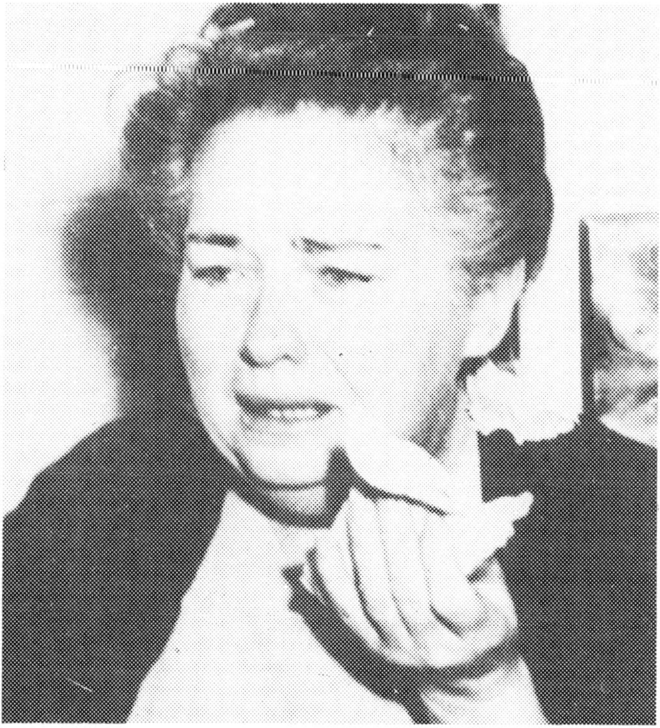

Louise Peete (above) burst into tears when she heard of the death of her husband (below) who had plunged down the stairwell of an office building

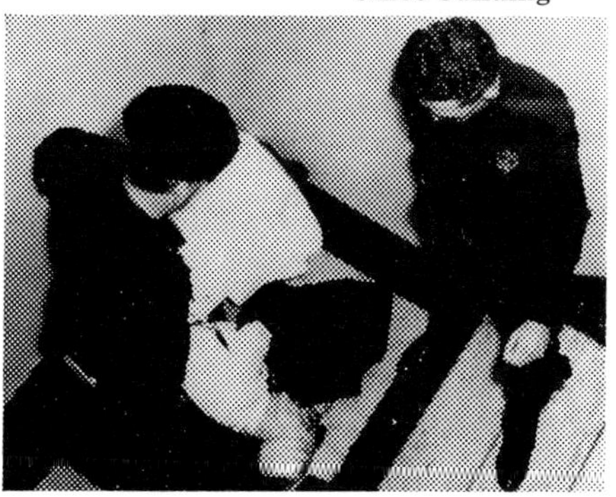

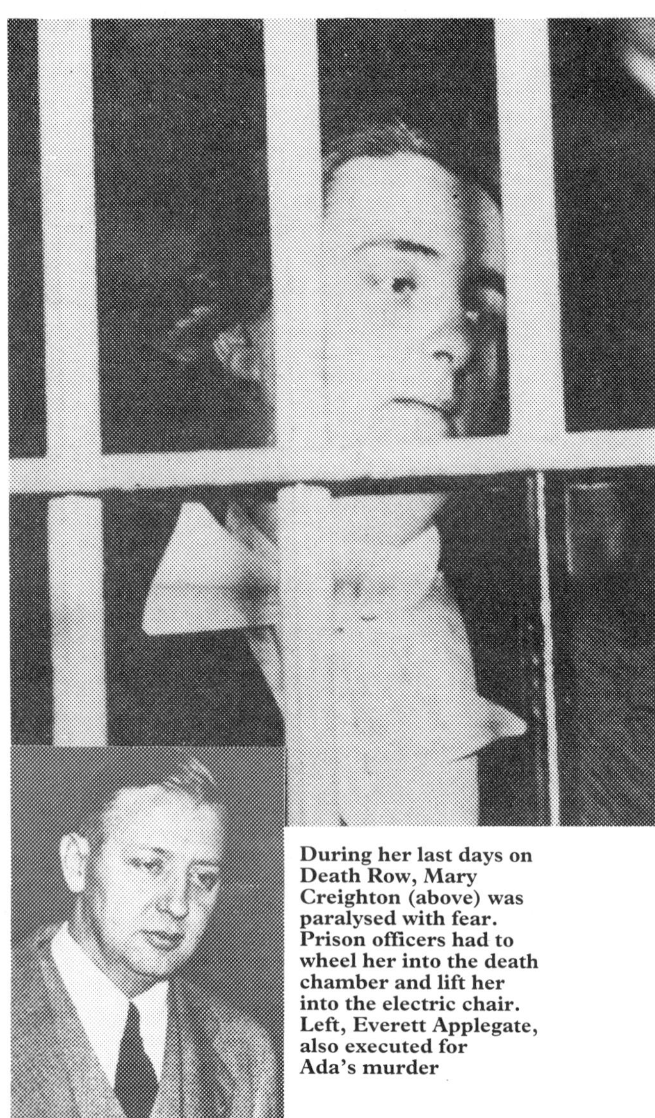

During her last days on Death Row, Mary Creighton (above) was paralysed with fear. Prison officers had to wheel her into the death chamber and lift her into the electric chair. Left, Everett Applegate, also executed for Ada's murder

Morgan City thereupon returned to its customary tranquillity. The bayou folk resumed their humdrum lives. The waters of Bayou Teche still run deep and black. On occasion, the evil currents in the heart of man run even deeper and blacker.

10

THE MUCH-WIDOWED BLONDE

Jean Eagen

"I could never hurt Jimmy Don. Nobody was ever as good to me as he was." — Betty Lou Beets speaking about the husband she was accused of murdering.

Buddies of Captain Jimmy Don Beets of the Dallas, Texas, fire department were stunned when they received the news that he had apparently drowned.

"It's a damn shame," one of his close friends said. "Just when he started living again, something like this happens."

He referred to how Beets had become depressed and morose after the death of his first wife. But all that changed remarkably after he met Betty Lou. She was a couple of years older than Jimmy, but she was just what the doctor couldn't order to cure Beets's depression.

It had been a brief courtship that had resulted in their marriage 11 months ago. They had a bash at the wedding reception. Jimmy, at 46, was his old jovial self again and filled with an exhilaration for living.

Some of his old friends felt that Betty Lou, a barmaid, could be a bit salty in her language. But she was certainly a looker and had Jimmy all fired up.

It didn't even bother him when some arsonist set a fire in his home in Glen Oaks. He couldn't figure out why anyone would pour gasoline from one bedroom to the other and then set it alight.

"It don't upset me much," Beets said. "I figured on selling the place as soon as I retired. This just makes it a little bit sooner — and I'm going to get in some darn good fishing."

Jimmy really got into the spirit of fixing up Betty Lou's mobile home at Cherokee Shores, on the lake. Betty Lou had a small garden out back. She told Jimmy that they could buy their vegetables at a market and he could lay a concrete slab over the garden and build himself a shed to hold all his fishing gear and other stuff.

When Jimmy completed building the shed there was another task. Betty Lou said she'd like to have a wishing-well in the front yard. Jimmy got right on doing it. He dug a deep hole out front, but after he got down a bit he realised that any water put into it would drain out to the lake, unless it was lined with concrete. And if he did *that*, the water would become stagnant and a breeding area for mosquitos.

But Betty Lou still wanted the wishing-well, so they eventually decided to fill it with earth and plant some flowers. Jimmy almost had it completed, using red bricks for the well.

On Friday evening, August 5th, 1983 Jimmy announced that he was going fishing. But when he hadn't returned by midnight, Betty Lou became concerned. She couldn't see Jimmy's boat anywhere in their part of the lake, so she contacted the Henderson County sheriff's office.

Deputy Johnny Marr came to the mobile home. Betty Lou expressed her fears, but Marr allayed them, suggesting that Jimmy possibly had motor trouble. He said they'd look for him in the morning, if he still hadn't returned.

On Saturday morning, people at a marina some distance down the lake from Cherokee Shores spotted a boat drifting. There didn't appear to be anyone in it, so they went out to check.

It was Jimmy's boat. The drive unit of the motor was out of the water and the propeller was missing. Inside the boat was an open tool kit, Jimmy's glasses and a bottle that had contained nitroglycerin tablets. Jimmy had a slight heart problem.

To the police, it was pretty obvious what had happened. Jimmy must have hit some submerged object that sheered the propeller-pin. He had removed the propeller to put in a new sheer-pin and apparently had suffered a heart attack.

They started a search for Jimmy, but all they found in the lake was his baseball cap. On Sunday the big lake was filled with boats as the search continued.

Beets's fire department buddies were determined that they would locate the body. Those with days off came to the lake every morning. The dragging continued. It went on for three weeks.

"It beats the hell out of me," one of the volunteers said. "The water isn't *that* cold. And unless it was weighted down, gases forming in the body should have brought it to the surface long before this."

A month after Jimmy disappeared from his boat and his body still hadn't been found, one of his close friends at the fire department came in to see Sheriff Charlie Fields.

"I'm damn sure Jimmy Don isn't in the lake," the friend announced.

"What makes you think that?" Fields asked him.

"I've been out there at the lake almost every day for a month," the other explained, "and I've used a grappling hook and covered almost every square inch of it."

The friend said there were a couple of other things that convinced him that Jimmy hadn't had a heart attack and fallen out of the boat, as everyone supposed. For instance, he knew that Jimmy had suffered a mild heart attack after the death of his first wife. A physician had given him the nitroglycerin tablets, in case he should feel another attack coming on.

"Jimmy Don told me only a while back that he hadn't used any of the tablets in more than a year," the friend said. "He carried them around with him, but he didn't need them."

He also knew that Jimmy needed glasses only for reading. While on duty he carried them around in his pocket. "Now, if he was out there fishing in the dark and sheered a pin, why the hell would he put on his glasses?" the friend asked. "And if they were in his pocket, they'd have gone overboard with him."

The friend had another point to make to Fields. Jimmy had undergone a recent medical by the fire department's physician and had been pronounced to be in excellent physical condition. He was also known to be a strong swimmer and an expert fisherman.

Fields listened to the information given by Jimmy's friend. "I'll agree it's strange that his body hasn't surfaced," he said guardedly. "But what else could have happened to him?"

The friend explained that when he first became suspicious that Jimmy might not have drowned he had done some checking. He learned that Betty Lou's former husband, who had owned the mobile home at Cherokee Shores when she married him, had deserted her. She had obtained a divorce.

"Now just suppose that this former husband came back and wanted to get it together with her again?" the friend said. "She wouldn't buy it, because she was happy with Jimmy Don. His solution might be to get rid of Jimmy Don."

Fields mulled over the theory. There were a couple of flaws in it. Betty Lou had said that Jimmy had gone night fishing. If someone got to him while he was on the lake, why wouldn't they have dumped the body into the water?

"With possibly a couple of bullet holes in it?" the friend challenged. "I haven't got all the answers, but I'm damn well convinced that somebody did Jimmy Don in and put his body someplace other than the lake."

Sheriff Fields said that he and his deputies would do some checking and see what they could come up with. They began by talking to Betty Lou. She completely discounted the theory that Jimmy had met with foul play. She was as confused as everyone else about *why* his body hadn't been found, but felt sure that he'd had a heart attack and had fallen into the water.

She said she'd had a number of men friends before meeting Jimmy, but none who were jealous enough to have killed him. As for her former husband, he had simply walked out on her and she hadn't heard from him since the day he left.

Fields assigned the case to his chief investigator, Jim Brewer, to work with District Attorney's Investigator Mike O'Brien to see if they could make head or tail of it. It took them a while to come up with all the information, but they uncovered some interesting facts concerning Betty Lou Beets. Jimmy was her fifth husband and, along the way, she'd had a few live-in boy friends.

Her first marriage had lasted 13 years and produced five children before the divorce. And then, after Betty Lou got a job in one of Dallas's less elegant bars, her personality took on a complete change. She was popular with the customers, capable of swapping sharp-tongued jibes and telling dirty stories. She increased her vocabulary with salty words.

Some said that Betty Lou was generous with her favours, but she had a wicked temper. It was displayed not only with her razor-like tongue, but sometimes physically.

Her second marriage was short, stormy and loud, lawmen learned. Neighbours agreed that it was more entertaining to hear the screaming, vituperative voice of Betty Lou, sometimes mingled with physical violence, than it was to watch television.

A couple of months after the divorce Betty Lou called the Dallas police to report that husband number two had come to the bar where she was working and had given her a hard time. She told him to leave, or she would have the bouncer massage his skull with a baseball bat.

Arriving at her apartment at 1.30 in the morning, she told police, husband number two had come to the door and demanded to be let in. When she told him to leave, he started banging on the door. She got her .22-calibre pistol and when she opened the door and he threatened to harm her, she shot him.

The police found husband number two lying in the parking area of the apartment complex, two slugs in his back. He was rushed to the hospital in a critical condition, but later recovered.

Admitting that she shot him, Betty Lou claimed it was self-defence. She said that after the divorce husband number two had wanted to marry her again and threatened: "If I can't have you, then nobody is going to."

Husband number two's version varied considerably from Betty Lou's account. He said that he had been at home watching television when Betty Lou called him and asked him to come to her place. When he asked what she wanted, he claimed she told him: "I have a surprise for you."

The surprise, he found out when he came to the door, was the weapon Betty Lou had in her hand. Knowing her temper, he took off and Betty Lou put two shots in his back as he ran. But he had no idea why she wanted to shoot him.

The fact that he had been shot twice in the back and made it as far as the parking area before falling flat on his face led investigators to believe his story might be more accurate than the one told by Betty Lou. She was charged with attempted murder.

Prior to the trial, husband number two said he didn't hold a grudge and would refuse to testify against her. So, without a witness, the prosecutor made a deal. The attempted murder charge was reduced to a guilty plea to misdemeanour and aggravated assault. The court ordered her to pay a fine of $100.

A smiling Betty Lou paid the fine and then demanded that the court return her weapon to her. As she was legally entitled to the gun, it was returned to her.

To the surprise of almost everyone acquainted with them, Betty Lou and husband number two got married for the second time. It was shorter, stormier and louder than their first bout — and it ended, predictably, in a divorce.

Husband number two later died of a heart attack, which some said was aggravated by his marriage to Betty Lou and the couple of slugs she had put in his back.

The investigators were unable to learn much about husband number three, except that the couple had lived together as man and wife for a short time. But they could trace no records of a marriage licence, or of divorce proceedings. Husband number three simply disappeared. No one knew where he went, or how he might be found.

Husband number four was Doyle Wayne Barker. A couple of years younger than Betty Lou, he was a building worker and owned the mobile home at Cherokee Shores.

Neighbours said that life became more interesting after Betty Lou moved into the mobile park. Her shrill voice was often heard hurling bitter insults at her husband. Then, during November, 1981 Barker failed to show up for work one day.

At the end of that week, Betty Lou came to the building firm to collect the back pay due to Barker. She said that she and her husband had had a serious disagreement — and he had just upped and left her.

Yet no one heard that Barker intended to leave — and no one heard from him after he left. When Betty Lou sued for divorce on the grounds of desertion, the court awarded her the mobile home.

Jimmy Don Beets was husband number five. Neighbours said that Betty Lou appeared to have found at last the man she had been waiting for. They got along splendidly. Jimmy gave his bride almost anything she wanted and did a lot of work around the mobile home.

The investigators took the information they had gathered to Sheriff Fields and District Attorney Jack Layton. They commented that it showed Betty Lou had lived an interesting, if hectic, life. But it didn't offer any clue as to where Jimmy Beets might be found.

Investigator Brewer was more convinced than ever that Jimmy hadn't suffered a heart attack and fallen out of the boat. He pointed out that there would have been plenty of time to take a body almost anywhere while the search was going on at the lake.

"Supposing she *did* do him in. What's in it for her?" Layton asked.

Brewer pointed out that Beets couldn't be considered

wealthy. But he did have property, a tidy sum in the bank, life insurance policies — and there was a pension for a fireman's widow that would pay Betty Lou $792 a month for the rest of her life.

Of course, Betty Lou couldn't collect on it until Jimmy was found, or declared legally dead. Still, she had already petitioned the court to have him declared legally dead and herself appointed administrator of the estate and sole heir to his property.

"Where do we go from here?" Fields asked.

O'Brien shrugged at the question. "Unless somebody stumbles onto a skeleton someplace, I'd say we're sitting behind the eight ball."

Then, on May 29th, 1985, just short of two years after Beets was thought to have drowned, a series of strange events took place. First, Betty Lou reported to the police that someone had slashed all four tyres on her car. She had no idea who could have done it, or for what reason. She hadn't been threatened and knew of no enemies.

At 2.30 the following morning as Betty Lou returned home from her barmaid's job, she stopped at the security office by the entrance to Cherokee Shores. She told the security guard about the tyres being slashed on her car and said she was fearful that someone might be attempting to harm her for some reason.

The guard said he would go to her mobile home with her and check it out, just to be on the safe side. Just as they were leaving the guard's office, they saw Betty Lou's home burst into flames.

The fire department responded quickly and were able to extinguish the blaze before it completely consumed the home. Damage was confined to the kitchen, hallways and two bedrooms. It was definitely arson, as established from the path of the fire and the remains of a plastic bucket apparently used by someone to pour out a flammable fluid and set it alight.

The fire chief said it was fortunate that whoever started the fire had closed the door, and that all the other doors and windows in the house were shut. The fire had practically extinguished itself when it burned up the oxygen inside.

When informed of the tyre-slashing incident and the house fire, Sheriff Fields asked the investigators: "Now, what the hell is this all about?" And Brewer pointed out that the fire in the mobile home was almost a replica of the fire set at the Beets's home in Glen Oaks, when he and Betty Lou had lived there.

"What's the connection?" Fields asked the detectives.

Brewer offered a possible explanation. He said that he and the other investigators were of the opinion that the fire in Beets's home that had destroyed the two bedrooms might have been set so that Jimmy and Betty Lou would have to move out to her mobile home.

He said that Betty Lou was well aware that he and the other investigators had been checking on her. If there were some bullet holes or bloodstains that hadn't been completely removed or patched, it would seem a good idea to turn them into ashes.

"But *she* didn't start the fire," Fields said. "She was with the security guard at the time."

"I know," Brewer said. "And we've already checked and found that she had been at work until the time she stopped at the guard house. Somebody else torched the place, but nobody out there saw anything. They were all asleep when it started."

"I don't know how much more weird this can get," Fields said. "What are you planning next?"

"I guess we just keep nosing around until we can locate Beets's body," Brewer answered.

It was a week later that the investigators had some interesting information for Fields. They had located a witness who told them that around the time Betty Lou's fourth husband, Barker, deserted her, she had dug up a small section of the yard behind her mobile home.

"It sort of surprised me," the witness recalled. "She didn't seem like the sort of person who'd be interested in gardening. And she didn't strike me as the kind of person to do the work herself."

He had noticed that she was digging the area rather deeply. "I told her that at the most a foot deep would be enough for a garden. She told me that it wasn't any of my damn business what she was doing. Knowing her temper and her sharp tongue, I agreed with her."

The witness said he hadn't thought much about it at the time. He did note, however, that shortly after Jimmy and Betty Lou came to live at the place, Jimmy had laid a concrete slab over the garden and built a shed on it.

He related that there had been talk around the mobile home park that the police had been asking questions after Jimmy was thought to have drowned, and that they suspected, since the body hadn't been found, that he might not be in the lake. The witness said that it brought to mind the fact that he had seen Jimmy building a rather large wishing-well in the front yard of the house. He had dug it deep and lined it with concrete and bricks.

"I talked to Jimmy Don at the time he was building it," the witness recalled. "He told me he was going to fill it with water and use an electric pump to drain it out into the lake, so that the water wouldn't become stagnant."

However, after Jimmy was thought to have drowned, Betty Lou had filled the wishing-well with earth and planted petunias.

"It's been bothering me for some time," the witness continued. "I keep wondering if maybe Jimmy Don might just be fertilising those petunias."

After hearing this, DA Layton asked: "And you guys think that Beets may be in the wishing-well and that fellow Barker under the shed?"

"That's exactly what we *are* thinking," O'Brien responded. "What we need is a search warrant to find out."

Layton pointed out that there was no positive evidence that the bodies might be buried and, if they destroyed the property and didn't find anything, they could be faced with a law suit.

"We can start with the wishing-well," Brewer said. "And

if we don't find anything, I will personally pay for restoring it."

Fields was equally insistent, saying: "After this length of time, we can assume that Beets is not in the lake. And if we don't open up that wishing-well, we may never know what happened to him."

So Layton drew up a search warrant and had it issued by the court. The Saturday morning of June 8th, 1985, was hot and humid when Fields, with a number of deputies and members of the local fire department, arrived at Cherokee Shores.

The number of men and equipment immediately attracted a large crowd of onlookers. A police line was set up around the mobile home as the men began to dismantle the wishing-well. Betty Lou was not there. Someone said she had left the house earlier that morning.

The men had dug only a couple of feet into the well when a terrible odour permeated the air. They were down just a little over three feet when they came to what they were looking for. It was a mouldy sleeping bag — and it apparently contained the remains of a decaying body.

"Hold it, fellows!" Fields called out to the men, who had taken turns digging and then backed off for a breath of fresh air from the stench. And D.A. Layton, who was on the scene, hurried back to his office to prepare a warrant for the arrest of Betty Lou Beets.

It was early evening before the remains were brought out of the wishing-well and placed in a body-bag, to be taken in for a post-mortem examination and identification. Looking into the sleeping-bag, one of the technicians said: "We may have trouble identifying this guy. There's no teeth in the skull."

"That should show that he's Beets," Brewer pointed out. "Jimmy Don had false choppers."

Fields questioned whether they should wait until morning when it was light to find out whether or not a body might be buried under the concrete floor of the shed. And one of the firemen said they had a truck that was used to fight fires when the power lines had been cut. It was equipped with a generator and floodlights.

"Bring it in and we'll go for it," Fields told him. He directed a deputy to locate a backhoe, a mechanical digger.

It was a grim, eerie sight for the growing group of spectators who ringed the mobile home as the operator of the backhoe demolished the building and began to skim away the concrete floor.

Meanwhile, the warrant had been issued for Betty Lou and an alert was out to police agencies for her arrest. Sergeant Mike LeMoines spotted the pickup truck she was driving near Mansfield, Texas. There was a man in the vehicle with her.

Informed that she was being taken into custody on a murder charge, and that a corpse in a sleeping-bag had been found buried in the wishing-well at her home, Betty Lou expressed surprise, saying: "I've no idea who it could be or how it could have got there."

The man with her was more vocal. He identified himself as her boy friend and said: "I've been sleeping out there off and on for the past six months. And, I'll tell you, if I had known there was a body buried in the front yard, I would've had nightmares."

Back at the Beets property, after moving the shed and scraping off the concrete, the operator of the backhoe went down about two feet. He was called off the job and men with shovels began to dig. They were down three feet when they unearthed another sleeping bag with skeletal remains in it.

Pathologists were later able to determine that these were the remains of Doyle Wayne Barker, Betty Lou's fourth husband. There were two bullet holes in the skull. And Jimmy Don Beets had also died from two bullets fired into his head.

With first-degree murder charges filed against Betty Lou Beets for the murders of her fifth husband, Jimmy Don, and her fourth husband, Doyle Wayne Barker, it appeared that the mystery and all the excitement for the residents of

Cherokee Shores was over.

But that was not so. There would be more startling developments in the case.

The trial of Betty Lou Beets began on Monday, September 23rd, 1985. Only those who arrived early and queued up were able to get into Judge Jack Holland's court.

Prosecutor Billy Bandy began the state's case with a routine recital of evidence and witnesses he would present to prove to the jurors that Betty Lou Beets had slain her husband of 11 months. He added that he would ask for the death penalty.

He said the prosecution would show that on the night of August 5th, 1983, after Jimmy Don had gone to bed, the defendant shot him twice in the back of the head.

"After shooting him, she draped his body in a sleeping bag and placed it in an ornamental wishing-well in her front yard. She filled it with earth and planted flowers, so that no one would disturb it and find the body," Bandy told the panel.

He said that he would prove that, after killing her husband she set his boat afloat on Cedar Creek Lake, with the drive of the engine up and the propeller missing, then scattered his heart medicine around inside the boat.

"She later reported that he had been fishing and drowned," Bandy continued. "And then she went to court to have him legally declared dead, so that she could inherit his considerable estate and benefits as the widow of a fireman."

Bandy concluded his opening statement by saying: "The evidence will shock and appall you, but it is a necessity that it be brought forth."

News reporters and spectators sensed that Bandy had something that had not previously been revealed. But the first days of testimony provided no clue as to what that might be. The prosecution covered the marriage of Jimmy to Betty Lou, the weeks of searching the lake for his body, then locating it in the wishing-well. Forensic pathologists testified to their findings and a deputy testified that the shell casing of the bullets used to kill him had also been found in the wishing-well grave.

Bandy then called as a witness an attractive 26-year-old woman. There were some gasps among the spectators, who quickly recognised her as a married relative of the defendant.

"Will you please relate to the court a conversation you had with the defendant in November, 1981, prior to the time the defendant's husband, Doyle Wayne Barker, was reported to have deserted her?" Bandy asked. Defence Attorney Ray Andrews sprang to his feet, shouting an objection.

Judge Holland had the jurors taken out of the courtroom while the attorneys argued whether or not the testimony was admissible. Andrews argued that he represented Betty Lou not only in the murder case being held, but would also represent her when she was subsequently brought to trial for the murder of Barker. He pointed out that any testimony heard concerning Barker in this case would taint it for a later trial.

Bandy, however, argued that the testimony was relevant, since it would show that the defendant was capable of plotting and carrying out a murder. Judge Holland ruled in favour of the prosecution and the witness was allowed to answer the question.

When the jurors returned to the courtroom, spectators were literally on the edge of their seats straining to hear the testimony, now that they realised of the relationship of the witness to the defendant.

With her eyes averted from the defendant, the witness related that Betty Lou had phoned her at her home, complaining that she was tired of the continual verbal and physical abuse she had been taking from Barker. "I'm going to kill him," she quoted the defendant as saying.

'I told her not to talk silly," the witness said. "If she couldn't get along with him, she should get a divorce."

The witness said that Betty Lou told her Barker owned the mobile home they were living in and, if she divorced him, *he* would have the house.

"I thought she was just talking," the witness said. "You know, like when someone is angry and says, 'I'll kill you' — only they don't actually mean it."

The witness related that Betty Lou came to her house the following day and said: "It's done and over with." When she asked what she meant, Betty Lou told her that she had killed Barker.

Bandy interrupted the recital to ask: "Did she tell you *how* she killed him?"

The witness nodded. "She told me that she had waited until he went to bed and was asleep. She put a pillow over his head, but when she tried to shoot him the pillowcase got caught in the trigger. She told me she was fearful that she had awakened him and backed off. But when he continued to sleep she came up to him again and shot him twice in the head."

The witness recalled that the defendant had confided to her that she had started to dig a grave in the back of the house *before* she killed Barker, had completed digging it and then put the body into it.

Bandy asked the witness: "Would you please tell the court about a phone call you received early on the morning of August 6th, 1983?"

The witness explained that Betty Lou had called her at 2.30 that morning and asked her to come to the house right away. Betty Lou did not say what the emergency was. The witness testified that when she got to the house Betty Lou told her that everything had been taken care of and that she should go home.

In response to a question from Bandy, the witness said that she was not aware at the time that Betty Lou had killed her husband Jimmy Don. But she learned of it later and knew that the body had been placed in the wishing-well.

Cross-examined by the defence, the witness stated that she had agreed to testify for the prosecution, after receiving a guarantee of immunity from prosecution for not having revealed the information to the police earlier.

Bandy had another surprise in store: he called to the witness stand a 21-year-old man, who also identified himself as a relative of the defendant. Bandy asked this witness to recall the events that had taken place on the Friday night of August 5th, 1983.

The witness related that he had been at the home of the defendant. He claimed that Betty Lou had told him that she was going to kill her husband Jimmy Don. And she told him to get lost for a while.

"I was shocked when she told me she was going to kill him," the witness testified. "I did not know for sure that she would kill him, but I suspected that she *might.*"

Bandy asked him if he was aware at the time that the defendant had killed her former husband. The witness said he hadn't known about that.

The witness related that he took his motorcycle and rode around for a couple of hours. When he returned to the mobile home, he spotted a sleeping-bag with a body in it lying outside the back door. Betty Lou told him that she had already killed Jimmy Don, who was now wrapped up in the sleeping-bag.

"She asked me to help her drag it around out front," the witness testified. "We put it in the wishing-well and then covered it with earth."

He said Betty Lou had some potted flowers she had purchased earlier, so they planted them on the top of the makeshift grave. Then they went down to the lake where Jimmy Don kept his boat, the witness related. Betty Lou told him to take the propeller off the drive unit, while she scattered some of Jimmy's heart medicine inside the boat. Then they pushed it out into the lake.

Later on, the witness explained, Betty Lou called the sheriff's office and told them that she was concerned because Jimmy had gone fishing and hadn't returned. Then, when a deputy came to the house to take down a report, the witness had been scared stiff and stayed out of sight. But Betty Lou had carried it off well and appeared to be really concerned that her husband was missing.

When the witness was questioned by the defence why he had not informed the police about the murder, he explained that he felt he was duty-bound to protect his relative and would not have revealed what had happened if the police hadn't found out about it on their own. He also stated that he had agreed to testify for the prosecution, after being assured that he would receive immunity from prosecution.

When it was the defence's turn Attorney Andrews called to the witness stand the defendant, Betty Lou Beets. A murmur of surprise went through the courtroom.

"What now?" a reporter whispered. "Bandy will crucify her on cross-examination."

Betty Lou, between dabs with a handkerchief to her damp eyes and occasional sobs, began her story of what had happened.

She related that she and Jimmy Don had been away on a vacation for three weeks prior to the night he died. She said that when they returned home they found that an older male relative was at the mobile home and had been staying there while they were away.

"Jimmy Don went down to his boat," she said. "He found that it had been hot-wired and the propeller was broken. There was also a flat tyre on my truck."

She said that Jimmy Don had been drinking during the day and became loud and angry with the relative for having taken his boat out without permission. They argued, and he became more angry when he learned that the relative had quit his job and planned to move in with them.

They were having it out with each other, with Jimmy Don calling him "a lazy, worthless bum," Betty Lou testified. She said she had tried to calm them by saying they could talk it over in the morning.

"Jimmy Don went into the bedroom to get ready for bed." The relative went into the bathroom, while she remained in the living-room.

"I heard them arguing again and then I heard the shots," she testified, and began to weep.

She said that when she went into the bedroom she saw

Jimmy Don lying on the floor, blood coming out of his head and mouth. She said the relative told her: "I'm sorry. I didn't mean to do it. Will you help me?"

Betty Lou related that the relative was on probation for six years and she knew the police would not believe that it had been an accident. She told him to leave — and that she would take care of it.

"While Jimmy Don was lying there on the floor I told him how much I loved him and what I was doing and why," the widow testified. "I knew, if he could have heard me, he would have said that he understood."

Andrews interrupted the recital to ask: "Are you owning up to the fact that you covered up for your relative?"

Dabbing her eyes with the handkerchief, Betty Lou answered: "Yes. I could never hurt Jimmy Don. Nobody was ever as good to me as he was. I loved him very much."

Questioned by the prosecutor, Betty Lou stated that she had told her younger relative that she herself had killed Jimmy, so that he would not know that the other relative had actually done the killing.

Surprisingly, Bandy questioned her only briefly. He waited for his closing speech to make the assertion that Betty Lou had been lying when she said a relative had done the killing and that she had only covered up for him.

Bandy told the panel: "You will remember that at the very start I told you the State would prove beyond a reasonable doubt that the defendant is guilty of the charges brought against her. Certainly, the evidence you have heard bears that out."

He began by reviewing the evidence, then said: "Two men were buried in the yard at the mobile home. The common denominator is that both were at one time married to the defendant, Betty Lou Beets."

He added: "Picture two men fighting. It isn't likely that one of them is going to be shot twice in the back of the head.

"The defendant has accepted that her husband was dead. She buried him in the wishing-well and planted flowers to keep anyone from discovering the grave. There is need for justice in this case. You are the only persons who can provide that."

Andrews' address to the jurors stressed the fact that his client had testified voluntarily. "I didn't *have* to put her on the stand," he said. "Who knows what a person will go through to protect a relative they love? Who knows?

"It wouldn't bother the person she said shot and killed her husband one little bit to see her rot in jail, or to see her put on a table and have a needle put into her arm to take her life. He's cold-blooded. Don't convict the wrong person for this crime, whatever you do."

Judge Holland gave these instructions to the panel: "If you have reason to doubt the charges against the defendant, you must acquit her. And if you do not believe beyond a reasonable doubt that the defendant killed her husband for remuneration, you may also find her guilty of the simple charge of murder, as opposed to capital murder."

The panel retired for their deliberations early on Friday afternoon, October 11th, 1985. They were out for five and a half hours.

Then a buzzer sounded from the jury room, indicating that they had reached a decision.

The defendant and her attorney returned to the courtroom. Spectator seats were quickly filled. The eight women and four men returned to the jury-box. Judge Holland came in and was seated at the bench.

There was a hushed quiet in the courtroom as Judge Holland called out the name of each of the jurors to ask if they had agreed a unanimous verdict. Each of the jurors responded that they had. Judge Holland then asked their foreman to read the verdict they had reached.

"We, the jury, have found that the defendant Betty Lou Beets is guilty of the crime of capital murder, as charged," the foreman stated.

Betty Lou brought her hands up to her face. Then she dropped her head on the table, sobbing. But she did not utter a word

Judge Holland addressed the panel that had been coquestered during the trial and told them that they would be required to return at 9.30 on Monday morning to deliberate the penalty, which could be life imprisonment without parole, or death by lethal injection.

When the jurors returned on Monday morning they heard brief pleas from the prosecution and defence. Bandy complimented the panel for their deliberations on Friday, in which they returned the guilty verdict. He asked only that they consider the evidence and return with a verdict recommending the death penalty.

After Andrews made an impassioned plea for his client's life, Judge Holland instructed the panel that they had only two special issues to decide. If one or more jurors answered no to either issue, the defendant would be sentenced to life in prison.

The first issue to be decided was "if the conduct of the defendant was done with the deliberate expectation that death would result." The second issue asked "whether there was a probability that the defendant will commit future acts of violence that would constitute a continuing threat to society".

Surprising almost everyone, the panel was out only 45 minutes before reaching a verdict. They returned with the recommendation that Betty Lou Beets be executed by lethal injection.

She remained silent and without tears as judgment was passed by Judge Holland. Then she was taken to the Texas Department of Corrections in Gatesville, where she joined three other women awaiting execution on Death Row.

11

THE LETHAL LADY

Michael King

"I only buried her, that's all!" —
Louise Peete protesting her innocence.

It is possible that "Lethal Louise" had never read the horror stories of Edgar Allan Poe. She may have thought that her spine-chilling pattern for murder and the concealment of her victims' bodies was entirely original. Unfortunately for Louise, the man who was to become her nemesis was an ardent reader of the Poe murder stories. He recognised the pattern. And because he did the Belle of Bienville, Louisiana, became the second woman in California history to die in the San Quentin gas chamber.

Her list of victims comprises two official murders, one unofficial killing, four men driven to suicide, and at least three suspiciously convenient deaths written off as natural. The deaths-for-profit attributed to her were not crimes of passion but coldly calculated horrors. It may be said that murder was her passion.

She was born Lofie Louise Preslar, in the little hamlet of Bienville in northern Louisiana, on September 20th, 1888. She was the daughter of a respectable middle-class family; her father was the publisher of a small weekly newspaper. She grew up in Coushatta, in the cotton country of Red River Parish, and acquired the conventional education for a young lady, with emphasis on music and the social graces.

By all accounts she was something of a beauty in her teens, with a wealth of glowing brown hair, creamy complexion and a lush, early-maturing figure. But Louise scorned the small-town swains with the same haughty contempt she was to hold for all men throughout her life, concealing it only when it suited her devious purposes to use them.

In this way she used young Henry Bosley, the first man in her life. Louise had no intention of becoming a back-country planter's lady. She longed for the great glittering world of the big cities. So when Henry, a travelling sales-man with eager ambitions blew into town, it was not he who ensnared the innocent village belle, but he who was trapped. On a spring day in 1903 — at the age of 15 by her own account and 18 or 20 by that of others — she married the adoring Hank who carried her off triumphantly to Shreveport.

But even love-stricken Hank Bosley couldn't remain blind very long to the character defect that his bride had managed to keep cleverly hidden in her home town: she just couldn't keep her hands off other people's property. She had a particular passion for jewellery and fine clothes and, before long their fellow-lodgers in Shreveport were openly accusing her of being a thief. But Louise always had some smooth explanation and Hank did his best to cover up for her.

Louise wasn't an undiscriminating kleptomaniac. She merely chose to steal luxurious things rather than save or work for them. She constantly berated her young husband for his meagre income. She urged him to take the easy way, to cut corners and to cheat on his employers.

Hank Bosley soon had enough. Perhaps he began to discern even at that budding stage of her career, behind his languorous little wife's slow smile and droopy-lidded grey eyes, the suggestion of a cold-blooded reptile ready to strike. At any rate, after brief "new starts" in Oklahoma City and Dallas they split up in 1905, and Hank gallantly allowed her to divorce him. Shortly thereafter he killed himself, presumably brooding over his disillusionment.

Louise made her way to New Orleans, where her sultry charm and sad story landed her a job as social secretary to a wealthy woman. Now she really was in business. No longer restrained by a scrupulous husband, in no time at all Louise made a tidy little stake by forging the names of her employer and society friends to store accounts and selling the merchandise, as well as by exercising her light fingers in the usual way. When things began to get hot for her she prudently left town a jump ahead of the police, taking with her a diamond ring belonging to her employer and a sheaf of forged letters of recommendation from the Crescent City upper crust.

She turned up in Boston as Louise Gould, 19-year-old New Orleans heiress to a large estate in Germany, just waiting for the legal red tape to be cleared. The forged letters opened the doors of Back Bay society to her, and she was soon installed in an exclusive girls' finishing school to pursue her musical studies.

Inevitably, her itching fingers betrayed her and she was exposed as the thief of valuables from lockers and also for leading astray some of the impressionable young ladies. She exercised to the limit her Southern charm and, for fear of scandal, the school authorities refrained from calling the police, provided she got out of Boston and stayed out.

Louise reappeared in Texas, this time as the widowed Mrs. Bosley. In addition to her musical bent, by this time she had developed an unladylike penchant for firearms, which was to play such a large part in her career. One night, according to her own story, she was amusing herself at a shooting gallery in Waco when a handsome well-dressed stranger expressed admiration for her skill. They got to talking and went for a car ride together.

An hour later Louise drove up to the sheriff's office to announce that she had killed the stranger with the little .32 she carried in her handbag for protection. "He tried to violate my honour," she explained.

Deputies went back with her and found her new friend lying stone dead beside the road, shot through the back of the head. Strangely, he had been robbed of his valuables, including, it later developed, a diamond ring. Clearly someone must have come along and robbed the corpse as it lay there.

Bemused by the young widow's languid beauty, the sheriff forcefully declared that no Southern woman should be prosecuted for defending her honour. He congratulated her on her narrow escape. Apparently no one ever questioned her account, or suspected her of the robbery.

In 1913 Louise was questioned by a Dallas grand jury investigating the fatal shooting of Harry Faurote, a clerk at a hotel where she was living. It seemed that both Louise and Harry had been suspected by the police of the theft of a $700 diamond ring. When the ring turned up among Harry's possessions Louise explained that she had found it and had given it to him for safe-keeping. The jury decided that Faurote had committed suicide, apparently convinced that he was disgraced and his career ruined by the unjust suspicion.

The turbulent year of 1914 found Louise living in Denver, Colorado. There, with the proceeds of her various enterprises, she started taking singing lessons. At about that time, she suffered a head and back injury in a car crash. This her attorneys were to make capital of later, trying to blame the blow on the head for her murderous tendencies.

In that same year Louise married for the second time. This husband was Richard C. Peete, a well-to-do pioneer car dealer. In 1916, their little daughter Betty was born. Louise apparently spent the war years quietly in their neat house on Adams Street, keeping out of trouble.

But Peete's health began to fail, and his fortune with it. When he could no longer supply her with the luxuries she demanded Louise sought them from other associates, cultivating a number of rich women friends. She moved out with the baby "to live her own life," although she and Richard were not divorced and remained on good terms. She rented from the local Belgian Consul a large house on Sherman Street, and took in selected lodgers.

In May 1919 Richard, hoping to recoup his finances, went to Singapore as representative of a tyre company on a two-year contract. It was understood that he and Louise would make another try at family life on his return.

In November of that year the Belgian Consul, M. Mignolet, whose distinguished name Louise had been using freely to enhance her credit, filed action to evict his fast-talking tenant. In addition to unpaid back rent and unauthorised sale of the consul's furniture, the charges involved noisy parties, shady associates and general bad repute in the locality. The harassed Belgian complained that he couldn't get Mrs. Peete to vacate.

Legal action resulted in an action against Louise for contributing to the delinquency of a minor by neglecting little Betty and exposing her to bad influences. She came before Judge Ben Lindsey, who handed the case over to a woman judge, Mrs. Gregory.

Louise turned on her persuasive Southern charm, with the result that not only was the case dismissed as a misunderstanding, but she and Judge Gregory, who was just about to retire from the bench, became good friends. Agreeing that they would both enjoy a change of scene, they decided to move to Los Angeles with Louise's baby and the judge's grown daughter. There they would share household expenses, and perhaps take in lodgers, until Richard Peete's return from the Orient.

However, in Singapore Richard's health worsened. He developed tuberculosis and, at the end of 1919 he gave up his job and came home. In February, 1920 he went to Phoenix, Arizona, for his health. Louise followed a month later with their child. But their reunion didn't last. Funds were short, and in mid-May Peete returned to Denver, taking four-year-old Betty with him, while Louise went to Los Angeles to go ahead with the plan of co-operative housekeeping with Mrs. Gregory.

On a spring day in 1920 Louise Peete made her first bow in the City of the Angels, which was then in the middle of its phenomenal post-war real-estate and oil boom. She also met Jacob Charles Denton, a ruggedly handsome 48-year-old man who had made his considerable fortune as a mining engineer in Mexico and Arizona. He was then a speculator in mining and oil properties.

Shy and reserved with women, Denton had had more than his share of grief. His first marriage went on the rocks; his wife divorced him and was living in Phoenix with their grown daughter, Frances. After having been single for a long time, only the previous year Denton had married a beautiful girl named Dolly, who finally brought him the happiness he had missed in his active life.

Although his own tastes were simple, he had bought a fine English Tudor-style mansion in the fashionable Wilshire district for his bride. Soon their bliss was crowned with the arrival of a baby daughter. But Jake Denton's hard knocks were not yet over. In February, 1920 the baby died. The grieving parents planned a long trip to try to forget. But they had hardly started when Dolly was taken suddenly ill and died in a few hours.

Jack Denton plunged into work. He couldn't stand living alone in the big house echoing with memories of his dead bride and baby. Arranging to go East by way of Texas on an indefinite stay, he advertised the house at 675 South Catalina Street for lease or sale. Louise answered his ad.

Doubtless she impressed the tough engineer with her appearance of shrewd capability and her tales of the property she owned in Denver. They talked over an arrangement whereby she would take over the $30,000 house, furniture and Denton's car, on lease, with the ultimate idea of selling them for a commission. She would move in at once, and Denton would retain one room for his own use until he was ready to leave, early in June. Denton thought a rent of $350 a month was fair. Louise reckoned it was too steep, but she moved in while they discussed the amount.

She wrote to Mrs. Gregory, telling her that she had found just the house for their co-operative boarding house enterprise, for which the ex-judge was going to put up the initial capital. On May 24th Mrs. Gregory and her daughter arrived in Los Angeles. Louise put them up at a hotel while she worked out final arrangements with Denton.

On May 25th Denton's niece helped her uncle and his new tenant make an inventory. On May 30th, Jake Denton blossomed out and escorted Louise to a beach party given by his niece. The following day he kept a business date with Everett B. Latham and told him that he would be leaving Los Angeles any day. By this time Mrs. Peete was fully installed, keeping house and cooking for Denton.

On June 2nd the usually punctual mining man failed to keep downtown appointments with three Texas oilmen, an insurance agent and an auto salesman. On June 3rd Louise called Mrs. Gregory and her daughter to announce that Denton had finally left, and the two women moved in with her.

During the ensuing weeks, when inquiries were made for Denton, Mrs. Peete said variously that he had gone to Arizona, to San Francisco, or to Seattle, and that she was handling his personal business in his absence.

When no one had heard from Jake Denton by the end of June, the inquiries became insistent. At the written request of the missing man's daughter in Phoenix, his old friend and attorney Judge Russ Avery undertook an investigation. He went to the house and talked to Mrs. Peete.

"I'll tell you the truth, Judge," Louise said confidentially, "although Mr. Denton doesn't want anyone to know. The fact is, the poor man got an infection in his arm and had to have it amputated in San Francisco. The right arm. You know how it is — he's ashamed of being crippled and he doesn't want to see any of his friends for a while."

"He's been in touch with you then, Mrs. Peete? Do you have any letters from him?" Judge Avery asked.

"No, I didn't save them. But Mr. Denton dropped in just about a week ago and told me to continue looking after things here."

Asked to produce papers showing her authority, she coyly explained that her agreement with Denton was only verbal. He'd had to leave before they could get around to signing a lease.

Judge Avery knew how close-mouthed Jake Denton

could be about his affairs, how informally he sometimes handled them, and how he would dislike prying. Also, the personable Southern matron had a way with her, and he was inclined to accept her story.

Further inquiries piled up. Denton had failed to pick up a new car he had ordered in Detroit. A big Arizona business deal had fallen through because of his absence. His regular remittances to his ex-wife and daughter had failed to arrive.

Meanwhile, Louise was cutting quite a figure in the Wilshire community, making friends everywhere and displaying new clothes and jewels. She and Mrs. Gregory gave up the idea of starting a boarding house and Mrs. Gregory went back to Denver. In August Louise followed suit, subleasing the house to a Mrs. Miller and turning in Denton's car to buy a new one, which she promised to return and pay for shortly.

In mid-September Frances Denton, convinced that something had happened to her father, went to an attorney friend in Phoenix and appealed to him for help.

The attorney forwarded the inquiry and various documents, including Denton's bank statements, which Judge Avery had sent to the daughter, together with a long letter to his associate in Los Angeles, Attorney Rush M. Blodget.

Blodget was a fan of the mystery master Edgar Allan Poe, and a great admirer of the cold deductive logic with which C. Auguste Dupin, Poe's great detective hero, solved his baffling cases. So, when the bulky inquiry from Phoenix arrived on the afternoon of September 22nd Blodget welcomed the challenge of a real-life mystery and put Dupin's methods to work. Totally unacquainted with the case, with Jake Denton and Louise Peete, Blodget spread the documents on his desk and studied them. He noted that no cheques had been drawn on Denton's fat bank account since June 10th. Yet Denton was supposedly living somehow and spending money. He had always paid his bills by cheque. Where were the cheques to the doctor and hospital for his arm amputation, which must have been expensive? And how did it happen that the energetic mining man, always devoted to his business deals, now totally neglected them?

"Jake Denton is dead," Rush Blodget said aloud to the walls of his office. "He's been dead since early in June!" Then, following the logic of Poe's Dupin, he mused: "Louise Peete says she saw him alive in July. She's lying. Why is she lying? Because she knows where he really is and can't tell. Louise Peete killed him!"

Obviously, her motive had been to take over his property. Where had she killed him, and where was his body? Since the corpse hadn't turned up anywhere, it was logical to assume that she had killed him in the house where they both lived and had hidden the body there.

A night's further reflection only reinforced the lawyer's deductions. Early the next morning he telephoned Judge Avery, told him what he suspected and urged him to join in a search of Denton's house. But the judge was hesitant. After all, this was mere speculation, he argued, and Jake wouldn't like their barging around.

A call to the district attorney's office met with the same unenthusiastic reception. By this time, however, Rush Blodget was thoroughly aroused and determined to do his duty by the Phoenix client as he saw it. He called his private detective friend A. J. Cody and together they drove out to Catalina Street. Mrs. Miller, the new tenant, was sure that there was no dead body in the house. But when the two men showed their credentials and insisted on making a search, she shrugged and told them to go ahead and look.

"Where do we look first?" Cody asked.

Blodget, in his role of Dupin, retorted with a withering glance. "Where is the logical place to bury a body? In the attic, do you think? In the basement, of course!"

In going to the basement Blodget was motivated not only by logic but subconsciously by the prickling recollection of Poe's *The Black Cat*. The dank, dark cellar was the natural place to head for.

The concrete basement floor seemed solid enough. But as they prowled among stacks of rubbish under the light of a dim bulb, the attorney found himself aping Poe's character and knocking on the walls, half expecting to be answered by the grisly howl of an entombed cat. At one point under the stairs he noted a hollow sound. Examination disclosed that it was the door to a small cupboard, completely nailed over with planks.

"Mr. Denton keeps his liquor there," Mrs. Miller explained. "He boarded it up, and Mrs. Peete told me not to touch it."

"Let's go!" Blodget told the detective. "Help me get these boards off."

Mrs. Miller provided the tools and stood by with a torch while the two men pried the clumsily-nailed boards loose and wrenched open the flimsy door. The torch beam showed not a store of precious Prohibition liquor but a pile of rusty stovepipe sections on top of some rotting timber. The little cupboard gave out a musty odour of decay.

"Nothing here but a lot of trash," Cody observed.

"Looks like it," Blodget agreed. "But why pile trash in a cupboard and then board it up and tell people to keep away? Here, give me a hand —"

They moved the stovepipes and timber aside to disclose a floor of loose brown earth. "Looks like this earth has been disturbed, and not too long ago," Blodget commented quietly. "Do you have a shovel, Mrs. Miller?"

So strongly did the suggestion of evil now grip all three that there was almost no surprise when the probing shovel turned up a soiled white tennis shoe — with a man's foot in it. Still clutching the torch, Mrs. Miller screamed and couldn't stop.

While Blodget took care of the hysterical woman, Cody phoned the police. Detective Commander Herman Cline was soon at the scene with Detectives Sidney Hickok and Louis Canto. Deputy coroners completed the disinterment of Jake Denton's pitiful remains, neatly swathed in a bloody quilt. There was no amputation of his right arm, Blodget observed. He had been shot through the back of the head.

Since Louise Peete had left California and extradition

might be difficult, the authorities kept their suspicions quiet while they completed their investigations. Bloodstains in the house showed that Denton had been shot as he sat in the breakfast nook, then apparently led upstairs to die in bed. The coroner estimated that he had been buried since about June 1st.

Detective Commander Cline's men and investigators from District Attorney Thomas Lee Woolwine's office piled up a mountain of evidence against Louise Peete. The last few cheques cashed to the victim's account, early in June, were clearly forgeries written by her. The bank recalled that Mrs. Peete had tried to cash further cheques, but they had been refused. In addition, she had forged Denton's endorsement to several sizable cheques that had been mailed to him. And she had been buying clothes and jewellery in the Wilshire Boulevard shops on the accounts of the late Dolly Denton, which the grief-stricken Jake had neglected to close.

She had pawned some of the Dentons' jewellery, and given other valuables to friends for safe-keeping, including Jake's cherished personal mementoes of his dead wife and baby. More directly bearing on the murder, she'd had a gardener dump a load of earth in the basement, explaining that in Mr. Denton's absence she wanted to bury some of his late wife's treasures for safety's sake. And before leaving for Denver she had ordered a quantity of cement, which hadn't been delivered in time.

With the newspapers headlining the murder, District Attorney Woolwine sent his most discreet and diplomatic aide, Charles A. Jones — later Los Angeles Chief of Police — to Denver to lure Louise back. Jones found her living quietly with her ailing husband and their baby. He explained that her testimony was needed, merely as a formality, for the official record on Denton's last days. Louise fell for it and accompanied him back.

Once inside California she was sunk. Under questioning by police and the D.A.'s men, she soon tied herself up in a network of lies. Woolwine filed a formal murder charge and she was indicted and held for trial.

The arrest of the cold-eyed housewife, who still retained her creamy complexion and could still be called beautiful, created a newspaper sensation. Richard Peete came to Los Angeles and announced that he believed in her and would stand by her.

Another who was convinced of Louise's innocence was an old friend from Texas, Margaret Logan, recently returned from several years in the Orient with her husband and then living in Los Angeles. Mrs. Logan generously volunteered to take care of baby Betty until things should be straightened out.

But there was little hope of Louise's escaping the murder charge by using her Southern charm. The evidence against her was too damning, too conclusive. She maintained that she was the innocent victim of circumstances. She claimed that the real killer was an unidentified Spanish woman, a jealous beauty with whom Jake had had trouble, and of whom he had been in mortal fear. As for the forgeries, her story was that Jake, with his infected arm in a sling, had asked her to sign his name for him.

Unimpressed, the jury of 12 men took only four hours to find Louise Peete guilty of first-degree murder. On January 28th 1921 Superior Judge Frank Willis sentenced her to life imprisonment — sparing her the death penalty because of the circumstantial nature of the case and the long tradition against executing a woman in California. Her appeals to higher courts were denied.

Still protesting her innocence, Louise was taken to San Quentin. The months went by, turning into years. Mrs. Logan was taking care of Louise's child, raising the little girl as her own and keeping the imprisoned mother posted. In 1924 Richard Peete, who had never recovered from the blow of his wife's conviction, shot himself to death in a hotel room in Tucson, Arizona. Louise remained a model prisoner, amicably sharing queenship of the San Quentin women's wing with hammer-murderess Clara Phillips.

In 1926 Louise reappeared briefly in the limelight with

a sensational appeal to Governor Friend W. Richardson. The governor was taking a hand in the reopened investigation into the murder in 1922 of famous silent film director William Desmond Taylor. Louise Peete climbed on the bandwagon with a statement that Taylor had been put out of the way because he "knew too much" about the real killer of Jake Denton. She knew who Denton's actual killer was, Louise said, but she couldn't reveal his or her identity because it would endanger the life of her little daughter.

A San Francisco physician declared that his ex-wife, a former friend of Denton, had told him a similar story. Another helpful informant said that Denton had been engaged in smuggling narcotics from Mexico for Taylor to distribute to film stars, and that both had been murdered by a rival gang. Los Angeles authorities duly investigated these tales, but found nothing to support them. Louise remained in prison.

In 1933 the aging Louisiana belle was transferred with the other women prisoners to the newly-established California Institution for Women at Tehachapi, where she enjoyed pleasant sunny quarters and easy work in the garden. "This prisoner works well," Tehachapi Superintendent Florence Monahan noted at that time, "and seems to co-operate, but is subtly critical."

From time to time, Louise applied for parole. She was able to produce a number of letters from respectable citizens in her favour, including Margaret Logan, to offset those opposing her release. But no one would go so far as to guarantee a job for her in the world outside the big wire fence, and the parole board delayed action.

In the mid-30s her daughter was safely married and left the Logan home to start a new life for herself, putting the shadowy family past behind her.

In 1939 Louise finally won parole. In view of her excellent prison record over the long years, the board, despite strenuous objection from the Los Angeles district attorney's office, decided that she rated another chance.

There was no job immediately available for her, but Mrs.

Emily Latham, women's parole officer in Los Angeles, agreed to take her into her own home until she could find one. By coincidence, Mrs. Latham was the widow of Everett Latham, who had been one of the last persons to see Jake Denton alive, and had testified against Louise.

It was further agreed that Louise could assume the fictitious name of "Anna B. Lee" in her new life outside. When the superintendent handed her the usual written instructions for parolees, directing her to report at regular intervals, she blithely tore them up. "I don't owe the world a thing!" she declared. But she promised to be good.

So on April 2nd, 1939, after 18 years behind bars, Lofie Louise Bosley Peete, now Anna B. Lee, walked out to freedom. She was then 51, by her own statement, but she may have been five or six years older. Her brown hair was streaked with grey, but her grey eyes and her slow smile were colder and more deadly than ever.

Mrs. Latham procured a job for Louise as a housekeeper. Other jobs followed, and 1942 found "Mrs. Lee" the respected superintendent of the soldiers' dormitory for transient servicemen on North Hobart Boulevard. Apparently she was behaving herself. At least, there were no complaints about her.

In August, 1943, Emily Latham, who had kept a constant eye on her protegée, was taken ill and employed Louise as her housekeeper at $25 a week. Three weeks later Mrs. Latham died of an apparently accidental dose of heart stimulant. Louise had her cremated at once. Perhaps Louise had hastened her end, perhaps not. At any rate, no suspicion was attached to her at the time, although it later developed that some of the widow's possessions had stuck to the housekeeper's hands.

Freed now from Mrs. Latham's friendly supervision, Louise went to see Margaret Logan, whom she had often visited in her neat home at 713 Hampden Place in Pacific Palisades, overlooking the ocean.

The Logans had always been fairly well-to-do, and Margaret, then 62, was a licensed real-estate broker. But recently the health of her husband, Arthur C. Logan, a retired Far East export-importer 12 years her senior, had been failing. Mentally as well as physically, he required constant care.

This drain on their finances, plus the wartime freezing of the real estate market, had spurred the active Margaret to take a temporary job in an aircraft factory. And now she welcomed the opportunity to give her old friend Louise a home, in return for help in taking care of Arthur and the household chores. She agreed to pay Louise $75 a month. So "Mrs. Lee" moved into the Logan household.

Louise soon began to urge Margaret to put her husband in a sanitorium. "He's not right in his mind," she kept insisting to Mrs. Logan and any of the neighbours who would listen. "He's dangerous. We may wake up some day with our throats cut!"

Although the mild-mannered old man had never shown any disposition to violence, his wife finally allowed herself to be persuaded, and had him committed to a private institution. But she was so lonely without him after their years together, and he was so unhappy in his new surroundings, that after a few weeks she brought him home over Louise's objections.

"He's my husband and this is his home," she told her housekeeper-friend.

In the spring of 1944 Mrs. Logan quit her defence job and went back into the real-estate business. One day she heard of a fine piece of property that was for sale for $50,000. She told Louise about it, wishing that she could swing the deal.

"I can help you, Margaret," Louise told her quietly. "I still have that $100,000 trust fund in Denver — or didn't you know about that?" And she smiled complacently.

Mrs. Logan happily put a $2,000 deposit on the property, to be bought in the name of "Lou Anne Lee," and advanced the money for a trip to Denver, which Louise wished to make to arrange for the funds.

But she returned from Denver without the money.

Margaret was shocked and disappointed. They apparently had some words and Louise left the Logan household. On May 2nd she married — secretly and in violation of her parole — Lee Borden Judson, a respectable widower in his 60s, a former advertising man now employed as a bank messenger, whom she had known for about a year. They moved into a hotel in suburban Glendale.

On May 19th, Lou Ann Lee Judson cashed a $200 cheque, purportedly signed by Margaret Logan, at a Santa Monica bank. Belatedly suspicious, the bank called Mrs. Logan, who immediately got in touch with Louise and demanded restitution. Louise promised to return the money very soon.

On June 1st — by a grim coincidence, exactly the same date on which Jacob Denton was killed — Margaret called her former friend and insisted on immediate repayment of the $200. She threatened to report her to the parole board. Louise promised to come out to see her that same night.

Six months later — on December 7th, 1944 — Mrs. Wave Walker, a women's parole officer from San Francisco, came to Los Angeles on the trail of a housemaid who had walked off with $50,000 in gems. Learning that the woman had been a friend of Mrs. Peete in prison, she looked up Louise's record and obtained Margaret Logan's address.

Calling at the Pacific Palisades home, she found no one at home. A neighbour volunteered the information that Mrs. Logan had been away since June, was supposed to be in a hospital somewhere, and that the Judsons were living there now.

Surprised and thoughtful, Mrs. Walker went back to the parole office, where she looked at Mrs. Peete's records again. Her superior, Mrs. W. F. Weibrod, agreed that Margaret Logan's signatures on the June, July and August parole reports — the regular monthly employer's forms required by law — were obviously different from previous ones.

A little further checking in Pacific Palisades increased

their suspicions and they laid the matter before District Attorney Fred Howser, who assigned investigators to look into the matter. Captain Thad Brown of Central Homicide was soon in the picture, and the picture was rapidly turning black.

The sleuths learned from the neighbours that neither Margaret nor Arthur Logan had been seen since the end of May. Early in June Margaret's friend Lou Ann had moved into the white house with her nice elderly husband, Mr. Judson. Lou's rather shocking explanation was that Arthur Logan had suddenly become violent and had bitten off his wife's nose. Arthur had been taken away to the psychopathic ward, where he had since died, and Margaret was in a hospital recuperating from plastic surgery, she explained.

They found that Arthur Logan had indeed been committed as insane on June 2nd, at the request of Anna B. Lee, who represented him as his foster-sister. And when he died at Patton State Hospital on December 6th, grieving and complaining that his wife had abandoned him, a telegram signed simply "Logan" ordered his body to be given immediately to a college for dissection. The telegram's contents had been telephoned from the Logan residence.

The detectives learned of the $200 forged cheque that never had been made good. There were other forgeries besides, and Louise had obtained $1,000 of Mrs. Logan's real-estate deposit, generously allowing the disappointed seller to keep the other $1,000.

When Captain Brown, with Detective Sergeants Harry Hansen, Roy Vaughn and other officers, rang the doorbell of 713 Hampden Place on the evening of December 20th they found Louise Peete in lounging pyjamas. She was going through a strongbox full of Margaret Logan's papers. Mr. Judson was reading his newspaper.

They took the couple down to the district attorney's office for questioning. Louise stuck to her story that Mrs. Logan was in a hospital "somewhere" and would be back soon. But under skilful questioning she became hopelessly confused.

Lee Judson was amazed and aghast. He declared that he'd had no suspicion that his bride was the notorious Louise Peete. He had accepted without question her story of what had happened to the Logans.

The homicide men went out to the Logan house again with a crew of technicians. Recalling the Denton case, Captain Brown led the way first to the basement. Nothing was found buried there, but he noted seepage of water at a spot on the basement wall, indicating that the earth outside was loosely packed.

They began to dig outside. Soon the shovels turned up the remains of Margaret Logan, buried in a shallow grave in a neat flower-bed under an avocado tree, just outside the window of the bedroom where Louise had been sleeping for six months. Like Jake Denton, she had been shot in the back of the head. In addition, her skull had been fractured, apparently by blows from a hammer.

Inside the house, Police Chemist Ray Pinker found bloodstains indicating that the murder had taken place in the living-room. And, hidden among Louise's possessions, they found two guns — a .25 automatic and a .32 revolver. The latter was identified as having belonged to the late Everett Latham, husband of the Los Angeles women's parole officer.

District Attorney Howser charged both Louise and her husband with murder. But at their preliminary hearing on January 10th, 1945 Municipal Judge William M. Byrne accepted Lee Judson's story that he had been completely unaware that a murder had been committed. The judge absolved him of any guilt, but he held Louise for trial in Superior Court on the murder charge.

Two days later Lee Judson, unable to erase the horror from his mind, leaped to his death from the 12th floor of a downtown office building. He was the fourth man driven to suicide by lethal Louise.

Louise wept when she learned of it. "We had such a happy time together," she sobbed. "He could not bear the disgrace I brought upon him." But she still steadfastly asserted her innocence in the death of the woman who had befriended her.

While Louise awaited trial Captain Brown investigated the deaths of Emily Latham and Arthur Logan. He considered the possibility that Logan had been the victim of a slow-acting poison. But at this late date nothing definite could be determined. And the body of Emily Latham had been cremated.

Another death he investigated was that of 60-year-old Mrs. Jessie M. Marcy, who had lived next door to Louise when she ran the soldiers' dormitory on North Hobart Boulevard. Mrs. Marcy had died on January 9th, 1943, after suffering painful injuries in two supposedly accidental falls within a month. She was known to have quarrelled with Louise. But again it was too late to uncover more facts.

On the eve of her trial Louise changed her story. She now admitted that she had buried Margaret Logan in the flower bed, after Arthur Logan had killed his wife in an insane rage. She had done this, and kept quiet about it, she asserted, because she knew that her record would lay her open to suspicion.

She repeated this story in her defence before the jury of 11 women and one man, but it failed to convince them. After deliberating for two hours and 40 minutes, they found her guilty of first-degree murder, with no recommendation for mercy.

And on June 1st, 1945, exactly one year after the murder of Margaret Logan, Superior Judge Harold B. Landreth sentenced Louise to die in the gas chamber.

Almost two years were to pass, however, before Louise reached the inevitable end of her incredible career. The public defenders who represented her made valiant efforts to obtain a reversal of the verdict, but their appeals were denied.

Meanwhile their client continued to protest her innocence. "I only buried her, that's all," she reiterated. "I was afraid they wouldn't believe my story, because I had been convicted of murder once before. I didn't kill Jake, either."

On the sunny morning of Friday, April 11th, 1947 Louise was awakened at 5.30 a.m. She was calm, although it was reported that she had slept but fitfully during the night. When Warden Clinton P. Duffy came to see her, she asked him what she should wear for the execution.

He told her: "Anything you wish." He pointed to neat brown dress. "That looks very nice," he said. "Why not wear it?"

When she was dressed the warden came back. "I'm ready," she said. "I've been ready for a long time."

Then, with two grey-haired guards holding her arms, she walked calmly into the green steel gas chamber. Outside she could see the 70 witnesses gathered. She made a faint, ironic bow towards them.

She sat down in one of the two steel chairs and swiftly the guards clamped the heavy straps about her feet, hands and body. Then, their duty done, the guards left the chamber.

One of them touched her shoulder as he passed, and said: "Goodbye — good luck."

And the other advised her: "Count ten — breathe deep."

"Thank you," Louise murmured.

Then the heavy steel door closed. It was 10.30 a.m. Her face turned towards one of the seven windows of the death chamber and she saw Warden Duffy. She nodded to him and her lips formed the words, "Let's go." He nodded, lifted a hand in a farewell gesture.

A motor whirred. Louise closed her eyes, breathed deeply.

At 10.43 the assistant warden said: "That's all, gentlemen. Please leave."

At noon, two guards wearing gas masks removed Louise's body and placed it in a pine box. It was delivered to unidentified "friends". The Belle of Bienville, Louisiana, had made her final bow.

12

THE LONG ISLAND BORGIA

Malcolm Carter

"Come on, let's mix her a good stiff one. I'm tired of her hanging on like this." — Mary Creighton speaking to her accomplice in murder.

The caller was a cocky little man. He wore an air of consequence and his strut seemed a blend of military march and drugstore cowboy swagger. In the outer room of the district attorney's office in Mineola, Long Island, county seat of Nassau County, he told the receptionist: "I want to see District Attorney Martin W. Littleton."

"Do you have an appointment?" she asked.

"If you'll just tell him who it is, I think he'll see Commander Applegate," the man said importantly.

"I'm sorry. Mr. Littleton isn't in."

"Then," said the caller, with sarcasm, "I'll see whoever does happen to be on the job this fine June day."

His manner was less aggressive when, after impatient minutes of pacing the outer office, he was ushered into the private room of a younger assistant district attorney.

"I'm Everett Applegate," he introduced himself. "You must have heard of me. Until just the other day I was Commander of the Second Division of the American Legion here in Nassau County."

"Sit down, Commander," the young attorney said. "What can I do for you?"

The caller took three plain envelopes from the inside pocket of his sports jacket. "Read one, you've read all three. Poison-pen stuff, aiming to injure me," he said. "I'm a candidate for the C.C. spot — you know, County Commander."

The attorney examined the envelopes. They were uniformly addressed:

"TO THE PEOPLE AT
12 BRYANT PLACE,
BALDWIN, LONG ISLAND"

He took out the three letters and placed them side by side. They were similar in wording and almost identical in appearance. The paper was of a cheap grade: three lined yellow sheets which, to judge by their torn and ragged top edges, had been ripped off a pad.

One of the anonymous missives read:

"I know I speak for your neighbours when I tell you that we are sick and tired of two people living on this street. You don't need to guess that I could only mean Everett Applegate and that fat Ada, his wife. Applegate is no good and never was. He is a wolf in sheep's clothing and is on the make for every woman he meets. As for his wife, she has a mouth as big as she is. She uses it to tell lies about the people she lives with and they are foolish to let her pull the wool over their eyes that way."

From the postmarks it appeared that the three letters had been mailed in Baldwin on June 17th, 18th and 19th. It was now Friday, June 21st 1935.

The assistant district attorney asked: "Who received them?"

Applegate replied: "Mrs. Creighton did. But since these insults are mainly aimed at me, she turned them over to me."

"You and your wife board with Mrs. Creighton?"

"My wife and I and our daughter reside with Mr. and Mrs. Creighton, who have two children of their own — a girl and a boy. That way, we split the expenses."

"You have no suspicions as to who would write such letters?"

"No, I don't. A man in my position makes some enemies. But not this kind."

"Then you don't associate it with the coming election of county commander?"

"No Legionnaire would do such a thing. But somebody else — someone who hates me and aims to wreck my chances — that's the person you've got to find."

The official frowned. "If these letters were obscene, or if they threatened you, it would be a matter both for the county police and the postal inspectors—"

"You don't call this dirt obscene?" Everett Applegate's eyes nearly popped with incredulity.

"Not in the strictest sense of the law. The accusation is spiteful. The words used are not technically in the realm of obscenity."

"Rubbish!"

The young attorney's voice was cool as he said: "I'll show these to my colleague, Dick Brown. He'll take them up with Mr. Littleton. If we feel that an investigation is warranted, you'll be asked to come in and discuss it further. You'll let us know, of course, if any more such letters turn up."

Applegate stood up abruptly and marched out of the office.

He didn't return with any more anonymous or abusive letters. Nor did he press for the investigation which, the District Attorney's office decided on the basis of the evidence, would prove only a time-squandering futility.

Weeks passed. Applegate failed to be elected in Nassau as county commander of the American Legion. Then, on Saturday, September 28th, at 4 o'clock in the afternoon, Patrolman Joseph O'Conner approached the desk of Inspector Harold R. King, commanding officer of the Detective Divison of Nassau County.

O'Conner carried a brown cardboard cylinder some 19 inches in length and two inches in diameter. He placed it on the inspector's desk.

King dipped two fingers into one end of the cylinder and began withdrawing the stiff paper roll which was its contents. "Photostats," he said. "What's this all about, Joe?"

"Something over in Baldwin," the patrolman explained. "A Mrs. Ada Applegate of 12 Bryant Place died yesterday. Living at the same address is a couple named Creighton. Mr. and Mrs. John Creighton."

"I knew Mrs. Applegate," Inspector King put in. "I know her husband slightly, because he's been active in Legion affairs. Haven't seen his wife for at least a year, though. I didn't know she was ill."

"That's it, sir. Mrs. Applegate died rather suddenly. And that's why I have these photostats," O'Conner said. "Mrs. Creighton, it seems, had some trouble with a neighbour of hers in Baldwin — a Mrs. Olive Salket. Mrs. Salket learned that 12 years ago the Creightons had been involved in a murder case in New Jersey. She went to the library, found reports of the trial in the newspapers, and had these photostats made. She called this morning and gave them to me."

King examined the photostats. A couple named Creighton had been on trial in Newark, following the mysterious death by arsenic poisoning of an 18-year-old youth named Raymond Avery. He was Mrs. Creighton's brother.

The Newark prosecutor had contended that young Avery was murdered from a motive of greed. His sister stood to collect on him. However, the State's case rested wholly on circumstantial evidence and it was not strong enough to convince the jury. The Creightons were acquitted.

Inspector King looked up from his reading. "What does Mrs. Salket have against Mrs. Creighton?" he asked.

"Well," O'Conner said, "she alleges that, several months ago, a sum of money disappeared from her purse while Mrs. Creighton was visiting her home. Mrs. Salket suspected her, but Mrs. Creighton managed to convince her that she could not have taken the money and that she was a devoted friend.

"Then, one day, Mrs. Creighton brought Mrs. Salket a cake which she said she had baked especially for her neighbour. Mrs. Salket ate a piece. Almost immediately she became ill, with nausea and vomiting.

"As soon as she felt well enough, she went to Mrs. Creighton and accused her of trying to poison her. She says Mrs. Creighton just laughed and said, "Better not repeat that, Olive, or you'll be very sorry. That was tried on me once, over in New Jersey. Just accuse me, and I'll sue you. I'll win such damages, it will take the last cent you've got to your name."

Inspector King nodded. "So that's why she went to the library to find out about the New Jersey case."

"That's it," the patrolman agreed. "And Mrs. Salket suggests that there may be something odd about the death of Mrs. Applegate. She says there's been a lot of gossip already. And she herself is afraid of Mrs. Creighton."

"Neighbourhood spite, perhaps?" King suggested.

"Maybe so, maybe not," O'Conner said. "Mrs. Salket claims that she was terribly sick after eating Mrs. Creighton's cake."

"We'll look into this," King promised. As the patrolman left, he summoned Detectives Bert Bedell and Joseph Hizenski. He told them what O'Conner had reported.

"Get hold of Applegate," he directed. "Find out what he knows about the Creightons, but don't let them know of your inquiry. They may not be the ones who figured in the Newark murder trial. But if they are, and Applegate doesn't know it, he ought to be put on his guard."

The inspector added: "Ask if there were any suspicious circumstances surrounding Mrs. Applegate's death. Get the ascribed cause of her death and the name of her family physician."

When the detectives reported back to him, they said that Everett Applegate had talked to them freely about his wife's death and about the Creightons. They were, he admitted, the couple that had been involved in the arsenic poisoning case in Newark. Applegate said he had known about it and had even discussed it with them. Mrs. Creighton had convinced him that it had been a frame-up, and she told him that she and her husband had been exonerated.

As for Ada Applegate, her husband said that she had been quite ill for almost a year and there had been nothing suspicious about her death. Ada had died as a result of gall-bladder trouble, with complications.

Bedell and Hizenski also brought back the name of the attending physician. He lived in nearby Malverne and had signed the death certificate late that same afternoon, Applegate said.

"Why this afternoon, when she died early yesterday?" King wondered aloud. He picked up the phone and called District Attorney Littleton, who happened to be working late. Then he hurried through the underground passage-way which connects police headquarters at Mineola with the Nassau County courthouse. He soon acquainted Martin Littleton with the facts presented by Patrolman O'Conner and the two detectives.

"One moment," Littleton said. "I think this has a tie-up right here in this office." He called in Assistant District Attorney Richard H. Brown. "How about it, Dick? Isn't there something in the pending file concerning a Baldwin resident named Everett Applegate?"

"You mean those anonymous letters?"

"Of course. The three letters." Littleton explained to Inspector King about Applegate's visit to the county prosecutor's office on June 21st.

King was shown the letters, which he read carefully. "I would think," he remarked, "that these could have been written by Mrs. Salket, except that the attack is on the Applegates. The writer seems to sympathise with the Creightons."

Littleton asked Brown to accompany King, who was going to call immediately upon the Malverne physician. The doctor was at home when the two investigators arrived and he listened thoughtfully to Brown's explanation of their errand.

"So there are ugly rumours being spread about Mrs. Applegate's death?" he said.

"You don't seem surprised, Doctor," King said.

"No, sir, I am not."

"Yet you signed the death certificate."

"Only a few hours ago. And against my better judgment. When I am treating a patient for one thing, and she unexpectedly dies of something else, my first impulse is to insist on an autopsy."

"Proper enough. But why didn't you insist on it, in this instance?" Brown asked.

"Everett Applegate and the others dissuaded me. They argued that it would cause a lot of talk and rumours and that no end, save medical curiosity, would be served. I finally gave in and signed the certificate, so that they could hold the funeral on Monday, as planned."

King and Brown questioned the doctor closely. Thus they developed a mystifying, almost sinister, survey of recent events at No. 12 Bryant Place in Baldwin.

The doctor stated that Ada Applegate had become his patient about a year ago. She was in her 36th year and weighed 269 pounds. He had begun treating her for obesity.

However, nine days before — on September 19th — he had been hurriedly summoned to treat her for violent attacks of nausea. He diagnosed her complaint as an acute disorder of the stomach and gall bladder. But when Ada Applegate's terrible retching and vomiting did not abate during the next 48 hours he ordered her removal to the South Nassau Community Hospital in Oceanside.

"And here is the curious thing," the doctor said. "Once in the hospital, the patient immediately responded satisfactorily to my treatment."

"The same treatment to which she had failed to respond for two days in her own home?"

"Precisely."

King and Brown exchanged glances. The physician added that four days later Ada Applegate had so recovered as to be discharged from the Oceanside institution. But she had not been home for more than five hours when the violent seizures and vomiting resumed.

Treatment which had seemed to cure her in the hospital was likewise resumed, the doctor said, but to no avail. Nausea continued to rack Ada Applegate until, at 6.30 a.m. yesterday — the 27th — her husband telephoned him frantically: "Doc, come as quick as you can. I'm afraid Ada's dead."

She was dead when the doctor arrived there. He said the cause of death seemed to be coronary occlusion, blood clots in a vital artery leading from the heart. But his analysis had troubled him, because Ada's fatal condition would not have been produced by the ailment for which he had been treating her — the treatment to which she had responded satisfactorily while hospitalised for an unknown ailment.

"When she was at home, who took care of Mrs. Applegate?" Brown asked.

The doctor said: "Usually, I think her friend Mrs. Creighton". He added that, whenever he visited his patient, Mrs. Creighton was at her bedside.

"When she was in the hospital," Brown asked, "was Mrs. Creighton or any of the family permitted to bring her food or delicacies?"

"No, indeed. Because of her acute attacks, I had confined my patient to a very strict hospital diet."

"A final question, Doctor," Inspector King said. "Would the introduction of arsenic into the diet of Mrs. Applegate have caused her to die in the way she did?"

"Arsenic?" The doctor looked startled. Then he said slowly: "That could be it. Yes, Inspector, arsenic could have caused not only the coronary occlusion but also the violent nausea and vomiting. Arsenic poisoning would give an answer to every conflicting circumstance or symptom which has puzzled me."

The two officials rose and thanked him. "Please say nothing of this," Brown urged. "We're only at the start of what may prove to be a long investigation."

At his desk in the Mineola courthouse District Attorney Littleton listened to the report of King and Brown. "That's enough for me," he said. "Inspector, have your men bring in the Creightons and also Everett Applegate."

It was close to midnight when the three detectives dispatched by King to Baldwin returned with the three persons named. Mrs. Creighton was a large, dark-eyed woman in her late 30s. She appeared to be an average housewife, neat and comely.

Was this, Inspector King wondered, a woman who would poison her young brother? A woman who would stoop to filch a few dollars from a neighbour's purse, then send her accuser a poisoned cake?

John Creighton, the husband, was a pleasant, unassuming man, his eyes puzzled, his easy-going manner belied by the heavy lines of care in his face.

Littleton began by asking them casual questions about the Newark case.

"But I explained all this before," Applegate interrupted. "Only this afternoon, I told those detectives that the whole Jersey business was just a filthy frame-up."

"But, Ev, if Mr. Littleton wishes to discuss it, that's his right and duty," Mrs. Creighton intervened with a disarming smile.

She explained coolly that her brother, Raymond Avery, had killed himself slowly by taking arsenic. It was suicide, because of his deep depression. He was physically underdeveloped to a degree that would prevent his ever marrying.

"Your brother suffered from extreme nausea before his death?" Littleton inquired.

"Mr. Littleton, he certainly did."

"His illness, then, resembled Mrs. Applegate's?"

Mary Frances Creighton did not seem to notice the tension all around her. "Yes, poor Ada's illness seemed quite like my poor brother's."

"What did that suggest to you, Mrs. Creighton?"

"Why, nothing. I remember asking the doctor. He told me that many forms of sickness produced these awful fits of vomiting."

John Creighton, when questioned, was frank. He said that he had been working right here in the Mineola courthouse for the past seven years as an employee in the county engineer's office.

Everett Applegate was abrupt in his replies and sounded patronising. He was employed by the Nassau County Veterans' Bureau, checking merchandise orders made by veterans on relief, he said. Since this job did not oblige him to keep very regular hours, he had been able to come home frequently to assist Mrs. Creighton in her devoted care of his ailing wife, Ada.

Mrs. Creighton stated that she or Everett Applegate had prepared all the sick woman's meals both before and after her four-day stay in the hospital at Oceanside. She conceded that she knew Mrs. Salket. But she was sure that she had given this neighbour no reason to feel unkindly towards her, particularly with regard to so trifling a favour as a gift of cake.

"The truth is, Mr. Littleton," she smiled, "I'm afraid I'm a wretched cook. I seldom bake a cake."

The prosecutor questioned each of the three separately. In this way, he began to get a picture of domestic arrangements that were strangely involved.

The Creightons were the original occupants of the small stucco dwelling on Bryant Place. Then, the preceding November, Everett and Ada Applegate arranged to double up with the Creightons. This placed seven persons under a roof meant to shelter but four.

The two bedrooms on the ground floor were taken over by Mr. and Mrs. Applegate and Mr. and Mrs. Creighton, respectively, a young girl boarder, Evelyn, sharing a room with the Applegates' 12-year-old daughter. The Creightons' son, 11, was given a cot on an enclosed porch in the rear.

On one occasion the Creightons had a couple of overnight guests. They were given their hosts' bedrooms downstairs. The Creightons took over the girls' attic quarters. The Applegate daughter joined the Creighton boy on the enclosed porch. Evelyn, now 15, shared the bed with Applegate and his ponderous spouse.

Asked why he did not have his own daughter move in

with him and his wife in the emergency, Applegate answered smugly: "But Evelyn's just like another daughter to me. I like the kid." Then he blurted: "Say, what are you guys driving at? If there was something going on between that child and me, you don't suppose we'd be in the same bed with my wife, do you?"

Martin Littleton let this pass. He handed Applegate an official form and a pen, and told him to sign his name.

"What for?" Applegate demanded.

"That's an authorisation by you for an autopsy on your wife." Applegate glared angrily at the attorney, but he signed the paper.

The order was passed at once to Dr. Carl A. Hettescheimer, medical examiner of Nassau County. Meanwhile, in another room of the courthouse, the Creightons had also been given pens. They were asked to set down in their own words their recollections of the last illness and fatal seizure of Mrs. Ada Applegate.

These two signed statements were taken in to Littleton and King. The reaction of both men was nearly instantaneous.

"Do you see what I see?" the inspector queried.

"I think so," Littleton said. He reached over to a tray on his desk and took out the three anonymous letters which had brought Everett Applegate to those same offices to complain, some 14 weeks ago, on the 21st of June.

No mistake about it! The strong, free-flowing hand which had just filled in and signed Mrs. Creighton's statement was the same strong, free handwriting of the three anonymous letters addressed: "To the People of 12 Bryant Place, Baldwin, Long Island."

At Littleton's nod, King went to the door and threw it open. "Mrs. Creighton," he said, "the D.A. wants to have a word with you."

As the woman came in, serene, her dark eyes bright with interest, Littleton said directly: "You wrote these anonymous letters. The handwriting is unmistakable."

"Is it? I'm not good at disguising things," Mrs. Creighton shrugged.

"You wrote letters to your own home, denouncing someone living in the same house? Why?"

"I wanted the Applegates to move out. I couldn't get my husband to tell them to go — he's so good-hearted. And I didn't know how else to manage it."

"Then, in these allegations naming Everett Applegate, you simply trumped up something to embarrass him?"

"Mr. Littleton, you could fill pages with stuff like that about Ev."

"You were concerned about Evelyn, the young girl?" Littleton asked.

"Ev Applegate's a bad influence to have around the house."

"You thought that if he stayed on there would be some trouble involving the girl?"

"Wouldn't any woman worry a bit?"

"Tell me, Mrs. Creighton," Littleton said, "weren't you moved to write those anonymous letters last June because there already had been trouble?"

"Over Evelyn? Heavens, no! The girl's only 15 years old. I was there, too. I love my husband. And I got sick of Ev's making passes at me. Always coming home in the afternoons or at odd moments. His job gives him plenty of leisure time and he's got big ideas about not wasting it."

Littleton excused himself, saying that he had to make a telephone call. He had Mrs. Creighton go into an adjoining office to wait — not the same room, however, in which her husband and Everett Applegate were sitting.

Littleton put through his call. It was to New York and it aroused in the middle of the night a long-time friend who was also an eminent psychiatrist.

The prosecutor was about to send for Mrs. Creighton again, when his telephone rang. It was the county medical examiner.

Dr. Hettescheimer explained that he had removed Ada Applegate's liver and kidneys and would also remove her stomach and brain. He had found the kidneys swollen to twice their normal size. The liver was badly inflamed. Arsenic, the medical examiner disclosed, has a predilection for the liver and kidneys and would act on them in precisely this way.

"Thanks, Doctor. We'll keep closely in touch," Littleton said and put the phone back on its cradle. Turning to Inspector King, he repeated what Hettescheimer had told him, adding: "He is going to submit the organs for chemical analysis."

King and Littleton resumed their questioning of Mrs. Creighton, but now they found her reluctant to enlarge upon any of her few admissions. No, she said, she had not been personally afraid of Everett Applegate. Rather she had been afraid for him. She had known that her husband would angrily resent the brazen and improper advances.

That was why she had decided — no doubt foolishly — to send the anonymous letters.

She said she hadn't thought it necessary to attempt to disguise her handwriting. She had never written to either Ev or Ada Applegate, and her writing was not familiar to them.

Mrs. Creighton was released, and a distinguished-looking grey-haired gentleman was ushered in by another door. This was Dr. Richard Hoffman, a well-known psychiatrist. Littleton wanted this specialist to examine the psychological complexities of the Creighton-Applegate household.

He particularly wished to have Dr. Hoffman talk with young Evelyn.

It was 5.30 on a drizzly Sunday morning when Dr. Hoffman, in company with Inspector King, Mrs. Creighton and Detective-Lieutenant Jess Mayforth, commander of the Homicide Squad, arrived at the small stucco dwelling on Bryant Place.

Mrs. Creighton, who had chatted casually with her three companions on the drive from Mineola, led them into the house. King asked her to send for Evelyn.

With a thin robe thrown over her sheer nightgown, Evelyn looked more mature than her 15 years.

"This is Dr. Hoffman, and Mr. King and Mr. Mayforth. They want to talk to you alone," Mrs. Creighton said casually.

Evelyn merely said: "How do you do?" and seated herself.

Mrs. Creighton offered to prepare coffee. The detective and the psychiatrist assured her that they were not in need of refreshment. But Inspector King seated himself so that he could be sure she went into the kitchen and stayed there.

Dr. Hoffman soon got on good terms with Evelyn. By degrees, he led the conversation round to the man whom Evelyn called Uncle Ev — Everett Applegate.

"You say you are quite fond of your Uncle Ev. My dear, does he kiss you?"

"Oh, yes. Uncle Ev often kisses me."

"And you like to have him kiss you?"

"Yes."

"Kiss you on the mouth?"

The girl blushed, but answered: "Yes, sir."

"It's all right, my dear. I'm a doctor and you needn't be afraid to talk to me. You like to sleep with your Uncle Ev."

It wasn't phrased as a question. And, though the girl's colour mounted, she offered no denial. The psychiatrist next asked her how long she had been having relations with Everett Applegate.

"Since last June," came the answer.

Mrs. Creighton came in with coffee. Nobody accepted any.

Inspector King said sternly: "Did you know, Mrs. Creighton, that Evelyn has been having improper relations with Mr. Applegate?"

"Why, no," the woman answered. "Evelyn, did you tell them that? It isn't true."

The girl looked genuinely astonished. "Of course it's true. You've known it all along."

"She's impossible at times," Mrs. Creighton said to the

visitors. "I would have put a stop to it if I'd had any idea such a thing was going on." She stalked from the room.

"She knew," Evelyn said.

"You told her at the time?"

"She caught us." This, she disclosed, had occurred in the Applegates' bedroom, soon after Evelyn first succumbed to Uncle Ev's seductive wiles. Their first intimacy had occurred in a motion picture projection booth during a social affair of the Legion.

"You say Mrs. Creighton knew of these happenings," the doctor said. "Did Mrs. Applegate know, too?"

"Aunt Ada knew. She was awfully mad. But not at me — at Uncle Ev."

"Did he tell you that he loved you?"

"Often."

"Did he say that he would like to marry you?"

"He said that all the time."

Following this interview, Detective-Lieutenant Mayforth informed Mrs. Creighton that he wanted to search the house.

"Go ahead," she said.

Mayforth found some bottles in a medicine cabinet and removed them. He also removed a writing pad, which he found marking a place in a book belonging to Evelyn. There were a few sheets left on the pad, and their colour and texture seemed identical to that of the three sheets of lined yellow pad paper on which the anonymous letters had been written.

Mayforth found nothing else in the house which seemed pertinent to the investigation.

It was past 8 a.m. when Dr. Hoffman, accompanied by King and Mayforth, returned to the courthouse in Mineola. District Attorney Littleton was still at his desk.

The psychiatrist gave his professional opinion. "In my view, Martin, the girl is telling the truth," Dr. Hoffman concluded. "She's too young to comprehend all this evil. She's a strange, beguiling youngster, with an air of innocence and honesty."

Littleton turned to King. "Do you agree with the doctor?"

"That the girl told us the truth? I do."

"If you believe her, then you disbelieve Mrs. Creighton?"

"There's a cold-minded, cold-hearted woman," King said.

Mayforth said: "The woman claims that she knew nothing of Applegate's romancing of the girl. Well, I agree with Dr. Hoffman and the inspector. She did know. The kid's under age. Mrs. Creighton could throw the book at him. But all she does is write anonymous letters. Why?"

Littleton said: "My guess would be that Everett Applegate has something on her."

"My guess, too," said King.

"I'm releasing Applegate for the present," Littleton said. "John Creighton, too, of course. He strikes me as a dominated husband and is, I think, at least in this sordid business, an innocent bystander. However, all members of the Creighton-Applegate household must be kept under surveillance until we learn the findings of Dr. Gettler in New York."

The surveillance was begun at once. Then, early on Monday, the prosecutor and Inspector King sent out teams of men to check on any arsenic sales made either to Mrs. Creighton or to Applegate, in Baldwin or some nearby community, at about the time that Mrs. Ada Applegate had been stricken.

Also on Monday morning, two of the county's detectives, Bert Bedell and Charles Jones, were dispatched to Newark. Inspector King instructed them to obtain information concerning the 12-year-old arsenic poisoning of young Raymond Avery.

They learned that the acquittal in the Avery case had been due, as already determined from Mrs. Salket's photostats, to the weakness of the evidence introduced by the Jersey prosecution. But the two investigators learned that Mrs. Mary F. Creighton had been accused not once, but twice, as a killer who killed with arsenic!

Not long after her acquittal in the Avery case, the woman stood trial alone in the case of the alleged murder of elderly Mrs. Walter Creighton, her husband's mother. Again the lethal dose was said to have been arsenic. And again, the motive of the poisoner was said to have been greed — to collect insurance money.

But in this case, too, a jury made cautious regarding circumstantial evidence where it might invoke the death penalty had listened to an ingenious defence rather than to the judge and prosecutor, and had brought in the second acquittal.

These trials of more than a decade ago had resulted in the Creightons moving from New Jersey. In due course the family, which now included an infant son as well as a young daughter, settled in Baldwin, Long Island, and had pretty well succeeded in living down the uneasy past.

"That woman," King exclaimed, "never breathed a word to us about having been charged with the poison-murder of her mother-in-law!"

Meanwhile, the officers checking on arsenic sales spread their inquiries wider, but without result. The medicine bottles which Detective-Lieutenant Mayforth had brought from the cabinet in the Creighton-Applegate home proved to contain only the medicines that their pharmacy labels specified.

The yellow-lined paper of the anonymous letters was proved to be the same as the paper on the pad which Mayforth had found in the house. The crudely-torn upper edge of one of the three letters exactly fitted a thin upper-edge residue of paper still glued to the top of the pad. However, since Mrs. Creighton had admitted writing and posting the letter, this confirmation was incidental.

King's men were covering the Baldwin cottage and its occupants. But nobody made any suspicious moves. The funeral was on October 1st. It was well attended, not only by friends and mourners, but by the morbid, idle, curious … and the police.

On Saturday, October 5th, 1935, exactly one week after

Patrolman O'Conner brought the Salket photostats to Inspector King's desk, the report came through to Dr Hetteschiemer, the county medical examiner, from Dr. Alexander O. Gettler, a celebrated toxicologist in New York City.

Littleton summoned King. "We can go ahead now, Inspector," he said, showing him the result of Gettler's examination. "There was enough arsenic in Ada Applegate's body to have killed four people."

It was after dark on October 5th, a windy autumn night, when the Creightons and Everett Applegate, surrounded by detectives, were again brought to the District Attorney's office.

Littleton read to them a summary of Dr. Gettler's findings. "What do you say to this, Mrs. Creighton?" he demanded.

The woman turned to her baffled-looking husband and rasped: "You going to sit there and let them accuse me?"

Littleton signalled to detectives to escort Creighton and Applegate from the office. The woman sat alone now, staring at the floor. Littleton walked around his desk and stood in front of her.

"Tell me," he said, "just how long have you been having intimate relations with Everett Applegate?"

Her answer came slowly. "That's over, Mr. Littleton. Ever since I discovered that he was having such relations with Evelyn."

"Then you admit now that you knew about it?"

"Yes. I caught them."

"In your own case, when did this thing start? I want you to tell the truth and tell me the whole story."

"There's little to tell. Ev and I were intimate in that way — well, almost as soon as he and Ada came to live with us," she answered calmly. "I love my husband and always have. I tried to resist Ev. Being home a lot during the day, he was always coming into my room. You see, he had found out about our having trouble over in New Jersey. He knew I didn't want Evelyn or our son to know about the trials. But he said he would tell both children all about it unless I listened to reason. So what could I do?"

"You say you have not had relations with Applegate since last June, when you found out about him and your young boarder?"

"Only two or three times since then."

The district attorney stared at the woman incredulously. "And your husband learned nothing of all this?"

"He never learned. He's had nothing to do with any of it."

"Wasn't he suspicious when the letters arrived? He would know his own wife's handwriting, I should think."

"It didn't seem to occur to him. John's a good soul. And, remember, we have all been under Ev Applegate's influence. Ev easily convinced my husband that there was only malice in the letters. No truth to them whatever."

Littleton conferred privately with Detective Jones, who had been questioning Applegate. The detective reported that the suspect was now less patronising and self-assured, and that he admitted having had illicit relations for some time with his friends' 15-year-old boarder, even though he knew her to be under age.

Then Littleton returned to his interrogation of Mrs. Creighton. "I detect a certain note of admiration whenever you speak of Applegate, although what you say is meant to sound hostile," he said.

"Ev's not too bad a sort. There's good fun in him. Except, of course, that he's a beast about women — any woman. Doesn't matter who. He was so terribly unhappy in his marriage. I expect that explains some of it."

"You hated Ada Applegate?"

"She had a mean mouth for gossiping. She was going to make bad trouble in the community about Ev and the girl."

"So you hated her."

"I expect I did."

"And your good friend, Everett Applegate — he hated her?"

"He certainly did. He told me he just couldn't stand the

sight of her."

Littleton paced the room, allowing the tension to grow. Suddenly he stopped. "When you couldn't get rid of the Applegates, then you wanted him to be able to marry Evelyn?"

"I didn't want her to get pregnant and no husband—"

"Is she pregnant?"

"No. But with Ev so crazy for her, the danger was always there." Mrs. Creighton's dark eyes flashed and she drew herself up proudly. "What kind of a woman would I be, not to worry about her?"

Martin Littleton's words became hammer strokes. "Then it was like this: Applegate wanted Evelyn. He wanted Ada dead. You wanted Ada dead. Then he would be free to marry the girl, in the event there was trouble. And that, Mrs. Creighton, is why you put poison in Ada Applegate's food."

Dropping her assumed dignity, Mary Creighton wavered. Her cool nerve was cracking at last. "Yes, that's why," she murmured. "And Ev helped me."

Littleton then adroitly guided her through the complexities of this sordid intrigue. She answered freely now, without reservation or apparent thought of self-preservation. One night in mid-September, she said, Ev had lovingly embraced Evelyn in her presence. The others, she said, were in bed and asleep. "I'm simply nuts about that kid," he had told her, as Evelyn ascended to the attic bedroom which she shared with Applegate's daughter.

"Why don't you marry her?"

"If I could only get rid of that tub of a wife —"

"Easy. We give her a dose of Rough On Rats. That'll fix her."

And, when Applegate was doubtful, Mrs. Creighton explained that Rough On Rats had "fixed" her brother, Raymond, and her husband's mother, old Mrs. Walter Creighton. You could pick it up easily in a cut-rate drugstore, and without having to sign your name.

"I'd do it in a minute," she quoted Applegate as saying

to her, "if I thought we could get away with it."

And she told him: "We can get away with it, Ev. You know how it was with me over in Jersey. They couldn't prove a thing. And it should be even more of a cinch with Ada — she's always sick with something or other."

There was no more discussion of his wife's murder that night, Mrs. Creighton said. Late the next evening, however, Applegate had touched upon the subject again. The following afternoon they drove to a cut-rate drugstore on Merrick Road. He waited outside in the car while Mrs. Creighton went in and paid 23 cents for a box of the rodent exterminator. Rough On Rats, a combination of white arsenic and lamp-black.

Later, that same day, when preparing dinner, Mrs. Creighton whipped up a bowl of chocolate pudding, a dessert of which Ada Applegate was inordinately fond. The only problem lay in making sure that no one but Ada ate any of it, since it had been generously spiked with Rough On Rats.

In puddings, in gravies and sauces, in coffee, this same poison was administered to Ada thereafter. She became very ill, and her doctor was called from Malverne. Mrs. Creighton described how dismayed she and Applegate had been when the physician, baffled by his obese patient's condition, insisted that Ada be removed to the hospital.

Mrs. Applegate so improved there that she was discharged from the hospital — discharged to her death. The solicitous Mrs. Creighton and Everett Applegate promised their victim "a nice glass of egg-nog, and a dish of your favourite pudding," before the car in which they returned from the hospital turned into Bryant Place.

By the evening of Thursday, September 26th, Ada had been fed so much arsenic tainted egg-nog, junket and broth that she was in a hopelessly weakened condition.

Mrs. Creighton said to Applegate in the kitchen: "Come on, let's mix her a good stiff one. I'm tired of her hanging on like this." And when the enfeebled Ada moaned, "I'm sorry, Ev, but I can't take any more just now," Mrs.

Creighton urged, "But you've got to take this, Ada. You need it, dear, to give you strength."

The "good stiff one" did its work.

Littleton glanced at King, then asked: "Mrs. Creighton, did you put some of that same poison in the cake that you gave to your neighbour, Olive Salket?"

"Maybe a pinch or two," came the cool response. "But that woman had it coming to her. She accused me of stealing a few measly dollars from her purse."

Everett Applegate and Mrs. Mary Creighton, were indicted for the murder. John Creighton was completely exonerated of any connection with the death of Ada Applegate.

The joint trial of Everett Applegate and Mrs. Mary Frances Creighton began on Thursday, January 16th, 1936, with Judge Courtland A. Johnson presiding.

The trial lasted a little more than a week. On January 25th Applegate and Mrs. Creighton were found guilty of murder in the first degree. Judge Johnson sentenced the convicted pair to die in the electric chair.

A series of legal manoeuvres followed. There were various appeals to have the verdict set aside and to obtain a new trial. All these efforts failed.

On July 16th, 1936, less than 10 months after the murder of Ada Applegate, Mrs. Mary Frances Creighton and Everett Applegate were put to death for their crime. When the night of execution came, Mrs. Creighton could not walk the last mile.

For days she had lain in her cell, semi-conscious and paralysed with fear. Death Row attendants were obliged to lift her into a wheelchair and trundle her into the grim chamber of execution. She had to be lifted from the wheelchair and placed in the electric chair, where she could not hold herself upright but, according to eye-witnesses, sagged like a sack of meal. And thus the woman who became notorious as the "Long Island Borgia" went to her appointed death as one already dead.